FIDDLING WITH LIFE

The Unusual Journey of
Steven Staryk

FIDDLING WITH LIFE

The Unusual Journey of
Steven Staryk

Thane Lewis
with
Steven Staryk

Mosaic Press
OAKVILLE, ON - NIAGARA FALLS, NY

Canadian Cataloguing in Publication Data

Staryk, Steven, 1932-
Fiddling with life

ISBN 0-88962-613-8

1. Staryk, Steven, 1932-   2. Violinists-Canada-Biography.
I. Title.

ML418.S72L48 1999   787.2'092   C96-930828-0

Published by Mosaic Press, P.O. Box 1032, Oakville, Ontario, L6J 5E9, Canada. Offices and warehouse at 1252 Speers Road, Units #1&2, Oakville, Ontario, L6L 5N9, Canada and Mosaic Press, 4500 Witmer Industrial Estates, Niagara Falls, NY 14305-1386

Mosaic Press acknowledges the assistance of the Canada Council, the Ontario Arts Council and the Department of Canadian Heritage, Government of Canada for their support of our publishing programme.

Every effort has been made to identify the sources of all materials, photographic and other, utilized in this book. Any omissions will be gratefully acknowledged.

THE CANADA COUNCIL | LE CONSEIL DES ARTS
FOR THE ARTS | DU CANADA
SINCE 1957 | DEPUIS 1957

MOSAIC PRESS, in Canada:
1252 Speers Road, Units #1 & 2,
Oakville, Ontario, L6L 5N9
Phone / Fax: (905) 825-2130
E-mail: cp507@freenet.toronto.on.ca

MOSAIC PRESS, in USA:
4500 Witmer Industrial Estates, PMB 145,
Niagara Falls, NY., 14305-1386
Phone / Fax: 1-800-387-8992
E-mail: cp507@freenet.toronto.on.ca

"A modest man is generally admired, if people ever hear of him."
Aristotle

Acknowledgements

To the following individuals, my thanks for their assistance in exhuming details of Mr. Staryk's past: Ms. DeLeur of the Concertgebouw in Amsterdam; Mimi Kwok, archivist of the Toronto Symphony Orchestra; Frank Villella, archivist with the Chicago Symphony Orchestra; assorted Librarians at the Interlibrary Loan Office, Suzzallo Library, University of Washington; and Tim Ramos, Interlibrary Loan at the downtown Seattle Public Library. Thanks to Erik J. Macki, Department of Germanics at the University of Washington, for his Dutch translation, and much gratitude to Neil Bacon, Angelo Calcafuoco, Larry Starr, and my wife Lisa Michelle Lewis for their suggestions and general advice. Special mention goes to Ron Drummond for his highly sympathetic and transparent editorial work in the eleventh hour. And finally, thanks to Gwenlyn Setterfield for her extensive research and interviewing and for her generosity in allowing us free use of the resulting manuscript, to which this book is indebted. What has evolved out of these efforts is something of a hybrid: part autobiography, part biography and part memoir.

Thane Lewis

Thane Lewis is a violist with the Northwest Sinfonietta and performs regularly as a freelance musician in Seattle. He serves on the Applied Music Faculty of Northwest College. As a member of the Pacific Chamber Group, Mr. Lewis is also Artist in Residence at the Magnolia Performing Arts Center. His early musical training included studies with Camilla Wicks at the University of Washington, the Philadelphia String Quartet at the Olympic Music Festival, and with Eugene Drucker of the Emerson String Quartet at the Aspen Music Festival. He also studied in Vienna with Elizabeth Kropfitch at the Hochschule Für Musik ünd Darstellende Kunst. After graduating with honours in English Literature from Whitman College, Mr. Lewis worked as the editor of three monthly computer software publications before completing graduate studies at the University of Washington School of Music with Steven Staryk, earning a Master of Music Degree in Performance. Thane Lewis shares a house with his wife Lisa, and two children, Justin and Emily.

Acknowledgements

The existence of this book (after earlier ill-fated attempts) is due primarily to the patient prodding of my student, colleague, and friend, Angelo Calcafuoco. His persistent belief that this was a worthwhile project motivated me and softened my rather cynical attitude toward producing 'yet another book.' Howard Aster of Mosaic Press, who repeatedly reset deadlines, must surely be the 'runner-up' in this test of patience and belief. Gwenlyn Setterfield's original manuscript, *Without Compromise: Steven Staryk's Life In Music*, of over a decade ago has been invaluable to the enterprise, as was the enthusiasm and professional assistance of an old colleague and friend, Campbell Trowsdale. The flexibility of author Thane Lewis with respect to our limited schedules was admirable, though the inevitable pressures of this project must have led to doubts and regrets many a time over the past three years. Mr. Lewis is a former Graduate student of mine, whose writing gifts I discovered during one of his Master's exams. I was struck by his sensitivity, style, and insight, and hope that he will forgive me for having entangled him in what seemed to become an inescapable web. He has my ever grateful thanks for his efforts in probing my thoughts and feelings, researching my career, and hopefully enlightening any who have been curious about some of the enigmas of my professional life.

Steven Staryk
Scottsdale, Arizona, April 1999

To the many individuals who have affected my fiddling and my life that we were unable to include in this book; my concern, or excuse, was that the covers might grow too far apart.

Steven Staryk

TABLE OF CONTENTS

PART ONE

A Prologue in Three

AN ENCLAVE OF THE IDEAL

It is Spring Convocation, June 1995, at the University of Washington in Seattle, where violinist Steven Staryk has taken his place in a procession of colleagues to formally accept the University's Distinguished Teaching Award. But in the fluid realm of Staryk's mind and memory, York University's June 1980 Convocation in Toronto, a celebration fifteen years past, is recalled and superimposed over the events of the day.

"At York, as in Seattle, I shuffled along to the strains of Elgar's *Pomp and Circumstance*," recalls Staryk, "as images from an Ingmar Bergman film, *Wild Strawberries*, came to mind. For those unfamiliar with the movie, Bergman portrays a formal convocation ceremony:" gentlemen in white tie and tails, their lapels decorated with medals and ribbons, walking together in a procession regulated by solemn music. The procession climbs stone steps and enters into the gloom of an old chapel. Once the assembly is seated, the master of ceremonies rises, moves to a central dais, invites Dr. Isak Borg to join him and intones a Latin text. And within a context of rightness, order, and ease, the aging doctor bends his gray head to receive his honors. Later, we learn through fragmentary glimpses into Dr. Borg's troubled past that his formal austerity and composure is only an appearance.

Years later, memories of this film mix with the immediacy of the present for Staryk, whose thoughts are as turbulent as the crowd assembled in Seattle: this once serious and solemn ceremony is now animated by the shouts and antics of the graduates, and a few balloons lost and floating in the air add to the impression that this is a carnival rather than a convocation.

Once again, memory imposes itself on the present: Professor Norman Penner rises as the representative of York University's Glendon College to present the citation: "Steven Staryk, a distinguished musician, performer, and teacher, has brought great honour to Canada . . . "

Staryk came to both convocations with a strong sense of the ironies and enigmas underlying such events. "Would it have meant my teaching was average or only passable if I had not received the award?" he muses. "Would it be inferior simply for lack of recognition? 'The world seldom notices who the teachers are; but civilization depends on what they do and what they say.'" Those who are officially recognized often play a significant role in the politics of their own awards. Lobbying for promotion and tenure is as much a reality in academe as in the real world, with recognition existing as a political prize for political animals. Not surprisingly, recognition is a routine which in many instances is far removed from actual achievement.

Professor Penner continues: "His parents were among the thousands of Ukrainian immigrants who came to Canada and contributed so much to the building of our country. They brought with them, among other things, a passionate love for liberty and progress, and a culture that has helped enrich our spiritual life."

Suicide, cancer, and dementia within Staryk's family formed the backdrop to his life on stage. Staryk had at one time seriously considered going into the medical profession, and given the amount of time he spent visiting hospitals, hospices, and nursing homes, he feels that it may have been more practical to have worked in them. Yet the profession that Staryk did pursue, with energy, purpose, and integrity, left him in the end with a surprisingly small listening public and very few momentos of his work. The Canadian Broadcasting Corporation, with whom he has extensively recorded, has deleted all but one or two of his recordings from their catalogue.

"Steven Staryk is a Canadian of whom we are very proud. He has accomplished so much already and will accomplish much more in the coming years."

An account of Staryk's life must depict extraordinary achievement coupled with chafing dissatisfaction. The near perfection, temperament, and intensity of his playing, displayed throughout an international career, has elicited the respect and awe of colleagues. Yet this reputation is divided among a small group of musicians and remains, for the most part, among those musicians. In terms of popular recognition, Steven Staryk, the violinist's violinist, is virtually unknown.

"It is indeed an honour for us at Glendon College, York University, to offer him the highest award which it is within our power to confer, and to have him accept it. Mr. Chancellor, we ask you to confer on Steven Staryk, master musician, the degree of Doctor of Letters."

Hidden

There is an underlying current that we sense running through our lives, at times strongly, at other times less so, tying events and people together, guiding, pushing, and quietly instructing. The idea of fate belongs to the mystical; the Taoist observes fate as Tao; Ludwig Wittgenstein condemns discussion of it to silence: "About which one cannot speak, one must remain silent." Perhaps fate is glimpsed peripherally, like the star which can be seen only by looking slightly to the side or with unfocused eyes. For most, fate's path is clarified by hindsight. Observing the course of Steven Staryk's career, one is tempted to speak of fate and of a pronounced element of irony.

Within the trappings of success.

The University of Washington's Kane Hall, Seattle, 1995. Chocolate-covered strawberries gleamed on silver trays. In the mid-June, mid-afternoon sun slanting through the tall windows of the reception room, the strawberries, arrayed on a series of buffet tables, settled deeper into their cushions of brown. A crowd of students and professors milled around these tables; finals were drawing to a close and the atmosphere was festive.

At 4:30 a bell tolled and the crowd emptied into a high-ceilinged corridor, spilled down two flights of stairs to the ground level of the building, pooled in the atrium around the entrance to Roethke Auditorium, and drained neatly into the rows of chairs within. Student violinists from Brazil, the United States, Canada, Great Britain, Germany, Russia, China, and Korea settled into the chairs of row N. Some still sipped from wine glasses as the President of the University stood and addressed the assembly.

The gathering honored the recipients, both student and faculty, of several of the University's awards for research, scholarship, and, for the faculty, excellence in teaching. After a number of introductions followed by grinning acceptance speeches, applause, and more introductions, the President finally (to the delight of row N) introduced the first of three faculty to receive the Distinguished Teaching Award: Professor of Violin, Steven Staryk. The President then embarked down the path of a *vitae* that is the stuff of musical legend. At age 24, the youngest concertmaster in the history of the Royal Philharmonic Orchestra under Sir Thomas Beecham, and, subsequently, concertmaster of three more of the world's greatest orchestras.

"Mr. Staryk is a recording and concert artist with a discography covering one hundred and ninety compositions on forty-five albums, of which sixteen are world premiere recordings of new music; this accomplishment places him among the most prolific recording violinists internationally. He organized Quartet Canada and toured through Europe, the Far East, and North America. Mr. Staryk has served as a jury member of the Tchaikovsky Competition in Moscow and is listed in *Who's Who in America*, *Dictionary of International Biography*, the *International Who's Who in Music*, *Discopaedia of the Violin*, *Encyclopedia Canada* and *The New Grove Dictionary of Music and Musicians*. Professor Staryk's honors include the Ukrainian Shevchenko Medal, an Honorary Doctorate of Letters from Toronto's York University, the Queen's Silver Jubilee Medal, and arts awards from the Canada Council. He has often been likened to the incomparable Heifetz and acclaimed by a host of prestigious publications, such as *Gramophone*, as 'among the great ones.'

"Rave reviews are nothing new for Professor Staryk, but it is his long and dedicated career as a teacher that we celebrate here today; more specifically, the eight years he has spent at the University of Washington. His impact on the individuals lucky enough to have been his students and on the musical life of the University has been profound. Student tributes to Professor Staryk have four common themes: his inspirational qualities, his gift for analyzing and solving technical and musical problems, his insistence born of his own long experience that students understand and prepare for the practical realities of a life in music, and his lavish expenditures of time and care on students. Teaching posts which Professor Staryk has held include those at Oberlin College (the youngest full Professor in the history of the school), the Amsterdam Conservatory, Northwestern University, and the American Conservatory in Chicago. He was Head of the String Department of the Music Academy of Vancouver, Head of the String Department of the Royal Conservatory of Music, Toronto, part-time faculty at the University of Toronto, and held visiting professorships at the Universities of Victoria, Ottawa, and Western Ontario, and is now Head of the String Division here at the University of Washington. This is the first time in the history of this University that a faculty member of the School of Music has received the Distinguished Teaching Award." Applause.

From his front row seat Staryk rose and moved to the stage with an energetic swiftness that belied his gray hair and slightly stooped physique. Once at the microphone, he paused briefly to put on glasses, then began his acceptance speech.

BEGINNINGS

The proverb says that 'the half is greater than the whole,' but we may go further and say that the beginning is greater than the whole, for the beginning clears up many obscurities together in the matter we may be investigating.

- Aristotle, *Ethics*, Book One

In 1929, at the sixteenth Conference of the All Soviet Communist Party/ Bolsheviks, Stalin introduced his program for universal collectivization; by 1930 all peasants were to be gathered into *kolkhozes*.[1] When peasants in the Ukraine resisted, Stalin deported many of them, intending to settle Russians in their place to keep the valuable land in use. Between 1930 and 1932, over three million Ukrainians were sent north to Siberia or into camps.[2] At the same time Stalin eliminated the intelligentsia: "This first wide-scale campaign to liquidate potential opposition claimed as its victims in Ukraine not only the forty-five writers, scholars, and national and religious leaders who were put on trial as members of the Union for the Liberation of Ukraine [an organization fabricated by the Party to incriminate their targets], but also tens of thousands of teachers, agronomists, cooperative directors, clergymen, and students. Most of them were shot in 1930 or were slowly exterminated in prisons and camps."[3]

This accomplished, Stalin manufactured a famine. Moscow began demanding impossibly high grain deliveries from Ukraine, setting quotas that doubled the amount that could reasonably be expected from a successful year's planting. The peasants fell behind with their deliveries, then further behind. Soon they had nothing to keep for themselves and soldiers were sent to confiscate stores of grain from earlier years. The soldiers were thorough, sweeping up every last kernel of wheat and destroying backyard garden plots and searching under the floorboards of villagers' homes for hidden supplies. Stalin covered the protestations of Ukrainian leaders with a thick and cynical layer of propaganda that placed the blame for the famine on the peasants themselves. From 1930 to 1933 six million[4] Ukrainian peasants died of starvation.

It was in 1929, the year of Stalin's compulsory collectivization, that Marynka Staryk left the village of Buczacz in the province of Ternopol (Western Ukraine) for Canada. She left little behind; Marynka's father Teodor had died when she was still an infant, and her mother, Tekla, when she was thirteen. Since the death of her mother, she had stayed with an older sister, Varvara, teaching herself to read and write and working in private homes as a domestic. Marynka's journey to Canada followed that of her brother Nycola and sister Pauline. Dotted across the United States and Canada were new-world islands of Ukrainian existence, and since Stalin's act of genocide was draining Ukraine of Ukrainians, their culture was better preserved in Toronto and Vancouver than in Kharkov.[5] In order to join her siblings, Marynka chose Toronto as her destination.

Shortly after arriving, she married Peter Staryk, a distant cousin. On April 27, 1932, Stefan Staryk was born. It was the Depression and Stefan's father was unable to find work and, in an act of despair, took his own life; Stefan was two. After this, mother and son lived alone at 89 Mitchell Street in downtown Toronto, in a neighborhood crowded with Eastern Europeans: Czechs, Poles, Macedonians, Ukrainians.

Far from their homeland, the Ukrainians knit themselves into a tight community with the threads of language, music, food, and dance. It was an odd mixture of longing and pride, anxiety and determination, that compelled the individual immigrants to form a community, and once begun, the community centered its energies around the young. The members of the next generation, the first generation Ukrainian/Canadians, were shaped by their parents into the traditional Ukrainian image, yet dealt with the "promised land" and its language and ways with a competency and ease that their parents could never have managed.

The children inhabited two worlds. In their oscillating course through the days of childhood, they acquired from their surroundings an early awareness of class stratification; they were newcomers and despite the richness of their heritage (or to some degree because of it), the Ukrainian children were burdened with an unjustified sense of inferiority and a concomitant insecurity. This was especially true of those who became professionals and worked within a world of people from more privileged backgrounds. The Ukrainian emigrants who dispersed into rural areas of Ontario may have had a different experience. It has been observed that "Ukrainian patriotism has a peasant quality: it is firmly rooted in the native soil," and, in fact, the rural immigrants have enacted their love of the land to the extent that they are, as a group, some of the largest producers of Canadian wheat in Alberta and Ontario.

Marynka eventually remarried. Her new spouse was Michael Paidak, a Serbian immigrant, who became surrogate father to Stefan. With Michael's help, Marynka "not only managed to survive, but with an uncanny instinct, innate intelligence, and the sheer sweat of labor, insured that her child received love, comfort, and the opportunities of the finest education and teaching available."[6] The greater part of this education was musical and the first notes learned were sounded inside the Ukrainian community.

"Everyone got into music," recalls Toronto violinist Elsie Babiak, a child of Ukrainian immigrants who grew up around the corner from the Staryks. "It was the thing to do and it was how the community expressed itself. We all played in the community orchestras as well as studying dance, singing, and reading and writing in Ukrainian."

Though one of his first toys was a tin violin "bought at the Woolworth's on Queen and Yonge," Staryk's earliest musical interest lay elsewhere: "I wanted to play the accordion, but my mother, in her shrewd peasant way, wasted no time investigating the options. She concluded that as an accordion player my future lay in weddings and wakes." The violin was Marynka's choice for her son and with the assistance of Michael Paidak, an instrument was secured for Stefan: "He and his wife recognized the boy's precocious gifts when he was seven," reported the Toronto *Daily Star* in February of 1957. "The father worked on a tobacco plantation near Delhi, Ontario during the six-week harvesting to make enough to buy Stevie his first violin . . ."

Playing the violin represented a path away from the blue collar existence of most Ukrainian immigrants. "They saw the neighborhood teacher as a man who wore a white shirt, as a man who had a better existence than the factory workers," Staryk recalls. "To them, it was a respectable, if limited, job. They never talked about becoming a 'concert violinist.'" In this respect, the Ukrainian mothers may not have been as savvy as their Jewish counterparts at that time, or as their Korean counterparts today, but they did instill a durable work-ethic in their children. Elsie Babiak remembers, "Our mothers were working — they didn't have time to be stage mothers, pushing us from the wings! But they made sure that they knew what the teachers wanted, they kept us neatly dressed for all the concerts, and they made us practice, by threat if necessary!"

Staryk's first teacher was a fellow Ukrainian, a young violinist named John Moskalyk. Since he lived in the same neighborhood as Staryk and shared a common language and culture, he proved accessible to Marynka as she accompanied Stefan to his lessons and listened to the instructions given. The outbreak of World War II interrupted Staryk's training. But as Moskalyk prepared to depart Toronto to join the Canadian military, he advised Marynka to enroll Staryk at the Royal Conservatory and arranged his further studies with Elie Spivak.

Spivak, also of Ukrainian descent, left his homeland early in his life for studies in France. He was the concertmaster of the Toronto Symphony Orchestra (TSO) and well respected for his ability as a soloist and chamber musician. But despite Spivak's qualifications, Marynka was ill at ease with her son's new teacher. In contrast to her relationship with Moskalyk, she experienced difficulties relating to Spivak, whose early education in France and England had distanced him from his Ukrainian roots.[7] On top of this, Spivak was expensive: "The fee for ten half-hour lessons with Spivak was $40.00, while down the hall, another violin instructor, Chris Daffef, was teaching the same number of lessons for $15.00"[8] After ten lessons with Spivak, Staryk switched to Daffef.

Daffef began his musical career on the mandolin and didn't receive formal training until he reached Toronto from his native Bulgaria. After attending the conservatory of the Hambourg brothers in Toronto, "he began teaching door to door like a musical traveling salesman, but by the time Staryk came to him in the early forties, Daffef was well established, conducting the Macedonian and Ukrainian orchestras. From those orchestras came many of his students; at one time he had a class of 72 pupils at the Conservatory."[9] Daffef was an imposing teacher who once said of his own teaching, "I was hollering too much." Staryk has to agree: "Fear is what I remember, one hell of a lot of fear." Staryk kept a busy schedule with Daffef. There was language class, folk dancing, orchestral music, mandolin; Staryk remembers that he was "continually coming or going: reading, writing, dancing, plucking, or bowing."

With the heightened activity came a greater awareness of an extended musical community. Through the influence of his peers Staryk discovered Heifetz: "The first time I heard about Heifetz was at a Ukrainian Orchestra rehearsal at around age ten or eleven." When asked if he had heard Heifetz in performance, Staryk replied "Who?" The interrogator leapt on this opportunity: "My God, you study violin and you don't know who Heifetz is!?"

"How embarrassing! I began to listen, and to be much more aware of what was going on." What was going on at that time was radio: Toscanini and the NBC orchestra, the New York Philharmonic and opera at the Met, all of which contributed to Staryk's musical growth.

In 1947, the year he turned fifteen, the year he performed Mendelssohn's Violin Concerto in E minor, the year he won all the available scholarships in town to finance his conservatory training, Staryk felt it was time to switch teachers. He had three options at the conservatory: Elie Spivak, who had trained at the Paris Conservatoire and with Adolph Brodsky; Kathleen Parlow, a student of Leopold Auer; or Geza de Kresz, the former concertmaster of the Berlin Philharmonic under Nikisch. Each studio had its star pupil and the interclass politics were lively.

Staryk chose to once again study with Elie Spivak. This caused some hard feelings between Staryk and Daffef. (The experience was painful enough that Staryk has since been wary of the teacher/student relationship, establishing an atmosphere of independence between himself and his own students.) But the change seemed an absolute necessity to Staryk, especially after an incident that took place just prior to an April 1947 recital. The young Staryk, auditioning for a position in the conservatory orchestra, played for the school's principal and orchestra conductor, Ettore Mazzoleni, and failed the audition.

Staryk's training under Daffef had consisted largely of the romantic violin literature and basic technique; the bulk of the orchestral repertoire was left unaddressed. The audition for Mazzoleni alerted Staryk to the gaps in his education: "I became aware that my training, that the music I was primarily being exposed to, was not what I would have to sit down and play in a symphony orchestra, an opera orchestra, or practically any kind of orchestra." At this point, Staryk began the transition from student to autodidact: "After his disappointing audition, Staryk took responsibility for himself, doing his own research on all the orchestral excerpts, studying them with the same attention he gave the solo repertoire. Making lists, borrowing parts from the library, practicing, listening, Staryk prepared himself thoroughly. He never again failed an audition."[10]

Staryk progressed rapidly under the serious and courteous, if somewhat detached, Spivak. In addition to intensive work on the solo repertoire, Staryk remembers excellent chamber music coachings with cellist Isaac Mammot.

But Staryk's intense focus on his musical training inevitably created difficulties in the area of his general education as a high school student at Harbord Collegiate. Family and friends advised Staryk, for obvious practical reasons, to make the violin a hobby while pursuing another profession, but Staryk was set in his course and struck a compromise in which he left Harbord for night classes at Jarvis Collegiate. Within this arrangement, Staryk could devote his days to the violin.

"Most of his time, however, was spent either practicing or listening to music," writes Setterfield, "he was refining his technique, playing solo recitals whenever and wherever possible . . . Staryk and friends appeared all over the province, Cornwall, Simcoe, North Bay, gaining experience and collecting their first professional reviews."

Staryk's first major solo appearance was with the conservatory orchestra conducted by Mazzoleni in venerable Massey Hall, Toronto's equivalent to New York's Carnegie, on May 3, 1949. He played the first movement of the Paganini Concerto in D Major. A critic for the *Toronto Daily Star* reported that "A lad of 16 played with brilliance and feeling . . . The feat could be roughly compared to executing a ballet dance on a tight rope. The work is a veritable obstacle race which Staryk negotiated with a rare facility for one so young. When he came to the famous melody of the first movement, he gave it the melting sweetness it demands. The crowd applauded wildly."[11] Although an opportunity for significant exposure, the performance was undertaken at some personal expense to the performer, since Staryk normally played dinner and dance music from ten to one in the morning at the St. Regis Hotel in Toronto each evening, and was obliged to pay union wages to a replacement violinist.

Having established his name in the Toronto musical scene, Staryk, now seventeen, was again faced with choices regarding his education. His first priority was clearly practicing his instrument but this was followed closely by the necessity of making money: "I was helping my parents pay off debts, my George Heinl (circa 1948) violin, and the house mortgage." Supplementing the hotel job, Staryk played in the Toronto Philharmonic summer Promenade Concerts. After this, as time allowed, came schoolwork. The option of advancing into the Royal Conservatory's Senior School offered no prospect of significant musical advancement, and traditional education held no interest for him, so Staryk departed from the formal educational scene altogether.

"I graduated from nowhere," he says. "I quit academic and musical institutions and was looking for a more realistic and practical direction."

This orientation toward what is "real," basic, and honest came to characterize every aspect of Staryk's life and music making; it appears in his choice of fingerings, in his stage presence, in his relations with students.

Staryk's search for private instruction widened his circle of acquaintances. He met Paul Scherman, the assistant conductor of the TSO, who took an interest in the young violinist and pointed him toward New York. Radio broadcasts out of this city had introduced Staryk to a violinist named Oscar Shumsky, who played occasionally on NBC's *Firestone Hour*. It was to Shumsky that Staryk first directed inquiries. An audition was arranged in an empty NBC studio with Shumsky at the piano. Staryk played and was accepted.

Shumsky is one of those fiddlers who plays like a famous violinist but isn't. Somehow the necessary connections were not made and the man exists as living proof that simply playing amazingly well is not enough. "He was probably the first outstanding example of someone at that level that I was aware of who was unrecognized," says Staryk. Though relatively unknown, Shumsky proved to be the right influence for Staryk and the atmosphere of New York provided the spark of excitement: "I remember thinking, this is the big time, this is New York."

Despite the long distances to travel for lessons, Staryk chose to remain at home. "I decided it was easier to continue working in Toronto: it was cheaper and there were fewer distractions. I'd make the trip for the lesson, then come back and practice like mad until the next time . . ." Returning from Shumsky's home, Staryk would write extensive notes to himself on the lesson just past. Staryk credits many violinists as influences on his playing, and Shumsky stands out among them: "His influence was strong violinistically and was what I needed at the time. In all I had about fifteen two or three hour lessons; they came to an end when I suddenly had immigration problems, but they were good sessions. He is a great fiddle player, especially for romantic fiddle music." However, Shumsky's facility as a fiddler was not a guarantee of profound stylistic understanding: "Stylistically, for Mozart, Bach, and Beethoven, for instance, I would question his interpretation. He was a Russian Kreisler then, perhaps he has changed since."

Continuing his quest for more and better work in Toronto, Staryk eventually auditioned for the TSO, though he very nearly missed the opportunity. Staryk was sitting in a rehearsal of the Promenade Orchestra when he was informed that Sir Ernest MacMillan was expecting him at that moment for an audition. Having received no notice of the audition, Staryk nonetheless excused himself from rehearsal and rushed to Massey Hall. "They were probably sorry I turned up since I was just one more to hear; but I began with the Paganini concerto, playing with a vengeance. Then they gave me the Tchaikovsky Serenade and an assortment of orchestral excerpts. It was one of those days when everything just came off. I felt terrific and played up a storm, feeling very cocky. I was so flip about it that when they gave me *Don Juan*, I shut the book and went through the first page by memory."

Assistant concertmaster and conductor Paul Scherman recalls, "Steve came in looking very shy, even suspicious. When he started to play it was exciting and refreshing. The Paganini was enough to convince me that he was the one . . ."

Staryk was not immediately given a position, but neither was he forgotten, for within the year he was seated in the second violin section. A season later, he sat with the firsts; he was occupying the fifth stand when he lost his job.

Five other TSO members joined him in this fate: double-bass players Ruth Budd, Abe Manheim, and William Kuinka, principal flutist Dirk Keetbaas, and violinist John Moskalyk (Staryk's former teacher, whose surname was, in an untimely manner, anglicized to Moscow). The six were not fired outright, but their yearly contracts for the 1952-53 season were simply left unrenewed; oddly enough, these Canadians had become the victims of an American political disease.

AMERICAN COLD-WAR POLITICS
AND THE TORONTO SYMPHONY SIX

*Politics is the diversion of trivial men who, when they succeed
at it, become important in the eyes of more trivial men.*
                                    - George Jean Nathan

*It behooves every man who values liberty of conscience for
himself, to resist invasions of it in the case of others; or their
case may, by change of circumstances, become his own.*

                                    - Thomas Jefferson

American border officials in the 1950s were empowered by the McCarren-
Walter Act to discern between foreigners who were acceptable applicants
for entry into the country, and those who posed a threat. According to
the stipulations of the Act, officials could limit alien access to the States
on the basis of the applicant's political belief or *suspected* political belief
without supporting evidence. This rather haphazard tightening of the
nation's borders was only a symptom of America's developing paranoia.
Xenophobia characterized the popular mind-set and infected the political
climate in Washington.

In fact, Washington was buzzing with intrigue and intrigue's unsavory
residue, suspicion. Richard Nixon, then a House member, had recently
interrogated Alger Hiss before the House Un-American Activities Committee; President Truman, in an Executive Order, requested loyalty oaths
from government employees; Ethel and Julius Rosenberg were later tried
and put to death (1953) for selling military secrets to the Soviets. Americans suspected that Soviet hydrogen bomb tests would mature into a
nuclear offensive against the West; China and Czechoslovakia had recently fallen to communism, and it looked as though South Korea would
soon follow. Then, somewhere in the middle of this furor, a Junior Senator from Wisconsin, Joseph McCarthy, stepped into the whir and flash of
press cameras to announce that he was in possession of a list of 205 card-
carrying communists at that time employed in governmental positions in
the capitol.

Through Senate hearings, McCarthy spun webs of slander to satisfy America's thirst for identifiable enemies. The American people's response to McCarthy's red-hunt was overwhelming. The postal service

brought large bags of support mail daily to McCarthy's senate office. However, despite his precipitous rise to power, McCarthy's influence was short-lived and ended with his censure on December 2nd, 1954 with almost unanimous repudiation and derision from his colleagues in the Senate. Dejected and despised, McCarthy drank heavily. But before his death in 1957 due to liver failure, McCarthy had ended thousands of political, artistic, academic, and governmental careers through the heavily publicized Senate hearings and through blacklisting.

Back home

Sir Ernest MacMillan was carefully grooming the TSO for wider recognition, and essential to this in his view was international touring. In the Spring of 1952, when an opportunity arose to travel south of the border to Detroit, Michigan for an appearance the following November, he and the TSO management set about making preparations.

Trouble arose when standard visa applications for six of the Canadian musicians were turned down. The United States Immigration Service ruled that their presence in America would be "detrimental to the best interests of the country." Though not directly stated, the understanding was that the six were suspected of communist affiliations.

At an April 21st board meeting (which MacMillan did not attend), Jack Elton, the orchestra's manager, presented the management's response to the American prohibition: the TSO would fulfill the November engagement in Detroit with new members occupying the seats of the six suspect musicians. His rationale and, by extension, MacMillan's, was that "for artistic reasons there could be no substitutes for such an important concert, leading, as it might, to other American engagements." This, in spite of affirmations by Elton that "they are good instrumentalists, they have violated no Canadian laws, and there is no evidence that they are security risks." Staryk recalls hearing of his dismissal via the grapevine and through the press, never having been confronted directly by either Elton or MacMillan.

Both the Toronto Musician's Association (T.M.A.), then headed by president Walter Murdoch, and the American Federation of Musicians (A.F. of M.) stood in solidarity with the TSO. Murdoch, who was known for his dictatorial leadership style and anti-Communist leanings, found no shame in hiding behind the letter of the law in dealing with Staryk and his colleagues. The TSO's practice of hiring musicians on a yearly basis made it a technically clean and painless task to dismiss musicians, though there was generally an understanding between management and the players that those musicians in good standing could operate under an assumption of security. However, in a transparent evasion of more pertinent questions, Murdoch presented this aspect of TSO housecleaning to the press as "a straight contractual matter. The federation has always been keen on keeping contracts, but there is nothing wrong in the orchestra's not rehiring musicians."

Hollywood

Musicians were not the only artists to be affected by McCarthy era sentiment. Actors, writers, and directors in America's entertainment capitol also came under close scrutiny and persecution. The familiarity of their names, names like Bertolt Brecht, Charlie Chaplin, and Jules Dassin (*Never on Sunday*), is a reminder that none were immune to the political spirit of the times.

The events that took place in Hollywood in the 1940s and early 50s were in part a reaction to the fashionable political stance of writers, artists, and musicians in the 1930s. As George Orwell wrote in 1940, "it was considered eccentric in literary circles not to be more or less 'left.'" The instability of the political climate of those years did not elude Orwell's critical pen. "The Comintern slogans suddenly faded from red to pink," he observed, "'World revolution' and 'Social-Fascism' gave way to 'Defense of Democracy' and 'Stop Hitler' . . . Since then, of course, there has been yet another change of 'line.' But what is important is that it was during the 'anti-Fascist' phase that the younger English writers gravitated towards Communism." Jaap, a character in Harry Mulisch's book *The Assault*, describes his wartime affiliations in this way: "I'm no Communist, by the way. I'm an anti-Fascist. But because Communism is the greatest enemy of Fascism, I happen to be anti-anti Communist, that's for certain."

What was once a defensible political and intellectual stance — a shift to the Communist left against the rise of fascism across Germany, Austria, Italy, and Spain in the 30s — was viewed with suspicion by American propagandists of the Cold War in the late 40s and early 50s. The intelligentsia which had turned to Communism during the Spanish Civil War and the anti-fascist period had, for the most part, turned to other interests by the time the House Un-American Activities Committee (HUAC) organized hearings in Hollywood.

Emulating HUAC's original activities in Hollywood in the 1940s,

McCarthy's adherents returned to Hollywood in the 50s to conduct hearings under the HUAC umbrella, bringing the already beleaguered entertainment capitol under the spell of the junior Senator's necromancy. In a Los Angeles *Daily News* article, Janet Weeks describes HUAC's influence on the life of the late actor Will Geer, who played the part of Grandpa in the television series *The Waltons*. "A former union organizer, he had been labeled a 'subversive' by followers of Senator Joseph McCarthy," writes Weeks. "Geer's refusal to cooperate with the committee effectively destroyed his film career. His wife left him, he lost his home in Santa Monica and was forced to work as a gardener to make ends meet." The article goes on to mention some of Hollywood's best actors and writers, including Zero Mostel and Dalton Trumbo, "who spent ten months in a federal prison. Ironically, Trumbo won an Academy Award for the 1956 screenplay *The Brave One*, which he was forced to write under the alias Robert Rich."

Dalton Trumbo had a number of aliases, all formulated after his confrontation with HUAC, as one of the so-called Hollywood Ten. The ten men were known to be some of the most creative minds in their field and included seven screenwriters, two directors, and a producer: Alvah Bessie, Herbert Biberman, Lester Cole, Edward Dmytryk, Ring Lardner, Jr., John Howard Lawson, Albert Maltz, Samuel Ornitz, Adrian Scott, and Trumbo.

HUAC's proceedings were conducted by House Republican J. Parnell Thomas and began with the questioning of "friendly" witnesses. These were high-profile Hollywood figures, such as Ronald Reagan, Elia Kazan and Gary Cooper, who the committee could count on to give the right answers and who would draw the public's attention to the televised hearings. Novelist Ayn Rand appeared as one of the committee's "friendlies." Some of them adroitly named names when asked, and a Hollywood blacklist materialized, published as the "Red Channels" list.

The "unfriendly" witnesses included the Ten. It was necessary for the committee to publicly defeat these men in order to remove the core of intellectual resistance from the industry they were attempting to dominate.

But, as it turned out, this was a difficult task. Before arriving in Washington for the hearings, the ten had consolidated into a unit and agreed among themselves to use the protection of the Fifth Amendment to protest what they felt was an infringement upon their First Amendment rights to freedom of expression and political belief. During the course of the proceedings the ten dissenters were repeatedly disallowed in their attempts to read prepared statements in their own defense, and the hearings deteriorated into shouting matches punctuated by Thomas's pounding gavel.

The Ten were eventually indicted for contempt of congress and sentenced to spend from ten to twelve months in Federal Prison. The entire proceeding succeeded, as intended, in adding to the climate of fear and suspicion already existing in America. It strengthened support of the government's Cold War stance and helped pave the way for general acceptance of the Korean War. On an individual basis, it at least temporarily inflated political careers, perhaps most notably or lastingly that of committee member Richard Nixon.

Fear

The firing of the six TSO members was clear evidence that the pallor of suspicion and distrust permeating the United States was now seeping into Canada. Violinist Morry Kernerman, at that time a CBC staff musician, described the spirit of the times as "terribly conformist. People so often seemed afraid . . . and the people in control in this country perpetuated it. Oh, they all *said* it was terrible, but they did nothing to stop it."[12]

Fear which resided at the apex of political power was amplified among those who had reason to fear the loss of their ability to earn a livelihood. Blacklisted double-bassist Ruth Budd, one of the six, remembers the sudden shift in her relations with other musicians: "People with whom I'd been quite friendly . . . if they were walking on the same side of the street as I was, they'd cross the street in order not to be seen talking to me. They were really frightened."[13] Passing the women's dressing room one day, Budd overheard the comment, "She must be a Communist. Do you see how much she reads?"[14]

Even the conductor of the TSO, Sir Ernest MacMillan, must have been worried. Though it is unlikely that he was in any danger of losing his position, MacMillan probably did not want to broadcast information about his past to the American public, the intended audience of his fateful tour, or to his contacts with American orchestras and concert halls. In the mid-forties, MacMillan had been a member of the National Council for Canadian-Soviet Friendship. He subsequently resigned from the Council and distanced himself from other left-leaning groups like the Canadian Artists Assembly for Peace. In December 1950, MacMillan was invited to conduct an orchestra and singers at United Nations headquarters in New York. Anticipating trouble at the border, MacMillan paved the way for this stateside visit by confessing his former involvement with the Council for Canadian-Soviet Friendship in a letter to the American consulate in Toronto. "I need hardly say that I am not a Communist and have no sympathy with present Communist aims and that I have disassociated myself with the Council."[15] MacMillan was promptly assured that he would be welcomed at the border. In possession of considerable power and personally acquainted with the political dangers of the times, MacMillan was in an excellent position to help the Symphony Six retain their jobs.

Before the Law

Staryk was initially counseled to visit the Royal Canadian Mounted Police (RCMP). "I was advised to get 'cleared.' In order to do that, I was told one had to go to the RCMP. I went to the RCMP but was told they couldn't clear me. An officer, who was very polite, even told me that he had a relative in the Mendelssohn Choir [Sir Ernest's brainchild]. This RCMP officer said, 'If we cleared you and refused clearance to others it would imply that you were O.K. but others were not.' This kind of response was extremely frustrating because I was studying during this time in the States with Shumsky, and was constantly traveling back and forth between New York and Toronto." At first, Staryk was only temporarily barred from the States, pending hearings to determine whether a visa could be issued.

The hearings themselves took place at the American consulate in Toronto. Staryk remembers that "it was a grueling experience with a power-drunk official at the consulate. I was the youngest of the Six and I think he was hoping to get the list of all those 'reds under the beds' out of me. I was possibly the most vulnerable, the most naive, but I had nothing to offer. He repeatedly questioned me, asking for names, information, anything! He couldn't understand that I had never been a member of any organization except the A. F. of M. and the public library, the two institutions that I belonged to requiring me to carry a card!" Knowing that he was innocent and unable to finance a private attorney, Staryk did not hire a lawyer to represent him and balked at the apparent admission of guilt that using a civil liberties lawyer might signify.

Was the young Steven Staryk a communist in the fifties? No, but he was part of an ethnic minority, a first generation Ukrainian, and American officials were concerned about Staryk's contact with left-leaning factions within his community. In the west-central area of Toronto where he grew up, communist candidates had been a legitimate part of the political scene for years. This was quite normal as ideologies of the left, whether communism or socialism, offered Ukrainian emigrants something better than the *status quo*.

Staryk's parents survived under foreign rule in Western Ukraine and came to Canada to seek the opportunity to earn money for food, clothing, and a family shelter. "This was not the American Dream of 2.5 children, a dog and a cat," muses Staryk. However, despite Canada's open invitation and promise of plenty, North America had little more to offer than had the Ukraine. The governments of both countries offered little hope or assistance, and alternative sources of help were sought out of necessity.

One alternative which promised bread on the table as well as education and health care was socialism. "Whatever interest my family showed for leftist principles stemmed from purely emotional and physical needs and were in no way based on theoretical insight. My father and mother arrived in this country [Canada], a 'land of milk and honey,' in the middle of the depression. My father committed suicide as a result of endless unemployment and the frustration of having been misled into emigrating to a country where he was not even able to support his family.

"What anyone in the family believed was due to circumstances. People became very cynical. You gave up going to church because organized religion didn't help. The government didn't help. The fact of no bread on the table was more convincing than the fiction of 'pie in the sky.' There were protests because, at that time, it was the only thing left to do. My God, protests were going on all over the place because there was no work and no bread! It was the depression! Perhaps we were forewarned by the history of governing bodies and should have remembered Marie Antoinette's advice, 'let them eat cake.' Or there's the Italian proverb which, in juxtaposition to the Bible's 'He that humbles himself shall be exalted,' warns: 'He that makes himself a sheep shall be eaten by the wolf.' Is it surprising that one becomes cynical?

"I was involved emotionally with a Ukrainian community. I had my early education there. I learned the ethnic art of folk-dancing, language, writing and reading, simple kid's stories, and music. I played in the orchestra, I danced, I performed solos on the violin.

"I played everywhere. I was a youngster with some talent which comes with a necessary desire to perform, and therefore played whenever I got the opportunity. I performed for a lot of ethnic and religious groups: Ukrainian, Polish, Jewish, Macedonian, etc., in halls, in churches, and for any organization where music was supposedly appreciated, including the Red Cross. I was seeking stage experience, and opportunities to perform new repertoire as is only natural in the performing arts, and it appears to have been beneficial to my career. But politically, there was nothing. I didn't know about politics, nor was I brainwashed in this respect. They were a kid's years."

Staryk played frequently within the Ukrainian community and elsewhere and he had been the subject of a number of newspaper reviews. A diligent employee of the American immigration service collected these reviews (most likely with the help of the RCMP and/or other factions of the Ukrainian community) and pasted them neatly together. "They had an excellent scrap book of me — every time I had played for an ethnic occasion. They had all the clippings, reviews, my picture, everything. My personal scrap book was never good (past and present) and I had never bothered to include ethnic clippings, knowing these were of little use in a professional *curriculum vitae*. I should have *invented something* just to get the scrap book!"

Shuffled in among these clippings was an account of an Ukrainian event at which the young Staryk played a movement of the Mendelssohn concerto. Quite in contrast to his accuser's suspicions, Staryk as a fourteen-year-old seems to have been lacking in political savvy. "One of the Ukrainian concerts turned out to be an anniversary for Lenin. At the time I wasn't concerned about the event itself; it was an opportunity to play in Massey Hall, Canada's Carnegie Hall! I played the first or third movement of the Mendelssohn, so I must have been fourteen years old. That was the Mendelssohn year in my studies. The only reason I know now that it was a Lenin memorial is because of the interrogation."

The final decision of the American consulate in the case of Canadian violinist Steven Staryk, was "barred for life," from entry into the States.

The assistance of MacMillan, at first a tacit assumption for the Six, never materialized. Staryk found that "during this period, people like MacMillan were a total loss. Prior to that point, despite ample opportunity, he had not helped me in any manner in my career, and then in a matter of such grave consequences, where you think a man of such stature would do something, he did nothing!"

MacMillan, through his silence, had coolly separated his interests from those of the Six. This choice was odd, since in the realm of social and personal ethics, he seemed irreproachable. Responding to a letter of thanks from UN Secretary Trygve Lie, following an engagement to perform parts of the *Messiah* at UN headquarters, MacMillan wrote: "It seemed to me a most valuable reminder of the ultimate values that we must keep in mind in these troubled times."

In 1955, MacMillan spoke publicly of unity: "In music, whatever our origins, we speak one language and share the expression of thoughts and feelings common to all mankind. In the world of commerce and politics, divergent interests may make for division; in the world of Arts, the universality of human nature makes for union — the true Brotherhood of Man."[16]

But in 1953, Steven Staryk was out of work and struggling with an ulcer condition. Not surprisingly, he found MacMillan's "union" divisive, his "Brotherhood" alienating, and the man himself, in some respects, contemptible. "He was a knowledgeable musician who was very good with choirs and as an organist. He was an outstanding musicologist and could read a score with understanding. He was not, however, an orchestral man with a background of orchestral discipline or training. Nor was he a personality like Sir Thomas Beecham. Not quite a Beecham, as Toronto was not quite a London! Sir Ernest wanted to take his orchestra, a minor league orchestra at that time, and conquer the world; it was part of the human frailty of the man, the ego, which, I suppose, is a necessary ingredient in a conductor, but in this case it was a delusion."

Had the TSO been ripe for a tour, the decision of management to release the six players might have had more weight, and MacMillan's ambitions would have been something more than fantasy. Staryk summarizes the situation in this way: "To create out of an orchestra a major touring attraction requires the combination of a great personality, a major recording contract, and a touring schedule which includes major music centers (all accompanied by plenty of P. R. and hype!). Lacking these elements, the tour could just as well have been canceled without harming the existing status of the orchestra."

Precedent eases the way for imitation. During preparations for American tours in the early fifties, the Concertgebouw of Amsterdam was twice denied visa applications for some of its members. Conductor, board, and orchestra members supported the individual players by canceling the tour. Their actions spoke of integrity and solidarity: all or nothing.

In 1954 the Concertgebouw chose to compromise their politics on American soil, but retained their integrity in their homeland and on other points of the tour. Still unable to obtain visas for all members of the orchestra, the Concertgebouw traveled on an American tour with replacements for those players whom U. S. border officials felt posed a security risk; these remained at home on full pay. Ironically, when the tour left the States and reached Massey Hall in Toronto, the missing members walked onstage as a unit to rejoin the orchestra proper and received a standing ovation from their colleagues.

Admittedly, the Concertgebouw enjoyed prestige and was in a more comfortable position to make choices on principle. The TSO was struggling for recognition and foreign engagements. But the Netherlanders made an impression that the TSO would have done well to note, an impression that their politics were based on strong ethical underpinnings rather than deference to expediency or timely impulses toward self-preservation. MacMillan's decision not to support the Six displayed and perpetuated Canada's deferential political relationship to the U.S.; it exacerbated the already troublesome image of Canada as just another northern state, and gave the Canadian people, collectively, little hope that their rights to security and fairness would be defended in a similar instance.

In his biography, *Sir Ernest MacMillan: The Importance of Being Canadian*, author Ezra Schabas claims that the conductor sent two letters of appeal to the American consulate in Toronto, specifically on Staryk's behalf.[17] MacMillan never spoke of this to Staryk, and Schabas, whom Staryk knows personally, never contacted Staryk to confirm MacMillan's claim. At least one question arises: why would MacMillan defend the twenty-year-old Staryk, a fifth-chair violinist, without putting in a word for his ousted principle flutist, Dirk Keetbaas, another of the Six? Schabas's book deals with the Symphony Six incident, as well as other potentially problematic topics, only in passing.

Rebuked by MacMillan's silence, the Six turned to the local musician's association, which had previously allied itself with the TSO management. Would Toronto Local 149 of the A. F. of M. reconsider their decision to support orchestra management? No. The decision of the union was final, or rather, pre-ordained. Walter J. Murdoch, president of the Toronto Local, was hand in glove with James Caesar Petrillo, American A. F. of M. boss. As Canadian representative on the international Executive Board, Murdoch held close to the party line, sunk Canadian interests into the larger American pool, and took to heart certain clauses in the bylaws of the international organization which urged the union to "purge its membership of all subversive elements." Genuflection and blacklisting were not exclusively American activities.

The A. F. of M. and the TSO had developed a working relationship before the Symphony Six incident occurred. There was once a professional musician's union in Canada — the Canadian Federation of Musicians. In a move to protect his turf, Petrillo broke this union by ruling that no A. F. of M. member could perform on the same stage with a C. F. of M. musician. The TSO relied on big-name artists from the A.F. of M. in America to draw the public into Massey Hall, and so the Canadian union was destroyed with the help of Canadians.

Petrillo's hostile influence and Murdoch's partisanship convinced Staryk and his colleagues that pushing their case too strongly would have endangered the Six's chances for significant employment anywhere in North America. "The union was useless," says Staryk. "If we had pushed this any further we might have been expelled. The whole matter became very dangerous." A halfhearted appeal was made to the International Executive Board of the A. F. of M., which was rejected, and the pursuit of assistance in that quarter was abandoned.

The debate

There were several distinguished individuals and groups in Toronto who witnessed the plight of the Symphony Six and responded with direct action. Staryk remembers that "there was a committee formed. I recall certain people, like Gordon Sinclair, who were quite outspoken in supporting us. A. Y. Jackson, one of the 'Group of Seven' artists, attempted to come to our aid. I remember going down to his studio in Rosedale Valley, a studio built by Lawren Harris in 1913, where we had one of the meetings."

The committee Staryk remembers was the Toronto Committee for the Symphony Six, headed by Langford Dixon. Other committee members included musician Harry Adaskin, writer B. K. Sandwell, broadcaster/writer Gordon Sinclair, and, as mentioned, painters Lawren Harris and A. Y. Jackson. Gwenlyn Setterfield, a member of the Ontario Arts Council who is familiar with Staryk's career and this political entanglement, wrote on the topic: "The Committee solicited support from various organizations including church groups and the Association for Civil Liberties. Their brochure outlined the facts of the case, and an accompanying letter signed by Sandwell appealed to the sense of public responsibility of all Canadians to protest 'one of the most blatant examples of an ever-growing totalitarianism that threatens our Canadian way of life. By voicing our objection on an occasion like this we will determine whether Canadian democracy is to function or not.' Through its mailings and in newspaper advertisements explaining the plight of the Six, the Committee asked people specifically to write to the Board of Directors of the Symphony urging them to rescind the suspensions."[18]

Staryk himself worked feverishly, as Setterfield notes: "He had not touched the violin for months, as he tried to contact anyone who might be in a position to influence management. He worked from morning to night, licking stamps, addressing envelopes, getting up petitions, attending meetings . . ." Staryk remembers that "during the period itself, of course, many things happened to me — much that was depressing and negative, but also some that was good and positive. I did a hell of a lot of thinking and reading, more than I had ever done or thought to do, and I met a lot of interesting people, people who had character and guts, people who did stand up, aside from their political beliefs, for what they felt was right."

Setterfield goes on to mention that the committee did not succeed in garnering support from the important cultural institutions: "The Royal Conservatory of Music, for example, with which all of the Six had been connected, as teachers, students or performers, or in all three roles, took no public stand on their behalf." A few prominent individuals in the area, such as Dr. R. S. K. Seeley, Provost of Trinity College at the University of Toronto (stating that he would "henceforth forego the pleasure of hearing the TSO, as long as the directors insisted on putting dollars before principle"), and Canadian Senator Eugene Forsey, voiced their disapproval of the action. But on the whole, the public response lacked tenacity and eventually gave way to the inevitable forces of complacency and time.

In the press

The press made the dispute a topic of discussion in the editorial pages. The *Globe and Mail*, for May 22, 1952 printed an editorial which acknowledged the complexity of the issues, yet sided with the Six and lobbied for some action on the part of the Canadian government: "The choice made by the TSO was the only one it, reasonably, could make. But that by no means justifies the whole train of events. Because of the U.S. Government's stated policy in these matters, it will be commonly assumed that the six musicians concerned are tainted with communism or some other harmful ideology . . . That would be damaging enough in any case. In this case, it has had the additional effect of putting them out of work in their own country." The editorial concludes, "If any of these people have been done an injustice, it has been done to them by Washington. If that injustice is to be remedied, it must be remedied by Ottawa."

The editors of an American publication, *The Nation* (June 14, 1952), also wrote in support of the Six. "This seems to us about the most shameful in the growing list of indignities occasioned by the McCarren Act and the paranoid policies of the State Department. It is bad enough that six men [apologies to Ms. Ruth Budd] have been done a grave personal injustice; it is worse that no practical remedy is available . . . Incidents such as that of the Toronto six make it increasingly embarrassing for Americans to speak sneeringly of other countries' 'iron curtains.'"

A Canadian magazine, *Saturday Night*, on June 7th, 1952, complained that the employability of Canadian citizens was being determined by an entity other than their own government: "The idea that a certificate of admissibility into the United States thus becomes a condition of membership in the TSO, and even worse, that a refusal of admission to the United States becomes sufficient reason for dismissal from the TSO, seems to us fatal to good relationships between the orchestra management and its players. It means that all the players hold their positions simply by grace of the U.S. Department of Immigration; an authority before which they cannot appear to defend themselves, and which has no responsibility for doing them justice." Toronto's own *Daily Star*, on August 28, 1952, focused on the issue of management and employee relations, stating that: "The prestige of the TSO is being jeopardized in Canada and the United States among people who place high value on moral responsibility and loyalty between employers and employees."

But support for the Six was not universal. One *Globe and Mail* editorial by Frank Tumpane, entitled "Some Nerve" began: "For a flagrant example of consummate gall, you need search no further than the statement issued by the six musicians whose contracts were not renewed by the Toronto Symphony Orchestra."[19] Tumpane felt that the six, in asserting that the TSO should refuse its U.S. engagements on their behalf and as a point of principle, were acting on the impulse of "unadulterated selfishness." Tumpane tacitly equates the six to "Communist members of Toronto's Board of Education," and to certain union officials of the same ilk. He concludes with some thinly veiled slander: "Canadians enter the United States as a privilege and not as a right. If they are the type that are not welcome in the United States, then keeping them out is the business of the United States." Tumpane's expression of assumed guilt was probably shared discreetly by many colleagues of the six musicians, while those who might have thought differently were intimidated into silence.

Maclean's Magazine of August 1, 1952, in what seems the most morally offended response, spoke out for common decency and fair tactics: "the arbitrary sentence on the unspecified charge is a standard device of thought-control and its dismal runningmate, guilt-by-association, and it is profoundly disquieting to find a great Canadian cultural institution running in such incongruous company."

Fractured mosaic

"I never had the feeling of being at home in Toronto," Staryk explains. "There was always a sense of being on the outer fringes. I was part of a first generation ethnic minority with no religious crutch to lean on, and apparently in the 'wrong camps' within our community. I managed (with assistance and guidance) to get into the 'wrong camps' even within the Conservatory. The Symphony Six incident was probably the culmination of personal and social insecurities. If there had been any possibility of feeling at home in Toronto or Canada as a whole, it seemed shattered."

Staryk's ethnic minority group, the Ukrainians, composed 2.66 percent of the Canadian population at the time of the Second World War. Of other minorities, Germans formed 4.04 percent of the population; Scandinavians, 2.13 percent; Netherlanders, 1.85 percent; Jews, 1.48 percent; Poles, 1.45 percent; and Italians 0.98 percent.[20] These groups, along with the British and French, formed what sociologists describe as Canada's ethnic mosaic. This notion of a mosaic, more realistic than the American paradigm of the melting pot, refers to the tendency of Canadian ethnic groups to remain distinct and to think of themselves, either by conscious choice or by the force of social reality (or some combination of the two), as separate entities.

On the surface, the Mosaic is appealing. It offers emigrants the chance to establish themselves in a new country with democratic ideals while retaining comforting elements of their separate national cultures. Ideally, all cultures would be seen as an enrichment of Canadian culture in general. In reality, minorities were met with fear, distrust, and resistance. "They worried about the displacement of 'good' Canadians by 'strangers,' and the consequent flow of the former to the United States; the gathering of the foreign (that is, non-British) in certain parts of the country, the western provinces and urban centres especially; the predominance of young men among most groups of immigrants; the capacity of the land to absorb new immigration; the self-imposed segregation of groups

. . . 'little nations within a nation,' where members were 'disposed to retain their mother tongue, maintain old customs, harbour ancient prejudices and make little educational progress.'"[21]

Wartime nationalism deepened the schism between the ruling majority and ethnic minorities. Chafing over issues of national security, Ottawa undertook to bring the "Ukrainian Canadians into line with the mainstream [by creating] a national coalition committee representing all the Ukrainian-Canadian nationalist organizations."[22] Within this condensed committee, each nationalist group held veto power, thus creating a structure that guaranteed the committee would always be deadlocked. The government's fear was based on the belief that the Ukrainians would align themselves with Nazi Germany if Berlin chose the tactic of helping the Ukrainians attain statehood. And following the Nazi invasion of Polish territories, it seemed the Germans were favoring Ukrainian separatists over the Poles in a policy aimed at dividing the Soviet empire.

The Canadian police force responded to this perceived Ukrainian threat by stepping up surveillance activities in the Ukrainian community. The RCMP found that, as prospects for a Ukrainian state improved, the battle within the Ukrainian community between nationalists and the Ukrainian left wing intensified; this was a polarization which Canadian officials felt would jeopardize the war effort since a majority of the Ukrainian working class was employed in the war industries. Rather than working to understand and tolerate Ukrainian grievances, Ottawa adopted a tactic of "direct action and threat," with the result that "the government's inconsistent intervention into the Ukrainian-Canadian community. . . [left] much of this population uncertain about the status and future of their community in the wider society. A chance to strengthen the process of nationbuilding was thus squandered, leaving aside the opportunity to nurture a genuine loyalty to Canada."[23]

It is within the bounds of this larger Ukrainian experience in Canada that Staryk's experience of the Symphony Six affair must be understood. This early Canadian experience also deepens our understanding of the decisions Staryk made in later life. "My experiences in life, starting early in my childhood, led to an inevitable feeling of distrust and insecurity in this world." Staryk turned down an offer to lead the Berlin Philharmonic at one point in his career and he cites the influence of his Toronto experience as the motivation behind his decision: "As a result of the Symphony Six, my whole attitude toward many things became much more fixed. Most importantly, I acquired a drive to set myself up as independently as possible, particularly economically, trusting nothing, be it state, church, or any institution. I developed a tremendous distrust of any authoritarian regimentation.

"As for my 'home town,' I harbor no special feelings or sentiment for Toronto; it does not hold for me a greater sense of security than any other place in the world. Toronto and Canada happen to be the city and country in which I was born, but ultimate and meaningful recognition, encouragement, and support came primarily from elsewhere."

Coming up for air

The TSO affair took Staryk's attention away from music and the violin for a number of months. At the end of this period, no nearer to a satisfactory resolution, Staryk returned to playing the violin. He describes the evolution of his anger following the consulate hearings: "I was enraged, reading, thinking, and dreaming of traveling to the Ukraine to resume my studies on the fiddle. It seemed an ideal plan, as once again a wave of string players was coming out of Russia: Oistrakh, Kogan, Bezrodny, Rostropovitch, etc. In retrospect it was obviously an emotional vendetta.

"Why or how it didn't materialize, I don't remember. The family was not in agreement and couldn't settle whether I should leave or stay, since employment in my profession was now in question. We didn't know whether there would be a general blacklisting.

"I remember getting advice from various people, including Albert Pratz (one of my former teachers, and a former concertmaster of the TSO). Albert simply told me 'Forget about it all. Don't read books, don't get involved, just play the fiddle.' This is probably a good recipe for a simple, uncomplicated life. I have managed to put into practice only half of this advice. I try not to get involved and play the fiddle, but, unfortunately, can't stop thinking or reading books! Fortunately, my questioning, thinking and reading has undergone some change for the better. The Symphony Six experience was a rude awakening and an unforgettable lesson in protective stupidity, one of very many ongoing lessons in how individuals will 'fiddle' with life. My experience with bureaucracy worldwide is summarized by Barbara Tuchman's observation: '. . . bureaucracy, safely repeating today what it did yesterday, rolls on ineluctably as some vast computer, which, once penetrated by error, duplicates it forever.'"[24]

PART TWO

Staryk in Canada
A History in Three Acts

ACT I
Early Professional Development

Recovering from the turmoil of the Symphony Six period, Staryk worked feverishly to establish a name for himself in Toronto's freelance scene: "Eventually I was jobbing around Toronto, whilst trying to decide what in hell to do. In time it all began to fade away, bit by bit, as I busily arranged lessons, chamber groups, and just did whatever came around. I remember doing concerts with various singers and instrumentalists and even a fan dancer on one memorable occasion, and in the meantime, practicing constantly. Eventually, more work came my way since there were a lot of freelance gigs around. It was a good period in that respect. I auditioned and played for practically everybody in the field; there were more auditions than performances."

The Canadian Broadcasting Corporation was an important part of Staryk's early career. "What saved me was primarily the CBC. I managed to make a living freelancing, most of which was CBC, for example the CBC Symphony, musical and dramatic programs etc., and some outside work (not always artistically desirable) which could include virtually anything from weddings to wakes.

"At first, the freelance CBC work wasn't doled out to me; I wasn't one of the club at the time, and no one was too sure after the TSO trouble whether people were still being blacklisted, even as fellow-travelers. Ivan Romanoff was one of the exceptions. As jobs drifted my direction, I was playing literally everything from soup to nuts. "Songs of my People," the "Stage" series, background music to plays, "Latin American Serenade," and occasionally some serious music. These were all CBC productions of that period.

"I can still remember a show with Sam Hersenhoren that went on all day Sundays, starting at ten in the morning. Of course, some people did not always get to sleep on Saturday night. I was immediately punished for my sins on Sunday by being forced to stay awake while relegated to the monotonous off-beat second fiddle parts. It was a different kind of 'musical training' I was receiving to compensate for my overabundance of 'superficial technique.'

"One of the more challenging CBC productions I took part in was the *Trans Canada Matinee*, a weekday afternoon show produced by Sir Ernest MacMillan's son, Keith. My role in the ongoing program, which was a sort of "music while you work" show, was to present a series of mini recitals accompanied by monologues written by Keith. It was fifteen minutes long and I would both play and talk: first I would play the quasi-commercial theme 'Estrellita' by Manuel Ponce, so as not to frighten off my audience, and then launch into the thick of the fiddle repertoire: Paganini, Sarasate, Kreisler, Wieniawski — violin world for violinists. It was fifteen minutes of panic playing with breathless talking in-between. I used to knock myself out preparing the stuff every week (in addition to the regular orchestral work). It was an opportune way to break-in nerves, gain facility and exposure, and even make a little money. Robert Spergel, with whom I enjoyed many years of music-making, was the pianist.

"Later, I was asked to join the new CBC Symphony Orchestra, organized by CBC music director Geoffrey Waddington. The group included both TSO members and freelance players and broadcast once a week during a forty week season. It was a very good orchestra, with interesting programs and conductors. I was *very content* sitting at the tail end of the first fiddles *without a stand partner*."

During his period with the CBC, Staryk gave a Sunday afternoon recital at the Art Gallery of Toronto, with pianist Emil Debusmann. More than 2,000 people arrived at the gallery to see the exhibits and hear the program, which included Beethoven's Violin Sonata No. 7, op. 30, no. 2, Lalo's *Symphonie Espagnole*, a piece by Szymanowski, and Saint-Saens's *Rondo Capricioso*. One critic took special notice of the Beethoven:

> Although many of the audience were standing, they listened to this number with such evident satisfaction that it seemed to prove again the truth of what that excellent connoisseur of music, F. Bonavia, suggested years ago. He commented that sonata recitals would be more popular if more players had a sense of sonata performance. They forget that sonata playing is really a kind of chamber music.
>
> But Mr. Staryk and Mr. Debusmann remembered that well, and so each had individual honor while achieving delightful ensemble. It takes more than personality and technique to do that. There is a kind of proper confidence

and intellectual courtesy involved when it comes off well, and the gentlemen might well be complimented on the pleasure their Beethoven sonata gave yesterday . . . There was taste in all the readings, with quite brilliant work by Mr. Staryk, but it is the true sonata style of both players that stays in the mind.[25]

Albert Pratz, concertmaster of the CBC Symphony, was in the crowd. "I had studied with Albert in the past" Staryk recalls. "The next day when I arrived at the CBC rehearsal, my chair was moved up to the front row. Instead of being number thirteen, I was suddenly number three on a first desk of three players, Albert, Hyman Goodman (then concertmaster of the TSO), and myself. It was Albert's customary manner. I am sure some people resented this unorthodox promotion and I didn't want to make waves; I thanked him, said it was a nice gesture but I thought I should go back until there was an opening and then I would move up in the regular way."

On November 19, 1952, Staryk played the Haydn C Major Concerto in a CBC live broadcast with Paul Scherman conducting: "It was a very difficult situation, very complicated. I didn't have a decent fiddle at the time; I had invested in a good bow, but couldn't yet afford a good violin, so Paul loaned me his Gofriller and, as he was conducting, he expected that I would have some coaching with him, since I had been studying with him from time to time. However, at this time I was studying with John Dembeck. Well, there I was playing on the conductor's fiddle, and coaching with John, the concertmaster: suddenly my role changed from soloist to diplomat. When I came to the first rehearsal, Paul was obviously not happy. He rehearsed the lengthy opening *tutti* forever, as though he was preparing a symphony, and before I ever played a note.

"At the live broadcast itself, someone was turning pages for me when all at once the music went flying off the stand and onto the floor. Suddenly, no music. I played as long as I could and then just stopped playing. Silence. No bad playing, just no playing, except for the skeletal accompaniment, for twelve, maybe sixteen bars. The music was up again quickly, but to me, it was the end."

On January 7, 1954, Staryk again performed a full recital, this time at the Heliconian Club, a converted church in the trendy Yorkville district of Toronto, with pianist Gordon Kushner and such luminaries as Sir Ernest and his wife in attendance: "It was more than music, it was a challenge. I was out to prove, after the Toronto Symphony incident, that I was still around and fiddling! During my preparation for this recital I remember literally having the fiddle under my chin sixteen hours a day, between the jobs and practicing. With the experience I now have, I would question the program in more ways than one: Brahms's D Minor Sonata, the Bach Chaconne, the whole Tchaikovsky Concerto, and that was only the first half! Bad programming, it was all in the key of D! After intermission there were half-a-dozen Paganini Caprices, Szymanowski, Kabalevsky, Sarasate, finishing up with Wieniawski for encores. One only plays this number of notes in *mad* competitions."

Critic John Kraglund of the *Globe and Mail* wrote in the next day's review that "the driving force that makes [Staryk] play almost like one possessed should be sufficient to insure future concerts by him." Staryk suspects he was "possibly trying to waken Sir Ernest, who, I soon became aware as I played, was sound asleep in his chair near the front of the hall. I think it was the applause, not the music, that finally roused him."

Despite these efforts, the musical community in Toronto responded indifferently to Staryk's presence: "Toronto was known for its Hogtown mentality. In the profession, much that was good, or had potential, was discouraged; few would show they were impressed since it could possibly be misunderstood as low standards or lack of knowledge. Too many wished to mimic the 'Big Apple,' New York. No matter how much fiddle I played, there were always those who would denigrate through questionable comparisons; if I could play Paganini brilliantly, there would always be some guy in Brooklyn or somewhere who could supposedly play it faster. These types never considered the power that they had to encourage or discourage youth. They were concerned about one thing, dividing the pie — in not too many pieces — and the pie was filled with dollars and cents, not music." Margaret Atwood, in *Cat's Eye*, portrays Staryk's hometown in very much the same way: "Toronto the good, Toronto the blue, where you couldn't get wine on Sundays. Everyone who lived here said those things: provincial, self-satisfied, boring. If you said that, it showed you recognized these qualities but did not partake of them yourself."[26]

Without any definitive breaks coming his way, Staryk used his contacts with local professionals to further his musical education: "I studied with everyone, unlike a lot of kids today, who will snub what is around and don't produce much from going elsewhere either. I worked with Albert Pratz, Isaac Mammot, Paul Scherman, John Dembeck and colleagues whose brains I constantly picked: Stan Kolt, Robert Spergel and others. I also studied with Mischakoff when he came to Toronto, and

Oscar Shumsky at the time when I was allowed to get to New York.

"I listened to people outside the string world as well: wind players, conductors, and pianists; I was already being influenced by many people. The new principle flutist of the TSO was living at our house, so I had the chance to play with him and gather some insight into the musical perspective of a wind player. I was getting around to anyone who had anything to offer, and scratching away to find new inspiration and insight. I was eating, living, and breathing music day and night. So I was ripe for Alexander Schneider, the 'great second fiddler,' when he came to town.

"I learned more and more about music from this character. He, of course, had the personality of anyone but a second fiddler: theatrical, flamboyant, even a little bit mad. He was an excellent musician and had an impressive manner of playing and a tremendous musical background in the chamber music literature, despite lacking real "fiddle chops" or sound. His often gross exaggerations were ideal for students, as you simply could not miss the point."

Lacking the support of a flourishing musical community, Staryk had arranged his own musical underground: "I think that in Toronto, before I went to Europe, I created a circle in which at least something was happening with some colleagues. We'd use my parents' house for this involvement with musicians and all kinds of music. My mother would cook for musicians from the Virtuosi di Roma when they came to town (she cooked for everybody), Franco Gulli and company, and many others. My mother didn't concern herself about celebrities, just as long as they liked the cooking, and more important, if I was getting something out of it."

Setterfield, in her manuscript on Staryk's life, relates some episodes involving Schneider: "On other occasions, Staryk organized carloads of his colleagues to drive to Fort Erie, the closest Canadian town to Buffalo where the Budapest Quartet was based at that time. He rented a motel room and had Schneider come across the Peace Bridge to give classes in the temporary studio."

"It was marvelous," recalls Staryk. "One violinist after another played what they had prepared. We really worked through a lot of material. I will never forget one period of three weeks in which I had about seventeen lessons with Sascha. I think even he was boggled. I would come in day after day with a major work: the Brahms Concerto, the Beethoven Concerto, this sonata, that quartet, playing and questioning the whys and wherefores of everything.

"Sometimes I'd have Schneider at the house and my mother would make *borscht*; he loved it. He drank beer all the way through the lessons and then we'd take him to the airport at night, pie-eyed, stuff some money into his pocket because he would never name a fee. When the customs officer would ask 'have you anything to declare?' he'd point to his dirty underwear in the bag and reply 'just aftom bomb,' and away he'd go. This was the atmosphere."

Despite the valuable input of local musicians and those passing through, Staryk felt that he was at an impasse; the work to be had in the city kept Staryk clothed and fed, but he needed artistic sustenance, inspiration, and insight. Staryk was looking for a way out of Toronto and all that it represented to him, but he was trapped in the upper Northern Hemisphere by U.S. jurisdiction.

Setterfield writes "[Victor] Feldbrill, also a violinist and a conductor, was doing radio work with Staryk and sometimes drove his friend downtown. One early spring morning in 1956, as he was parking his car in a lot on Parliament Street in the old downtown section of Toronto near the CBC studio, the two violinists were complaining to each other about their lack of enthusiasm for yet another routine rehearsal of inconsequential show music which was scheduled that day. Both men had ambitions to do something more important and more rewarding in music, but neither was sure which direction to take. As he locked the car, Feldbrill looked across at Staryk. 'Why don't you get out of here?' Feldbrill said. 'Go to Europe — England, France, anyplace, but just go, what have you got to lose?' Staryk made no reply as the two, fiddles in hand, went on to the rehearsal, but he was thinking about his friend's advice."

"I had been considering going to Europe for some time, since the situation in Toronto appeared to be a dead end," says Staryk. "Also there are simply times when things pile up in one's life. I married in 1954 and, by this time, it was rocky; there were a lot of personal problems along with everything else. So I began making preparations: winding up my affairs in Toronto, writing to competitions in London and Geneva, and looking around for a better violin."

The next time Feldbrill and Staryk shared a walk together, it was four years later in Amsterdam, and Staryk was First Concertmaster of the Concertgebouw.

ON ORCHESTRAS AND CONDUCTORS:
LONDON, AMSTERDAM, AND CHICAGO

"He has to convince the men and women who are playing in the orchestra that, if there are six, seven, eight, or eighty, ninety, or a hundred, he knows more than all of them put together . . ."

Isaac Stern on conductors,
from the IMG/BBC/Teldec video,
The Great Conductors

"Thanks to his inconquerable egotism and innate stupidity, he will take a first class orchestra and after playing twenty bars he will stop and he will begin educating them; fancy educating a body of people like the Royal Philharmonic Orchestra, they already know the damn piece ten times better than he does . . ."

Sir Thomas Beecham on conductors,
from the IMG/BBC/Teldec video,
The Great Conductors

Once known in Germany as "the land without music," England, by the middle of the twentieth century, had become one of the foremost musical centers of the world. The London *Times circa* 1950 provides evidence: thirteen year-old Daniel Barenboim was giving recitals at Wigmore Hall; Vladimir Ashkenazy, the new Russian sensation, had recently moved to town; the young Isaac Stern was establishing himself as an international star; pianist Myra Hess was actively giving concerts; David Oistrakh premiered Aram Khachaturian's violin concerto, and was performing the Sibelius, Tchaikovsky, and Brahms violin concertos to packed halls. In the arts columns there were premiere reviews of Sartre's *No Exit* (1944) and of Charlie Chaplin's *A King in New York*. The list of conductors appearing in the concert notices of the Times read like a golden-age Who's Who: Klemperer, Hindemith, Krips, Furtwängler, Kempe, Horenstein, Kubelik, Toscanini, Karajan.

This was the stage set for the twenty-four year old Staryk when he arrived in 1956. His eventual success in London and beyond was considerable and, in some respects, unparalleled. By the age of thirty-five, Staryk had led three of the greatest orchestras of his day: the Royal Philharmonic Orchestra of London, Amsterdam's Concertgebouw, and the Chicago Symphony Orchestra; from *The Strad* magazine he earned the appellation, "King of Concertmasters."[27] (The Concertgebouw, that vehicle of instruction for Sir Ernest and the TSO management during the Symphony Six incident, toured with Staryk as First Concertmaster on a temporary permit, through fifty-five American cities in April and May of 1961. No questions asked.) In March of 1983 *The Strad* added that "As a concertmaster, Staryk's career has remained unparalleled to this day." Staryk's varied experiences of the orchestral world on three different musical continents places him in a unique position to evaluate and compare.

London

The London orchestral scene, from its beginnings, was tumultuous and fast-paced. Musicians worked freelance, without the stability of a seasonal contract, and the various orchestras operated in open competition for the best players for any given concert, and the players themselves for the highest-paying jobs. Thus, when a player received an offer for a more lucrative engagement, he would simply arrange for another musician to play the original job in his stead. This practice became known as the deputy system. "The standard joke," according to Harold C. Schonberg, "related the story of a conductor who, through four rehearsals, saw a constant, bewildering succession of new faces. But through all this sat the same first clarinet, solid, dependable, understanding. At the end of the fourth rehearsal, the conductor went up to the clarinetist and thanked him. 'At least you will understand what I am doing at the concert tomorrow.' The clarinetist looked at the conductor. 'I'm sorry I shan't be at the concert," he said. 'I'm playing elsewhere.'"[28]

Although the deputy system was defunct by the time Staryk arrived in London in 1956, the atmosphere was still somewhat frenetic. The best musicians were in demand as orchestras vied for predominance in a crowded field: "Orchestras changed personnel and each had its heyday. In my time the prominent groups were the Philharmonia with Karajan and the RPO with Beecham. The attitude was very pragmatic. Players attempted to do a good professional job, give the best possible performances with as little rehearsal time as possible, and to enhance the reputation of their orchestra in a highly competitive atmosphere. We undertook everything from film scores to opera at Glyndebourne."

Glyndebourne Festival Opera, founded by the wealthy Eton science master, landowner, and businessman, John Christie, is located in the Sussex Downs near Lewes. Christie's wife, the soprano Audrey Mildmay, assisted her husband in planning and designing a structure of modest dimensions which was to eventually produce the operas of Mozart (*Le nozze di Figaro* and *Cosi fan tutte* in its opening season of 1934), Verdi, Britten, Gluck, Rossini, Debussy, Strauss, Stravinsky, and others. The building is adjacent to the Christie manor house and originally accommodated 310 concertgoers. In 1958, Christie stated the principles upon which his opera house functioned: "1. we must do the work better than the others; 2. the work (not we) must be based on respect." By this last condition, Christie meant that the public must "take trouble" by dressing in evening dress, by arriving on time, and by remaining in their seats until at least five minutes after the performance was completed. Christie: "The essence of Glyndebourne is that it is an ideal." The inhouse orchestras have been the RPO (1948–63) and the London Philharmonic Orchestra (from 1965).

For the musicians, opera at Glyndebourne was a taxing engagement but one with many benefits, not the least of which was the opportunity to play under conductors such as Fritz Busch (to 1951), Georg Solti, Hans Schmidt-Isserstedt, John Pritchard, and one individual whom Staryk particularly admired, Vittorio Gui. "It was fascinating to work with Gui, Giulini's mentor; it was like meeting and rehearsing with an old master. And the great voices and casts that were involved were marvelous to work with since everything was well prepared, unlike the touring groups we would get in London during the season. Glyndebourne carried on the elegant traditions of Salzburg and Bayreuth, and participating in this was one of the most musically satisfying things I have done."

But Glyndebourne meant weeks of very hard work, rehearsing thirty hours per opera, launching one production in an evening performance, then rehearsing all day for the next. "Physically it was very taxing, there were so many hours of rehearsal, and sitting in the pit was something I was not accustomed to; it seemed like an eternity was spent under the stage, as though we would never get out to see the light. And this clearly had psychological effects: we were below ground, it was damp, and summer wasn't particularly warm in England. Then, if we weren't rehearsing for another opera, we often had recording sessions in London!"

Glyndebourne was roughly a sixty-five-minute ride by local train from Victoria Station and the program began late in the afternoon and was punctuated by an intermission that allowed for an elegant supper on the lawn, after which the program resumed. "Dinner was very sophisticated, with people dressed in their evening wear eating elaborate picnics on the grass with their best china and silver.

"The musicians, of course, lived under more humble circumstances. The orchestra was generally a Mozart-size group but for large productions, like Strauss's *Rosenkavalier*, the group overwhelmed the theater. In that small space the sound often rang in my ears long after the performance was over!"

Violinist Paul Scherman remembers a production of Strauss's *Ariadne auf Naxos:* "We had a very small orchestra with only six or eight fiddles. Steve had us all sit in a circle to play, which was very difficult. It meant that everyone had to be at his level; he was very tough."

Staryk concludes, "In all it was a fantastically demanding experience, but I was young and thought I had all the energy in the world to keep up with the rehearsal and performance schedule as well as to practice."

The Proms were another facet of London's musical scene. They constituted what Staryk has described as "one of the biggest musical farces of all time. First, the orchestra was literally sightreading the concert onstage because there was never enough time to rehearse. Everything in London is under-rehearsed, but these didn't even get a decent minimum, there was just too much music. The concerts began at seven-thirty and went very late, and were played almost nonstop, so the quantity of music performed was overwhelming. And all the tradition-minded Prom concertgoers crowded into Albert Hall with nothing of quality to listen to because of the poor acoustics; it was a classical three ring circus."

In addition to Glyndebourne and the Proms, Staryk's London freelancing included ballet, films, pops concerts, chamber music, BBC broadcasts, rock and pop recordings, Muzak recordings, and jingles. "There was a film in which I played half of Bach's Chaconne as background to a screaming scene between a couple *à la* Taylor and Burton." The hectic pace of Staryk's playing schedule led to some memorable days: "The morning began with an RPO rehearsal at the Edinburgh Festival. Later in the afternoon I was driven to Glasgow and performed a live broadcast of the Glazunov Concerto with the BBC Scottish Orchestra; then it was back to Edinburgh for the concert at the Festival that evening." Staryk played the London premiere of the Kurt Weill Concerto, and performed concertos by Sibelius, Brahms, Tchaikovsky, Mozart, and Paganini with various orchestras across the U.K., including the Hallè in Manchester, the Royal Liverpool, the BBC Symphony London, the BBC Northern, the London Symphony, and the RPO.

It was also on the London scene that Staryk first suffered at the hands of amateur conductors: "I don't know where all of the amateurs came from. But England has a tradition of amateurs, collectors, and hobbyists. Those who have the money are able to hire a hall, not some little church basement but the Royal Festival Hall, and a major orchestra like the RPO, LPO, the London Symphony, or Philharmonia, and they put on a concert.

"It could at times be absolutely demoralizing and degrading. I remember at one rehearsal things deteriorated so badly that I walked out, and initially refused to play the concert [this occurred at a time when Staryk was Leader of the RPO]. I subsequently relented and played, while this character stood on the podium trying to figure out how to read a score and flap his arms at the same time. Sometimes we just muddled through because the orchestra itself could carry the music along at a certain level. I will never forget one occasion (although I have forgotten the name of the infinitely forgettable conductor): Beryl Senofsky, the Assistant Concertmaster of the Cleveland Orchestra, had just won the Brussels prize in the Queen Elizabeth competition, and was making his debut in Festival Hall. He was waiting the long wait of the opening *tutti* of the Brahms Violin Concerto when the conductor managed to split the orchestra in half and completely grind the production to a halt! There was poor Senofsky — he hadn't yet played a note and the orchestra had come to a standstill! The musical scene in London has unfortunately always been an odd mixture of professional business and amateur pleasure."

Sir Thomas

The greatest amateur conductor, businessman, impresario, connoisseur, and wit London had to offer during Staryk's time was Sir Thomas Beecham. Beecham, a "short man who suggests tallness" and son of an industrial chemist made suddenly wealthy (The family wealth was based on the invention and subsequent popularity of a laxative pill: "Hark the herald angels sing, Beecham's pill is just the thing!"), entered the English musical scene in 1909 with the founding of the Beecham Symphony Orchestra, "a band of carefully chosen young players who gave adventurous concerts, toured, and played for opera and ballet."[29]

During the First World War Beecham used his inheritance to give financial support to three institutions, the Hallé Orchestra, the London Symphony Orchestra (LSO), and the Royal Philharmonic Society.

In 1915 Beecham formed the Beecham Opera Company and in 1932, after the conception and quick demise of his Imperial League of Opera, the London Philharmonic was born and rose quickly to the forefront of the orchestral scene, both in England and on the continent. By this time, Beecham had already introduced England to a profusion of unfamiliar music, much of it operatic; in a season of opera at Covent Garden, Beecham featured the works of such composers as Strauss, Delius, Smyth, and Hollbrooke.

The year 1940 found Beecham in New York, then Australia, on a concert tour. The remainder of the war years were spent leading the Metropolitan Opera and conducting concerts of the New York Philharmonic and the Seattle Symphony Orchestra. (Beecham once publicly dismissed Seattle as an "aesthetic dustbin.") Upon his return to England in 1946, Beecham formed the Royal Philharmonic Orchestra ("because there was no existing British orchestra of a high enough standard to maintain my reputation"), a group whose touring, recordings, and consistent quality at home brought international fame to its founder.

"He liked to perform good light music," notes Ronald Crichton in *The New Grove*. The *bonbons* — musical "lollipops," as he often described them — were closest to Beecham's heart: one London paper described a Festival Hall program which "contained Beecham favourites, Delius's *In a Summer Garden*, and a suite from Bizet's music for *L'Arlèsienne*. He has played them to us before, and he still loves them." Staryk acknowledges that "Beecham championed the music of Delius, but some of the pieces, the lesser known ones, were extremely boring. I suppose he was convinced of their value, but I always found it difficult to understand. I remember the title of one work, 'On Hearing the First Cuckoo in Spring,' being transformed, probably by the Dutch, to 'On Catching the First Herring in Spring.' This was one of his better works." Perhaps Beecham's empathy for Delius stemmed from their mutual dislike of J.S. Bach. Delius once told Beecham of an odd little bald man who came around to pay his respects, proceeded to play the scale of C major for half an hour on the cello, and then left.[30]

As Staryk recalls, "Beecham's interpretation of composers such as Haydn, Schubert, Berlioz, Wagner, Mozart, as well as many lesser composers, could be great; Brahms and Beethoven seemed to go on interminably. Beecham did not have a good reputation as accompanist, particularly with an outside soloist, but the times I played with him, I was generally happy because we had a rapport from working together. When I played Tchaikovsky, his concept was quite different from mine; we just heard it two different ways. I was following him for a period, then he would be following me. But with Mozart, fortunately, these problems did not exist.

"Our preparation for a Festival Hall performance of the Mozart G Major Violin Concerto was memorable for me. First I had a piano rehearsal with him, which, besides being most amusing, exposed his limitations as a pianist. He sat down at the piano, puffing away on the usual cigar, and began to bang out the accompaniment; few of the chords were even close! The only thing that was approximately correct was the rhythm and out of the corner of my eye I could see the manager and the librarian hiding in the background trying to subdue their laughter, as they realized that this was my first sampling of the Beecham keyboard technique. I just kept playing away, suppressing my laughter. There really was nothing to discuss because we agreed on tempo, phrasing, and style. I had played enough Mozart with him to know what to expect, and approached this composer in much the same way as he, except that my intonation was faring a bit better than his dischords. After we played through the piece, he waved his arms. 'Are you happy?' he asked. 'Yes, I'm happy,' I told him. 'Fine, then,' he replied. 'Then everyone is happy.' And that was that; once-through with the orchestra, and we played the concert, which turned out to be a fine performance."

"I would give the whole of Bach's Brandenburg Concertos for Massenet's *Manon*," Beecham once said, "and would think that I had vastly profited by the exchange." Beecham generally tried his best to avoid the three Bs: Bach, Beethoven, and Brahms. In fact he was known to feign sickness before performances of Beethoven's Ninth Symphony: "The *tiefste innigkeit* and *molto religioso* approaches are not for him . . ." explained the London *Times* of December 13, 1956. "Never mind about the *ethic* of music or what the composer means," Beecham would retort. "This is all nonsense, the consequence of Beethoven who was at times the Mr. Gladstone of music. Music should first and last have a beautiful sound, and every composer has a certain style." But to discern what that style is and how to draw it in each instance from the orchestra as they move from one composer to the next requires a conjurer and a man of catholic musical understanding and taste. On November 15, 1956, the *Times* chided Sir Thomas for his rendition of Beethoven's Second Symphony: "The music will, of course, take the elegance Sir Thomas bestows upon it, since it is still in the Viennese tradition of Haydn and Mozart, but somehow Beethoven is not immediately recognizable with his hair so well brushed."

Staryk, the consummate stylist, who led this concert from the concertmaster's chair, concurs with the *Times*'s assessment of Beecham's sense of style: "I entered the orchestra skeptical of Sir Thomas's abilities. Beecham was not an orchestral conductor or trainer in the truest sense; I saw him, rather, as an inspired and very talented amateur — a wealthy exhibitionist who could afford to take chances, creating headlines and scandals to attract attention. I had heard Beecham and the RPO when I first arrived in London, and although there was a magic that would happen with Beecham in certain works, his stylistic understanding of the bread and butter repertoire was limited.

"Beecham's perception of music was very melodic. He always centered his comments around the 'tune,' and since that was what interested him, it was the focus of our rehearsal time; if the music was beautifully done and phrased well, then that was it "by gad," as he would say. He saw a score horizontally, and didn't particularly bother to see it up and down as well, and in that sense he often missed the interesting contrapuntal inner voices. That is why, of course, he never played Bach. Even Handel's *Messiah* could be a trial to him; I remember a recording session for the work during which he offered some constructive criticism on the Chorus's rendition of "For unto us a child is born." 'Ladies and Gentlemen,' he said, 'if we dwelt more on the pleasures of conception than the pains of labor, we might, perhaps, get it right.'

"Beethoven was a very trying experience because he kept going over and over poor Ludwig, trying to decide which direction to take. The opposite was true when we were doing music he was comfortable with; then we would just whip through everything, do a little bit here, a little there." Beecham himself said on this point: "There is only one way to rehearse an orchestral piece, which is what I do. I take either a Mozart symphony, or a Strauss tone poem, I play the whole thing through, beginning to end without a stop, the whole blessed thing. The orchestra makes a few mistakes, naturally. I play it through a second time; the orchestra makes no mistakes. I then take just a few difficult parts, I pinpoint them, I emphasize them, I repeat those three or four times; I am ready to perform it."[31] For Staryk, "This brings to mind the story of the young flute player rehearsing with Sir Thomas. 'I've never played this before, Sir Thomas,' said the flutist, hoping for more rehearsal. But to no avail. 'Oh, you haven't?' came the reply. 'Well, you'll love it.'"

Beecham, whether in the press, the courtroom, or on the podium, was good entertainment and a steady attraction to Londoners, so much so that he was nearly a cult personality among the English. He traveled with a personal entourage and was the darling of the daily press, in which his ready wit was heavily quoted: "'Tommy,' we used to say in Fleet Street, 'is always good copy,'" wrote London journalist C.B. Rees in 1958. (American journalists concurred: a *Time* Magazine report of November 6, 1950, on the occasion of Beecham's American tour with the Royal Philharmonic, reveals some of the charming audacity of the conductor: "He was set to face U.S. audiences with an orchestra of his own — an enterprise 'I have undertaken in a becoming spirit of modesty and humility.' In fact, beamed Sir Thomas, he had come 'neither to educate nor to enlighten, but only to please.'" This largesse was maintained even after running the gauntlet of the United States's new Security Act to gain access into the country for his musicians: "Said Sir Thomas blandly: 'We're all British, thank God.'") Cultured, urbane, given to temperamental outbursts and extended huffs, Beecham's man-about-town persona was at odds with Staryk's workaday musical ethics.

"I was not one of the worshippers of Beecham," Staryk says. "After all, his world of affluence and glamour, his avid pursuit of 'the good life' was not part of my upbringing. As with my evaluation of all conductors and musicians, I had to be convinced by musical ability proven on the stage."

But despite differences in their personalities and upbringing (though they share an April 27th date of birth), Beecham and Staryk were alike in their devotion, or addiction, to hard work. Beecham once complained: "All sorts of things are said about my 'flair,' my 'temperament,' my 'genius,' but I seldom get credit for my main virtue and attribute — inexhaustible industry!" [32]

The audition

Staryk initially proved himself to Beecham in a tiny dressing room filled to overflowing with Beecham and his adherents. Staryk had prepared Paganini and unaccompanied Bach, due to the fact that he was to have no accompanist, and played the latter despite a shocked last minute warning from the orchestra librarian: "'Oh God, don't play Bach, he hates Bach.' What else could I do? I was playing in a dressing room, hardly bigger than a cupboard, with absolutely dead acoustics. There was no pianist, there was no piano, even if I had brought an accompanist! It was only logical to begin with unaccompanied Bach. The room was crowded with the usual entourage, and Sir Thomas puffing on the inevitable cigar, filling the room with smoke. I wasn't nervous: I was young, cocky, and not particularly anxious to resume my orchestral life at this time. He was in good spirits, waved the cigar at me with his usual 'Good Afternoon,' and signaled for me to begin. I think I apologized for the Bach, explained about the problem with the accompanist, then proceeded to play the D Minor Partita, including the Chaconne, right through, though without repeats."

Staryk's audition was followed by a trial period in which he played with the RPO alternately as concertmaster and assistant concertmaster, which in turn was followed by Staryk's signing of a contract with the managers of the RPO on the fourth day of January, 1957.

Several factors contributed to Staryk's desirability in Beecham's eyes. Adding to the reputation he had already gained as a freelance player were placements at two recent international competitions: runner up in the Carl Flesch International Violin Competition in London, and runner up and medal recipient at the Geneva International Music Competition. Staryk recalls the Carl Flesch competition, "The finals came around and there was a Czech violinist, Ladislav **Jacek**, playing, and very early in his performance, there was a power failure; the hall was in total darkness. Now, this is a tricky situation, as the accompanist can hardly be expected to have his part memorized. In this case, **Jacek** kept right on playing, as did the accompanist, with neither missing a note. They went on right to the end of the Sibelius, first movement, in the dark, which, of course, just knocked everyone over, and **Jacek** won. It's ironic that after that, **Jacek** went to Australia. He went to one colony and I went back to another.

"I was surprised when I reached Geneva," Staryk continues, "because I began to see that there were distinct likes and dislikes about music making, and that this spot on the continent was not necessarily internationally oriented or unbiased as I had expected. Geneva didn't always 'dig what I was doing.' Some didn't like the efficiency while others were impressed by these very same characteristics!

"I don't think there was anyone else from North America in Geneva that year; all the rest were continental players, or British, and the jury members were all continentalists, except for Isaac Stern, who was there for the first round only. I would have been knocked out then, except that Stern came out after they heard me and asked who was playing; he recognized in my playing a style that was familiar and to his liking."

Staryk clearly possessed the necessary star qualities to be one of Beecham's principle players. But an additional factor in Beecham's eventual choice was the fact that, as a twenty-four year old emigrant from the colonies and a newly discovered talent in London, Staryk must have awakened Beecham's joyful indulgence in the art of advocacy. The London *Times* summarized Beecham's beneficence when it described him as "a keen champion of musical waifs and strays." In Staryk's case, Beecham extended certain promises in exchange for a commitment to the RPO — promises that he would promote Staryk's solo career from his vantage point on the podium. Staryk had been taking a break from orchestral life at this point in his career and wasn't anxious to return to it; his feelings about the offer to lead the RPO were mixed, so the added incentive of solo work made the position more attractive. As for the sincerity of Beecham's offer and the possibilities of establishing a solo career in a fickle marketplace, Staryk admits that, "Though already somewhat skeptical, I was obviously still too naive."

For his part, Beecham, a veteran publicist, was known for unerring political virtuosity. As a case in point, London concertgoers and the members of the RPO may well have been groomed for Staryk's ascension to the concertmaster's chair. At the time of the Royal Philharmonic Society's initial concert of the 1956 season, Staryk was still playing with the RPO as a section violinist, though strategically seated behind the incumbent concertmaster, Arthur Leavins. The evening's program included three pieces by Richard Strauss: *Le Bourgeois Gentilhomme*, a selection from *Ariadne auf Naxos*, and *Ein Heldenleben*. The difficulty of playing these solo violin parts in a single program must have taken its toll on Leavins by the time he played the characterization of Mrs. Strauss in *Heldenleben*: "Mr. Arthur Leavins drew a fairly tame portrait of the excitable Mrs. Strauss," reported the London *Times* of October 17, 1956. Staryk now suspects that Beecham's machinations created the context for the disappointing performance, thus priming Leavins and the orchestra for a change of guard. "I think that such unusual programming would serve one of two purposes. It would either give a brilliant concertmaster the opportunity to shine, or it would push a weaker player over the edge."

An English concertmaster

"At the beginning, in the RPO, I first looked and listened. You have to establish your own credibility before you can make any moves as a new leader, and it's usually best if the conductor can program something that will immediately open up the situation. Everyone can hear you and can make their own evaluation. If you just sit there playing *tuttis* and never have a chance to either play a solo or one of the major cadenzas, it can take a much longer time. Your presence may be felt in a more subtle manner or sometimes not at all."

Staryk's first challenge as a newcomer was to participate in a recording of *Scheherazade*. "All the circumstances surrounding the recording were, for me, very difficult. In the first place, recording with Sir Thomas was sometimes hectic because he just simply would not have people wasting his time going over things which *he* already knew!

"Also, in the 'Aquarium,' [the control room], there were two more personalities to contend with: Victor Olof, from HMV, the first manager of the RPO, who was possibly another frustrated conductor, and who, at any rate, had his own ideas about The Thousand and One Nights; and Lady Betty Humby, Beecham's wife at that time, and a pianist who had what might be called a third conductor's point of view of what was coming across on tape.

"There I was caught in the crossfire of these three. I was the new man, not by any means accepted by everyone, and playing a major solo on a new fiddle, all the while trying to be as diplomatic as possible in agreeing with Lady Humby's argument with Sir Thomas about ensemble matters (in a section of the piece that he claimed he had never heard played properly in the fifty odd years he had been conducting, 'so why waste time now?')."

The recording was finally completed and for several months was no longer discussed. Then suddenly the parts reappeared at a recording session. Staryk remembers the event: "Beecham decided that there were some things he wasn't happy with. For instance, there was a bassoon solo at the beginning of the second movement that didn't come off as well as it might have. We were recording something in Paris at the time when suddenly, there was *Scheherazade* on the stand. I thought to myself, 'I've already finished this! I did it! It's over!' But no, I was expected to get on the magic carpet and do my tricks in the opening of the second movement, which ostensibly I did, but not as well as when the part was prepared in the London version."

Though it isn't mentioned in any of Beecham's biographies, this recording significantly added to the Beecham legend. New York critic Irving Kolodin wrote this review in the liner notes of The Franklin Mint Record Society's printing of *The Hundred Greatest Recordings of all Time*: "Also worth noting is the participation of Steven Staryk as a Scheherazade in pants. He is the only contemporary virtuoso-concertmaster who has recorded, on his own, a century-spanning compilation called *400 Years of*

Violin Playing. . . . As a matchless intermediary for the impulse of Beecham, whether sketching a portrait of Scheherazade, depicting a love scene, or painting a stormy seascape, Staryk had the once-in-a lifetime opportunity, for a violinist, to be a star soloist and the most cherished member of a string section simultaneously."

The *Scheherazade* session wasn't the only occasion on which Staryk was forced to perform a solo on a moment's notice for the sake of posterity. "For one of the big solos from the third act of Delibes's ballet *Sylvia*," Staryk recalls, "I literally walked into the studio cold, never having heard or seen the solo, and was told we were recording it. I was frantically bowing, fingering, and trying to get it to instantly marinate. So basically the recording was a sightreading session, which wasn't always so bad in a *tutti* situation, but to record a difficult solo under such conditions is a little awkward. That was the British way of doing things in those days. I hope the recording was deleted very quickly." The reviewer found Staryk's solo work "persuasive."

An initiation into the business

"In the RPO the role of Leader, as defined by my contract, was a difficult job. There was the expectation that you were to look after the shop when the shopkeeper was away (which was often, in the case of Beecham), and of course the Leader was particularly to look after the standard of the string section and act as liaison with all the guest conductors. My appointment was both my first concertmaster position and an initiation into a system practiced neither in North America nor Continental Europe; and as a further complication, the RPO's arrangements within this odd system were, themselves, unique."

Staryk's duties as concertmaster placed him in the position of having to introduce change into an entrenched and unacceptable *status quo* — to ruffle and enliven what has been described as the "cathedral ambiance of many English musicians." Staryk's unusual contract specified his exact duties, stating succinctly that "as Leader of the Orchestra, you are responsible for all matters of orchestral discipline and are entitled to audition players as and when necessary; in short, the standard of the Orchestra is in your keeping and you are entitled to do what is necessary to maintain this standard."

And apparently the standard did need maintainenance; before Staryk's arrival, the *London Times*, in the spring of 1956, reported that "the Royal Philharmonic Orchestra has been missing the inspiration of its chief conductor. The string playing in Schubert's Fifth Symphony was decidedly ragged. . . ."

"I knew some of the problems because I had been briefed on them," Staryk recalls, "and had heard them at first hand — both when I attended concerts and as I played with the section prior to becoming Leader. There were many positions to fill and few to fill them, considering all the orchestras and the amount of freelance work available to London players. In every orchestra, there was a core of dependable people who were traded around from one orchestra to the next like professional athletes, but there wasn't a large enough pool of excellent people to choose from, not in relation to the size of the city; so one of the first things I did was to arrange auditions. I'll never forget it. About a hundred and forty fiddle players turned up for those auditions, and, unbelievably, most were no better than those that we had; many were absolutely terrible. Can you imagine what it's like to listen to such a huge number of bad violinists? So I had to use other approaches. I bought some of the best players from other orchestras" — an uncommon practice in the musical world of Staryk's early years — "and tried sectional rehearsals.

"Not that the string playing in England was universally problematic; with the right conductor, you could at times get a brilliant response. For accompanying, an English orchestra was very special. There was never a danger of too large a sound or insensitivity, and they have a pianissimo which nobody else can match: it is a veiled sound, very soft, quite transparent. There is a tenderness you can almost touch, something a conductor can mold, and with this beautiful quality, this refinement, they can do a great deal. But they do not have the power, the physical presence. It just isn't there when you are there, in person, at a concert. On record, the engineers manufacture much of the end result with twists of the dial and slashes of the splicing blade, nowadays the punching out of a digitized note. Recording is a different game."

In contrast to the violins, the other sections of the RPO, headed by carefully chosen principals, were reliably excellent. The London *Times* reported on November 9, 1956 that "the Royal Philharmonic Orchestra, whose horn department was once again led to glory by Mr. Dennis Brain, sparkled in Haydn, melted in Delius, and blazed in Bizet's *Farandole*."

Staryk points out that "Beecham's choice of principle players was a reflection of his own character, so naturally it was a star situation. They referred to the winds in the RPO as the Royal Family, and I must say they were marvelous. The violas and celli were also excellent overall. The brass could best be described as sensitive. There were many stars, including Dennis Brain and Allan Seville, two great french horn virtuosi. With so much talent, a problem that inevitably arose was that sometimes Beecham's stars would outshine Beecham, a situation [reflected mainly in the press] which he didn't care for."

Such an occurrence was Staryk's Zürich debut on the 23rd of October, 1957, playing the Tchaikovsky Concerto. Zürich's *Tages-Anzeiger* covered the concert:

> Sir Thomas Beecham conducted Beethoven's Pastorale in the same easy manner that he walked onstage: with the carriage and composedness of a "signor." It is certainly agreeable to hear this nature music, conceived in the open air and untouched by a precious picture of the countryside, without any romantic *pathos*. At times, however, everything got faintly colorless and dim, and there was no danger of flooding by either the stream purling across meadows and woods or the thunderstorm. The English musicians, hindered by their conductor from loud outbursts of feeling, kept a cool distance from the mostly contemplative work and remained, despite all care in handling the sonorous details, in lulling passivity.
>
> To what degree of temper the community of the RPO can be raised could only be heard after the intermission. It was, naturally, a Russian who launched the "Sputnik" and got it rolling — a young Ukrainian whose violinistic art sparkled in the Tchaikovsky Concerto and revealed a sound musician's heart and the most lively sensations behind his rigid mask. The sound of Steven Staryk's violin is not especially big, but Slavically soft and elastic. One wonders at his easy bow and wrist techniques. The *finale* sped by at such a tempo that the conductor and his orchestra were brought running after in agitation.

If Beecham was bothered by this contrast, he didn't reveal his impressions to Staryk.

Another Beecham star was a violist named Frederick Riddle. In Staryk's first year with the RPO, Riddle played the Walton Viola Concerto, and the solo viola part in Berlioz's *Harold In Italy*: "with the rich, dark tones of Mr. Frederick Riddle's viola . . . and Sir Thomas's evergreen affection and enthusiasm for this music, it yielded nothing but delight."[33]

He also performed Rubbra's Viola Concerto: "Mr. Frederick Riddle was an eloquent soloist, never forcing the tone of his viola unduly but always giving great value to the intrinsic beauty in the music."[34]

Though Staryk confirms that Riddle was a very fine violist, "he was the one person with whom I could make no accommodation for a long time. He just simply was not happy about my being there as Leader, to lead and not be led. For one thing, he had been used to a situation where he was almost leading the orchestra from the violas. But, perhaps more to the point, he just didn't like my personal style. I was a little too casual for him, a little too tainted with the dress and manners of the colonies and at odds with his expectations for a concertmaster who should have been both violinist and 'gentleman.'"

It should be noted that Staryk was only twenty-four when he took over the responsibilities of concertmaster, while Riddle was middle-aged; the juxtaposition of ages may have, of itself, been grounds for a certain amount of friction between the two men. Yet Staryk eventually earned Riddle's enduring respect. "Many years later," says Staryk, "after Beecham died and Kempe was director of the orchestra, Riddle was in the invitation group, wining and dining me, trying to persuade me to come back and lead the RPO again."

But another player, the principle second violinist, wasn't so willing to give Staryk's reforms a chance, and soon offered his resignation. "I remember there were differences of opinion concerning the changes I was introducing: the principal second resigned; he felt he couldn't live with me. This didn't greatly concern me — my response was, 'So be it.' I wanted to tighten things up, felt that I was clearly justified in making the changes, and saw that he didn't agree with my way of going about it. We were basically at odds on matters of musical style. He was a very fine fiddler, very professional; an excellent principal second. But we didn't see eye to eye and so he went and found work elsewhere without any difficulty and I found another violinist to fill his position."

When in Rome

Sometime in Staryk's second year as Leader of the RPO, the question of Staryk's suitability for the position of concertmaster came into even sharper relief. The conflict centered around two main issues: Staryk's interpretation of his role as Leader, and his youthfully volatile temperament, especially as expressed through his manners and use of language.

As already noted, Staryk's contract with the orchestra management empowered him to do what he deemed necessary to maintain the standards of the orchestra. Like most individuals of strong will and quick intelligence, Staryk instinctively wanted to shape the situation to match his personal standards. And since the stipulations of his contract gave him discretionary power to achieve these very subjective ends, Staryk made use of his position to pressure the violin section when the playing was ragged: "I lost my cool once at Glyndebourne during Stravinsky's *The Rake's Progress*. We were nearly at the dress rehearsal stage and there were still unacceptable errors — so I turned around and in more-or-less North American lingo said, 'If you guys don't get this right, shit's going to fly.' In other words, 'a lot of you are going to get the pink slip.' Maybe I was heartless at the time; I don't think so."

Staryk viewed this measure as a minimal exercise of his duties, brought on by a lapse of discipline and musical standards: "If the conductor was not addressing the problem, or was not aware that the problem existed, it was up to the next person in the hierarchy to speak up, as in any organization. In the RPO, the next person in the hierarchy happened to be the Leader [concertmaster]."

Word of the incident reached Sir Thomas and evoked a response: "For sometime past I have been worried about the leadership of the Royal Philharmonic Orchestra," wrote Beecham in a memorandum dated September 16, 1959. "I have been conscious of a growing restlessness and irritation among both rank and file over Mr. Staryk's conception and performance of his duties."

"At the time," Staryk explains, "the atmosphere in the RPO was still very provincially British, even though we were in cosmopolitan London. My personal upbringing and professional style were not everyone's cup of tea. Pity! However, it was only a small minority whose feathers were ruffled. I believe that the issue was primarily the linguistic form that my criticism took, not that I was overstepping the bounds of my duties: my contract instructed me to create a very efficient orchestra while the behind-the-scenes nature of the arrangement prevented me from receiving the glory of doing so. I had no reason to believe that the contract and conditions originated only from the management and not Beecham. If my 'manners' were at the heart of the problem at Glyndebourne, I think that, later, other currents were stirring the waters."

On another occasion, a point of etiquette surrounding the use of public space for private practice was brought to Staryk's attention. The British at that time customarily did their warming up at home, or, on those rare occasions when it was done in public, discreetly and hurriedly:

"There's not too much warming up backstage, especially by the strings. They arrive for the gig, get onstage and then warm up during the first piece!" One day in 1959, during a break in a recording session at Abbey Road Studios, Staryk was practicing on the first stand when "Anthony Pini came up to me and in a typically British manner asked, 'Would you mind doing your practicing at home?'

"I had always practiced on jobs, between jobs, wherever possible," Staryk explains. "In London this was a necessity since a musician in demand was never home! This was one of the areas I was trying to influence by role modeling. Pini was obviously not aware of this, having recently been brought back to the position of principal cellist. (The position became suddenly available when John Kennedy left for Australia: The 'colonies' were offering better positions and conditions than the 'rulers!')"

Anthony Pini had apparently lost his position due to a drinking problem, and was rehired again primarily on Staryk's insistence. "It was ironic that he should complain to me. Pini was obviously not aware that it was by my grace and not God's that he was even there." Staryk, who was later described in *Time* Magazine (October 21, 1966) as an "articulate, supremely cool" concertmaster, responded to Pini's request (and his general attitude that practicing was, if not unnecessary, then a nuisance) with another outburst of temperament: "At that point I blew up and said, 'It would do a hell of a lot of good if you all started to practice!' And really, more than just venting a momentary reaction to the situation, I was voicing a deeply held conviction that those who work carry those who do not."

Beecham's memorandum continued: "Against Mr. Staryk, as a man and musician, I have no complaint to make. But I have grown to doubt if his talents lie in the direction of orchestral leadership, especially in the case of a British orchestra.[35] Furthermore, it is equally clear that Mr. Staryk himself is not happy or contented as things are. He longs for increased authority to make drastic changes in the personnel, and conspicuously in certain quarters with which under no circumstances would I permit interference. This frustrated ambition on his part has recently provoked him to more than one outburst of ill-tempered criticism which I am unable to treat lightly or overlook. In one of his less controlled moments he has taken upon himself to condemn the orchestra as a whole in language altogether unbefitting one who occupies such a position as his."

In a letter of response, Staryk denied any ambitions for greater authority and pointed out to Sir Thomas that his contract explicitly assigned to him the responsibility that he had been undertaking. In a second letter, dated 2 October 1959, Beecham expanded on his initial evaluation: "Our personal association has always been agreeable to me and your artistic accomplishment is beyond question. I attribute a good deal of what I have described as a growing unrest in the Orchestra to the ill-advised instruction issued to you by the late Manager when you first joined us. These instructions would never have been sent you in the language expressed had I first seen them. Briefly, the Management was delegating to you control and power which I had up to that time preferred to exercise myself. Out of this gross blunder a vast misunderstanding grew gradually until it reached a point which I considered to be prejudicial to the interests of the Orchestra . . ." Beecham again maintained that Staryk's efforts might more worthily be concentrated on developing a solo career: "I do seriously hold the opinion that your talents are more conspicuously those of a virtuoso player than an orchestral leader. It is for this reason that I do not think that your career will be halted in the slightest measure by your retirement from your present position. All things being equal you should have a highly successful future as a solo player and I shall always look upon it as a pleasure as well as a duty to do anything within my power to enable you to achieve this purpose."

Despite his conciliatory words, Beecham insisted that Staryk immediately resign. The youthful Shirley Beecham, Sir Thomas's most recent wife and his secretary, tried to carry the process through, but discovered to her dismay that Staryk would leave only on his own terms. Staryk's contract contained a clause requiring three month's notice for the dismissal of services and Staryk, with the help of British Musician's Union solicitors, eventually extracted £450 from the RPO management to cover the losses incurred by his pressured resignation. In the meantime he continued his practice of playing engagements elsewhere and was slated to take over responsibilities of leadership in Amsterdam's Concertgebouw Orchestra. "Beecham didn't like the fact that the Union lawyers settled matters in my favor," Staryk says, "but Shirley really took it harder because she was the new manager. In fact, she took it very personally: I wasn't leaving, I was working on the outside, then I was appointed concertmaster of the Concertgebouw, and *still* I wasn't going!"

Conclusions

Staryk feels that the RPO recordings made during his period with the group contain a bite and clarity in the violin section that isn't heard from the other English orchestras of the time or from the RPO at other points during Beecham's era. The critics writing during his tenure seem to support this view: Graham Paton of *Music and Musicians* commented in 1958 that "much of the credit for the enormous improvement in this orchestra must go to its vital leader, Steven Staryk. The RPO always did play efficiently; it now adds to sheer skill a musical zest in all sections which rivals that of the Philharmonia." And in the same issue Peter Heyworth found that "under their new leader, the strings of the RPO seemed to have gained in weight and warmth."

Despite the improvements he introduced in the orchestra, the paths chosen by Staryk in effecting change led, in turn, to his eventual dismissal. A social structure such as an orchestra can absorb change to a point, but will disintegrate if pushed too far: one too many pink slips and the general tension in the group becomes unbearable and the group suffers and is distracted from the task of making music. (One too few pink slips and the orchestra remains mediocre or handicapped by its weaker elements.)

Staryk, in his mid-twenties, may not have been fully empathetic in dealing with his colleagues. He was strong, overqualified in his position, and had high expectations for himself and his career as a soloist. Staryk may well have erred in making changes of personnel on a purely objective musical basis. And given that there were simply too many personalities, perceptions, and interests involved — too many variables for the equation to be fully understood, manipulated, and altered by one man — Staryk the politician and mediator might have done well to wrestle Staryk the violinist and artist into temporary submission. A further characteristic of Staryk's situation that might have cautioned a more seasoned concertmaster was the overarching, at times unstable, atmosphere created by Beecham's increasingly temperamental and authoritarian rule. Considered from these perspectives, Staryk acted without sufficient foresight.

On the other hand, Beecham took a political risk in putting a young "foreigner" in such a position of authority and should have anticipated the reaction of his players. In failing to support his Leader when that person carried out his duties and encountered resistance, Beecham showed himself to be inconsistent.

The young Staryk, eager to perform his duties to the best of his ability (in his first major appointment in the foreign professional world), found himself in a situation where the printed rules were not the actual ones. But given the fast-paced trading atmosphere of the times, Staryk feels that his actions were in accordance with what was generally ac-cepted: "In London they traded musicians in the manner that profes-sional athletes are exchanged; even principle players were traded. Gener-ally, in the British music scene of the 1950s, approximately sixty players were permanent while thirty to forty would come and go."

Additionally, there may have been an unstated reason for Staryk's dismissal that had little or nothing to do with his demeanor or his con-ception of duties: Beecham had apparently caught wind of plans to marginalize his role in the RPO. He was aging and some of the players had gathered in private to consider a move to offer Rudolph Kempe the principle conductorship of the orchestra, with Beecham operating as an emeritus conductor. It wouldn't have been the first time that one of his own creations turned him away.[36] Beecham may have caught wind of the plans, suspected Staryk's involvement, and dismissed him in a defensive gesture.

Time moves on. Staryk was already playing in the Concertgebouw by the time legal matters were settled, and on the 8th of March, 1961, Sir Thomas Beecham passed away.

Amsterdam

"The Concertgebouw is regarded as a major institution, like a museum, art gallery, or library," observes Staryk. "It is different from these institu-tions only in that it functions and produces here and now, like theater and opera. The orchestra is important to people there, as much as the other institutions; everyone is very involved in the daily functioning of the hall. The stage hands were often former members of the orchestra who were truly concerned about the orchestra and its traditions."

Newsweek of October 25, 1954 lends weight to this observation, commenting on the Concertgebouw's extended season and explaining that "the Concertgebouw's deficit is underwritten by the national, pro-vincial, and municipal governments. Its concerts are heavily subscribed, and the orchestra plays three to four times a week from October to May."

"I went twice to this famous hall during the week," wrote one London journalist on a visit to the continent in 1962, "but heard almost the same concert on each occasion, such is the Dutch system. There are 2,000 seats in the Concertgebouw, and the regular subscription concerts, given on most Wednesdays during the season are so popular that they must be repeated on the following day. Then on the Saturday a third concert is given, but of a more popular nature, though drawing on some works already heard in the middle of the week. (A system somewhat unfortunate, one may think, for those who wish to attend two or three concerts during the same week: but perhaps different concerts every night at the Royal Festival Hall make a Londoner too greedy in this respect.) Of course the Dutch system ensures that the works chosen are well pre-pared and, as happened during my stay, give a very large audience for a new, or seldom-heard, piece."

Dutch musicians and Netherlander politics

For obvious reasons, the people of the Netherlands were politically sensi-tive following the Nazi occupation of the Second World War. Concern surrounding a leader's political past has shaped relations between players and management ever since, and substantial segments of the Amsterdam public monitor the Concertgebouw's activities.

Consequently the orchestra, like a small nation within a nation, has constructed its policies in opposition to social injustice and fascist politics. In 1950, the management and players of the Concertgebouw responded to the restrictions of McCarthyism in the United States by canceling a tour to that country when visas were denied to two of their members. In 1949, according to *Time* magazine (February 12, 1951), the musicians of the Concertgebouw objected when management proposed to give a pension to "wartime conductor Willem Mengelberg, who played for the Nazis and now lives in exile." And the strength of Dutch convic-tion was revealed in an incident surrounding the engagement of native conductor Paul van Kempen to conduct two concerts on consecutive evenings for an ailing Eduard van Beinum, the orchestra's principle con-ductor at the time. Van Kempen, like Mengelberg, had conducted during the occupation for the benefit of the *Wehrmacht*. *Time* described the Dutch response to his reappearance as conductor of the Concertgebouw: "Inside, as the conductor raised his baton for the Verdi *Requiem*, someone yelled 'Down with Van Kempen.' Others took it up, adding '*Sieg Heil!*' to the chant. Two students began singing the *Horst Wessel* song, two others tossed bottles of tear gas." On the second night, "a woman screamed '*Naziknecht*' (Nazi tool) when Van Kempen raised his arm, and the old hall became a bedlam of cap pistols, noisemakers, yelling, whistling." The instrumentalists "got up from their chairs, stalked off the stage and went to their dressing room . . . when a vice president demanded they return or resign, not one of the 62 musicians moved."

The audition

Aside from the attraction of institutional security after the free-market pandemonium of London, the Concertgebouw excited Staryk's musical curiosity. There were questions of style and inflection in his mind, and the traditional European musical centers offered the possibility of informed answers. "I had read about the Concertgebouw, listened to the orchestra on recordings, imagined what it was like to play in the group. And I had wanted to experience continental music making, either in Amsterdam, Vienna, or Berlin, because it was generally regarded as being more authentic. I wanted to hear the sound, the inflections, see the approach, analyze it, and discuss it all, which I did.

"In Holland, as in Germany, the violins could sometimes be their weakest element. The violas were better, the cellos and basses good. But they just do not have the temperament for the light violinistic range; they create a dark, heavy sound that is marvelous for the music of Bruckner, Mahler, Beethoven, Brahms, and Bach; for music in the Austrian, German tradition, the Concertgebouw is a thrilling orchestra. It was in Holland that I first began to understand this. The Concertgebouw is not brassy, but has a thick string sound, and if a conductor tries to get them to play very softly it won't happen in the same way as in England. The approach in Holland is more earthy, less transparent."

In 1959, changes were taking place at the Concertgebouw. Conductor Eduard van Beinum had recently passed away and in his stead Bernard Haitink and Eugen Jochum were given joint responsibilities of leadership. "It seems that their policy was that one of the conductors had to be Dutch, and when Van Beinum died there simply wasn't anyone of that rank to replace him. So they hired Jochum from Germany, together with Haitink, supposedly as equals. But really, Jochum was the principal man as far as making music was concerned. If Haitink had been in complete charge the orchestra would have deteriorated badly because he was rather unsure of himself, insecure, playing safe. Undoubtedly, in my mind, if they had to have a Dutch conductor, the man who should have had the job was Van Otterloo, who was experienced. But he was apparently not of the right religion and had been divorced (not unlike the rest of the world). Despite their liberalism, the official Dutch liked the appearance of everything being right. Divorce was alright for outsiders perhaps, but within their own conservative house they liked things neat and tidy, even in small details. My wife Ida Staryk's second and current wife], for example, who was a member of the orchestra, was instructed that her long golden hair was not to fall freely, but was to be tied tightly in a bun! However, I think things have changed. Mr. Haitink has even broken with some of the traditions (in his personal life, in any case). Things in Amsterdam are different now."

In 1959, the orchestra's concertmaster for the past season, Jacob Krachmalnick, was looking west to the San Francisco Symphony and the committee for a new concertmaster was searching the world's music scene for a replacement.[37] Staryk's situation in London came to their attention. The management of the Concertgebouw received a strong recommendation on Staryk's behalf from Raphael Kubelik, as well as Krachmalnick, and soon the former Principal Second Violin and the orchestra's acting *Directeur*, Piet Heuwekemeijer, arrived in London for an initial impression of Staryk's playing. Staryk was subsequently invited to Amsterdam for the formal audition process.

"The audition was very revealing," recalls Staryk. "There were, of course, other candidates, both Dutch and foreign. All of the principle players from the orchestra were sitting in, and they could ask any candidate to play whatever it was they wanted to hear from a lengthy list. It was a very good audition, the standard routine which I think most major orchestras in the world go through when they are making such a change.

"The applicant had to prepare two or three concerti, and one of these had to be a standard concerto; you couldn't just walk in and play Baroque and avant-garde music.

"I played the Tchaikovsky and Mozart G Major Concertos, and had a third concerto, but was asked by Tibor De Machula, the principal cellist, to play some unaccompanied Bach. I proceeded with the *Chaconne*, but fortunately, was spared having to finish it. Then there were some of the major cadenzas to play, normal *tutti* passages from the repertoire and some sightreading of a modern Dutch work."

Rite of passage

Staryk was chosen and moved to Amsterdam. However, Staryk's acceptance among those who weren't present at his audition was gradual. His first "test-by-fire" before the Amsterdam public was an evening recital for the Society of Friends of the Concertgebouw. The recital program included: Beethoven's Violin Sonata No. 2 in A Major; Bach's Partita for Solo Violin in D Minor; a sonata by Dutch composer Hans Henkemans; and Prokofiev's Sonata No. 2.

Dr. Prisse, president of the organization, offered his public congratulations to Staryk at recital's end, and emphasized, "We are happy and fortunate that you have come through the front gates of the Concertgebouw to be with us." Yet the reviews were mixed, all of them agreeing that Staryk was well suited for the job of leading the Concertgebouw, but some complaining that Staryk's playing was too detached: "Steven Staryk is not only a great violinist but also a great artist," contrasted with "his shortage of temperament," "the neutrality of his mental status," "his rendering seemed a trifle impersonal here and there," "a certain diffidence." But the reviewers were already looking ahead to Staryk's next appearance as soloist, this time with the Concertgebouw itself, in Tchaikovsky's Violin Concerto.

This appearance, on the 25th of October, 1960, was a resounding success. In an article appearing in *De Typhoon*, entitled "The Orchestral Leader as Soloist," one Dutch critic, in a colorful but quirky and misinformed review, observed a turning point for Staryk:

> For the orchestra, and for that matter for the regular public as well, it is always a great occasion when the leader detaches himself from the orchestra in order to perform as a soloist for the first time. The atmosphere in which such an event takes place is different from the usual performance of a soloist.
>
> A certain tension hovers over the concert hall, mixed with a kind of pride, roused by the fact that suddenly a member of the orchestra is about to realize a dream, cherished by so many colleagues. He is no longer a part of the accompanying ensemble, but in fact sets the tone for it, as the one accompanied.
>
> Steven Staryk, the 28 year old leader of the Concertgebouw Orchestra, who in April succeeded Jacob Krachmalnick in this position, made his debut as a soloist last Wednesday evening with Tchaikovsky's Violin Concerto. The orchestra was conducted by Eugen Jochum, who from the beginning of the new season is becoming one of the permanent conductors of the Amsterdam orchestra.
>
> So far the impression made by Staryk has been rather vague. He appeared to be a good leader, a man with authority despite his youthful age, a violinist who, in the few solo parts he played up to now, was not very conspicuous, and who also, at the evening for chamber music which he

gave the other day, did not give the impression of being a great virtuoso. Consequently expectations for this maiden solo appearance with the orchestra were not very high.

But hark, Staryk — a quiet man without the attitude of a soloist — had kept back one formidable trump. And this he played on Wednesday evening. It was a trump card which, just to remain in the realm of card playing, procured him such a surprising victory, that both the orchestra and the audience rose, to a man, to honor him for a performance which in many respects was comparable to the most illustrious. The peculiar thing in this reproduction lay in a mixture of two widely divergent impressions obtained from Staryk's playing. On the one hand, especially in the first part, a hesitant soloist was heard at times, an artist who has retained something of the detachment but also of the uncertainty of the amateur. It seemed as if Staryk was wavering before finally committing himself to playing that most difficult concerto together with this famous orchestra. He played by heart, but concealed at the conductor's feet stood a little desk with his solo part, just in case . . .

This somewhat amateuristic way of acting was the more charming because Staryk's tone has a most personal enchantment. Also his instrument, a Stradivarius, which over 100 years ago was already played by the great Joachim, should be mentioned in this respect. But far more dominating and, on account of that, more surprising than this detachment was that other trait in his playing: a bewildering virtuosity. It seemed as if he had to surmount something. This done, he stood before us, a great master, a superior artist, who performed, for example, the final part at a dazzling speed, but controlled up to the most minute details.

Consequently, the frantic cheering at this surprising acquaintance was quite understandable.

The *Algemeen Handelsblad Amsterdam* was more concise: "On this remarkable evening, Steven Staryk surprised his audience by his sublime performance of Tchaikovsky's Violin Concerto. His enthralling playing, pure of tone and highly musical . . . sounded exceedingly brisk and natural."

This was the beginning of a busy schedule of solo appearances for Staryk, which, though it contrasted sharply with his experience in London ("it wasn't hectic unless I made it so"), provided him with opportunities to perform in recitals and broadcasts and to do solo work with Dutch orchestras: the Bruch G minor Concerto, the Prokofiev D major coupled with the Bach A minor, the Beethoven, and the Bach Double Concerto with oboe, in Amsterdam, in The Hague, and in the provinces.

The committee

Staryk quickly immersed himself in his work as concertmaster. "The role of concertmaster was different in Amsterdam," he says. "There was a very strong orchestra committee, management, and musical directors, so the demands on the concertmaster were of the standard musical nature; he was to lead the section, play the major solos, and participate in the audition process. Everything else, in terms of running the orchestra, was already taken care of."

If the orchestra is a microcosm of the state, then the orchestra committee might be considered its main political apparatus. And like any such organization in the world at large, a number of agendas were pursued within the Concertgebouw committee: "The orchestra committee was very powerful, controlling the orchestra from within, or trying to. Of course, there are good things about a committee: to protect people from the whims of some dictatorial characters who come along, and to see that people are treated with respect. But in Amsterdam, one could see the other aspect of it, where, in my time at least (and things might have changed), the weaker elements in the orchestra controlled the committee, with the result that there was a 'protectorate of the mediocre,' as Kubelik once put it. The committee did not always reflect the views of the whole orchestra, so there was a good deal of manipulating to try and impress or persuade.

"Usually they were concerned, of course, not with artistic matters but with housekeeping, time, economy, all kinds of things other than artistic matters. This type of committee exists in many orchestras. Then there are the 'Artistic Committees' made up of musicians from the orchestra, and these can try to either raise standards or protect mediocrity, depending on the quality of the committee itself and the amount of influence it has with the other committees, the conductor, and the management."

The Dutch sensitivity to fascism, voiced through the orchestra committee, at one point nearly caused a cessation of relations between the instrumentalists and conductor Eugen Jochum. During a rehearsal, a member of the orchestra removed a sticker from the front page of his orchestral part — music which belonged to Jochum's private library — and found an emblem of the Third Reich. The rehearsal was immediately halted and the orchestra committee convened to decide what action to take. Staryk remembers the event: "In the first place, I cannot see Jochum in an evil role. He was a deeply religious man who had lived in a monastery or seminary at times during the war, and continued this practice afterwards.

"But more to the point, the Concertgebouw had all kinds of German conductors, Klemperer, Krips, Leitner, Sawallisch, a long list who came to conduct, and in this respect, the organization undermined its own liberal aspirations. It was after all inevitable, living in a country right next to Germany, where they certainly turn out some of the best conductors. They had chosen Jochum knowing he was German, so the whole business with the stickers on the music was both meaningless and a show of double standards or selective conscience on the part of the orchestra members. Someone picking away at a sticker was obviously bored, and what better reward than finding a reason and an excuse for the committee to make a show."

Jochum was able to convince the committee of his innocence, but only after the parts were exchanged for Concertgebouw Library materials and the day's rehearsal time was spent.

In addition to acting as a political watchdog, the committee served to protect the orchestra players, including aging members. "What they [the committee] were about was not always good for standards," Staryk explains. "You couldn't demand anything, in terms of discipline or in terms of necessary changes. There were, for example, many older people in the orchestra, people close to retirement who were sitting up close to the front of the section who simply couldn't hear well anymore, who were playing badly even though they were trying their best. At the same time there were many young players, who were much better, sitting in the back getting frustrated and losing morale. I'm speaking now of the strings, because of course in the winds, when people could no longer play to at least some minimum standard, they were moved over, given an assistant's position, because it is much too obvious when a wind player is missing notes or playing off pitch. But in the strings it can be covered, lost in the 'mush,' depending on how lush a mush they make, and the Concertgebouw made a very lush mush, assisted by the great acoustics of the hall."

One of these aging players happened to be in the first violin section. "I discussed it with the manager and the conductor," Staryk says, "but the committee was not about to have this man moved. It was very humane, in the Dutch way; the man was getting old, it was understood that we would all get old so we were expected to put up with it. Eventually, however, long after I left, this man was moved to either the second violins or the violas, anyway to a position where he would not be affecting the intonation of the first violins, a problem which had possibly become obvious even to the committee.

"The ideal orchestra clearly doesn't exist. There are always weak links in the chain and people who are getting older with a variety of problems. There are also 'geographic' musical weaknesses, strangely enough. Different cultures have different aptitudes and it is not uncommon to find, for example, outstanding string sections attached to weaker woodwinds or brass. Each orchestra goes through stages; there are low points and highs when there is a lot of young blood (the Concertgebouw is currently at a high with an average age of 40). Generally what is obvious is also simple: weak people have to be moved from sensitive places."

The orchestra committee could also exercise influence over conductors. This was especially evident in the case of the youthful Bernard Haitink: "Haitink didn't want to create any tension; after all, he was only starting out his career and preferred to be liked by all. His nickname in the orchestra was the Dutch equivalent of 'Boy Scout': 'The Pathfinder.' Quite often, for example, you would see him lean over to the principal viola and his assistant, who was one of the strong figureheads on the committee, and ask 'Everything all right? Bowings okay?' things of that sort. It was so obvious that the others would laugh, and that was different from elsewhere. In the Concertgebouw, in those days, there was laughter without any holding back."

At one point in his tenure, Staryk himself became the object of the committee's displeasure. The occasion was a rehearsal with conductor Carlo Maria Giulini. "Giulini is a marvelous person, regardless of what one thinks of his musicianship. He is a noble man, refined, sensitive; if things don't work out he is almost in tears, but he will rarely say anything to anyone. We were doing the Verdi opera *Falstaff*. In opera, Giulini is marvelous and in this particular one he was fantastic; it was the kind of musical experience that you rarely encounter, even in the Concertgebouw. Giulini made a specific request a number of times with no response, and finally I could see that he was very disturbed. Aside from my responsibility as concertmaster, I felt sorry for him. Simply out of compassion I turned around, gave some simple and clear instructions, in a very correct manner, as the problem was in the violins. I reminded them of what he had just asked, and then made a gesture, pointing to my head, meaning 'use your brains.' (After my RPO experiences, I thought I would try sign language!) Well, they took it as an insult. So, the committee had to meet and discuss this latest crisis, and they decided to rule that no one should talk to me — they referred to it as 'sending you to Coventry.' It really was very funny; in the true Dutch fashion those who felt like talking to me did so, those who didn't have anything to say to me left me alone, and it was just the same as if there had been no rule!"

Discipline

The tolerant social dynamics of the Concertgebouw may have worked to the members' disadvantage when it came to putting together a concert program. Soon after his arrival, Staryk found himself adjusting to the drastic changes from London: "In terms of discipline, it was a Turkish Bazaar. After a while I did not bother to come in to morning rehearsals on time because they never started as scheduled. I more or less calculated that if I arrived ten minutes *after* the rehearsal was scheduled to begin, I would be in plenty of time to tune the orchestra. People would still be straggling onto the stage, with the personnel manager going around pleading, 'Please ladies and gentlemen, can we begin, please let us begin now.' Then, no sooner had they begun, especially if it was a program that required more effort than usual, or a conductor they didn't respect or who did not have much control, there would be calls of 'coffee, coffee!' and it would be time for intermission already!"

The Concertgebouw provided its players with lockers for their instruments inside the concert hall; as a consequence, many players rarely took their instruments home. The *Holland Herald*, magazine of the Dutch airline KLM, commented on the inevitable result: "To our shame, it must be admitted that the sad practice of misusing orchestra rehearsals to learn your part is more widespread in the Netherlands than in any other country with a comparable musical culture. Giulini is not the only conductor to have noticed this. He once remarked that whipping up a concert from the standard repertoire went a lot quicker in Chicago."[38]

Giulini and other visiting conductors and musicians reacted, each in their own way, to the unique social situation of the Concertgebouw. "I remember my student Michael Rennie," says Staryk, "who came to the

Concertgebouw from London, sitting there staring in disbelief; he just couldn't understand all the nonsense. In London he had to work hard — hacking it, running from studio to concert, and next morning to a film session — and here they were in Amsterdam comfortably putting in time, no one getting too excited. Eventually he opted for stress rather than security and went back home. There was also an English cellist who was principal of the second orchestra in Amsterdam. One day he just up and left; disappeared overnight. I don't think he even picked up his pay!"

Hans Rosbaud came to the Concertgebouw and found himself conducting and cajoling in equal measure. "Rosbaud specialized in modern repertoire," Staryk says, "although he also interpreted the classics beautifully. He was a great psychologist." He certainly needed to be for the recording sessions of Stravinsky's *Petrouschka*: "It was becoming monotonous and tense as we went over and over the problem spots, and there he was, trying to break the tension, telling stories, joking, and then asking, 'Shall we try it again?'. Inevitably there would be a bloop here, or someone would miss there, and we would have to go back. And it would be the same thing again, a cracked note here and a bloop there, particularly in the difficult brass passages; some of the brass simply were not with it (in this repertoire, and at that time). I have no idea whether they ever got that record together, or if it was ever released. Like many European orchestras they were not flexible enough musically to encompass a wide range of musical styles. They were either too bound to tradition, or lacking efficiency, or at the retiring age.

"Then there was a Yugoslav violinist from Paris, a very good player, who wanted to leave the madness of that city. Now if London was freelance, Paris was anarchy. A musician would do some of the rehearsals for a job and send in someone else to complete the engagement, just the same scenario as years earlier in London. So, this violinist came to the Concertgebouw because it was sane, but returned almost immediately to Paris! He couldn't fit in with so much complacency!"

George Szell, with his disciplinarian approach, entered this complacency and transformed it. Though officially the principal guest conductor, Szell was so often on the podium at the Concertgebouw that he was in effect the third mainstay, next to Haitink and Jochum. "Here was a situation with everyone only approximately doing the same thing, and then along came Szell. George Szell and the Concertgebouw made a very good combination. There were others, but Szell was outstanding. He tightened a loose orchestra. I had worked with both Reiner and Rodzinski in London, and I favored them for their discipline, even though they pushed this to the extreme and were tyrants as well as authoritarians — they were, in my opinion, great technicians. Szell, also an authoritarian, was less obviously a technician with the stick, but a great musician. There was very little nonsense at his rehearsals, but he did have a dry sense of humor, providing he made the jokes. If you did your job he was not impossible to live with because he appreciated your efforts. The others did too, but it is always more difficult to comment on conductors who come around as guests for just one or two weeks. It is completely different when they are the musical director, or around for a longer time as Szell was in Amsterdam."

"An extreme contrast to Szell was Istvan Kertesz. He was a very talented and very flowery Hungarian who couldn't stop telling the orchestra how thrilled he was to be there. 'Gentlemen, it's been my dream since childhood to conduct this great orchestra.' He went on and on; we could do no wrong. Now any orchestra likes to be flattered, but when it is carried to that extent some eventually become suspicious, especially if the man is in the running to become a permanent conductor or even to do a lot of guest spots."

After two years as concertmaster, Staryk realized he needed more freedom in order to pursue the possibility of a solo career, as many of his best opportunities were to be found in London. "I had not really made up my mind to leave, but I was definitely thinking of it," he says. "In the meantime, Piet Heuwekemeijer came to me with a most elegantly attractive carrot, a Guarneri del Gesù which I could use as long as I remained with the orchestra. It meant that I could sell my Strad, pay off my debts and live much better, which was important because in Holland, while there was excellent security, taxes were very high. There were so many deductions from the paycheck that I was getting nowhere financially. And despite the gloomy climate (it always seemed to be dark, overcast, even in summer), it was possible to actually *live* in Amsterdam because there was almost no freelancing. There was time to think, to have hobbies, to be with one's family. In the orchestra there were always eight weeks off during the year, a week at Christmas and Easter, and six weeks in the summer. It was a respectable way to live, and it showed me that it was possible to live in a country in which the musician is respected and treated with dignity."

Still, Staryk eventually decided to go. It is a sign of the esteem in which he was held that the Concertgebouw's formal notice releasing him from his contractual obligations ended with an official compliment: "[He has] fulfilled his duty as concertmaster from 1960-1962 with great meticulousness, also providing repeated evidence of his talent."

To ease the transition, Staryk continued his involvement with the Concertgebouw on a part-time basis through the summer of 1963, during which time he commuted from London to Amsterdam. "A problem of double taxation existed due to ill advice from my English accountant," Staryk recalls. "England and Holland were already two of the most highly taxed countries in the world. In order to ease the burden, it was necessary for me to make my residence back in London and commute to the Concertgebouw."

Another sign of the Concertgebouw's continuing esteem for Staryk came many years later, in the late 1980s: a reinvitation to lead the orchestra. A second invitation is uncommon, and points both to Staryk's abilities and to the need for a new generation of virtuoso orchestral leaders.

Chicago

It was George Szell who eventually suggested to Staryk that he should consider Chicago: "He persuaded and finally convinced me that it would be a good move. He recommended me to the management, who in turn, contacted Jean Martinon, who had been chosen as the new conductor, to arrange to hear me play in Europe. Meanwhile, Henryk Szeryng, whom I knew but who did not relish Szell, decided that he would also recommend me to Martinon, who was his friend." Staryk had already discontinued his fulltime association with the Concertgebouw and was pursuing some solo and recording engagements when Martinon listened to him play in London and, liking what he heard, offered him the position. And so, satisfied for the moment with his investigation of European music-making, Staryk returned to North America in the company of a former member of the Concertgebouw violin section, his wife Ida.

"I knew the Chicago Symphony from recordings and I respected it very much," Staryk says. "It was brilliant and one of the cleanest, most classical of orchestras in North America at the time; that's why on musical grounds I agreed to go there. In addition, there was the financial attraction and an attitude and type of playing which I had been accustomed to before I went to Europe. In the intervening years, I had changed, my attitude had changed, but still I was looking forward to it. I expected what Chicago turned out to be: a tight, very efficient, well-oiled machine. This was true from the very beginning. At the first rehearsal, I decided to come down early, warm up, look around. I arrived in what I thought would be plenty of time, more than three-quarters of an hour early, but over half the orchestra was there already warming up! I had never seen this in London or Amsterdam and don't know whether it continues today."

In 1963, The Chicago Symphony was composed of 106 players. The season began in mid-October and ran for twenty-eight weeks with weekly subscription concerts on Thursday evenings and Friday afternoons, twelve subscription concerts on Saturdays, and ten popular concerts also on Saturdays. In addition to the regular season, every summer a majority of the orchestra would travel north of the city to Ravinia Park in the suburb of Highland Park for the summer festival directed by Seiji Ozawa. In 1964 the guest conductors and composers included Robert Craft, Igor Stravinsky, Pierre Monteux, and Aaron Copland.

It was at Ravinia Park that French composer and conductor Jean Martinon first led the orchestra on July 19, 1960. Martinon was asked back for a three week subscription series in Orchestra Hall during March of 1961; the series included a well received performance of his own Second Symphony. Martinon returned to the Ravinia Festival on June 26, 28, and 30 of 1962. On October 10 of 1963 he appeared in Orchestra Hall in his inaugural concert as the newly appointed director, and sharing the stage that evening was Steven Staryk, the new concertmaster.

Martinon was entering the void left by an ailing legend: Fritz Reiner. Though an organization of long standing (the CSO was formed by Theodore Thomas in 1891), the orchestra crystallized into one of America's finest ensembles under Reiner's baton. He wielded an acerbic wit and was a feared tyrant. At the same time, Reiner was respected as a master of control, conducting with an oversized baton in minuscule and precise patterns and cuing entrances with his eyes, a trick he had learned from Artur Nikisch.[39] His RCA recordings with the orchestra are legendary: "The music that the Chicago Symphony made under Reiner was glorious," said one orchestra member. "Some of the players believe that it was better then than today; many believe that the records made for RCA during Reiner's regime . . . were the finest ever made, including those of the Solti era." In 1962 Reiner was seventy-three years old and failing in health. With a nine-year tenure behind him he chose to step down and trade the title "musical director" for "musical advisor," a role that would entail significantly fewer administrative responsibilities. The scramble was on to find a new director, and guest conductors Paul Hindemith, Paul Kletzki, Josef Krips, Charles Munch, Hans Rosbaud, and William Steinberg were engaged to fill the 1962-63 season. Martinon was appointed director in October of 1963. Reiner died in November.

Staryk found that the "Chicago Symphony was a typical American orchestra in many respects: marvelous mechanically with great flexibility. But at the same time, it didn't produce a typically American sound. You can hear it particularly on the Reiner recordings. There is clarity in spite of the weight. This, I believe, is due to the combination of Reiner, the acoustics of Orchestra Hall, the RCA recording technique, and the Germanic tradition of the group. Chicago was primarily brass-oriented, so their strings were never quite as beautiful as, say, the Philadelphia Orchestra. But it was brilliant. Actually it is very unusual to combine this brilliance with weight, but the Chicago Symphony did, and it created a powerful effect."

An American Concertmaster

The Chicago Symphony was an efficiently run organization and a disciplined ensemble. There were no managerial matters to look after, as in the RPO, and no conflicts with management. Staryk was overqualified in his role, but his personal style matched that of the orchestra. In fact, the streamlined clarity and precision that is heard in Staryk's performances suggest the CSO couldn't have chosen a more suitable concertmaster: "My approach, which eventually became businesslike and was always egalitarian, worked best in Chicago. The organization and efficiency within the management of the orchestra resulted in fewer extraneous problems and a greater sense of satisfaction for me personally. As for the players, almost everyone came prepared, and 'almost' is as good as it gets anywhere. They did the job and then went on about their business. Most (including myself) were teaching, freelancing, or doing other things; it was a very full schedule that left little time for socializing." Staryk's position as a visiting professor at Northwestern University, and his commitments to recording, playing chamber music, and performing as a soloist continued the pattern set in Amsterdam.

Staryk was immediately required to prove himself in his role as the new concertmaster: "The inevitable test came right away. One of the first things that Martinon scheduled was *Le Bourgeois Gentilhomme* of Strauss, which was not very humane. It is a very difficult solo, one of the most treacherous in the whole orchestral repertoire, and it was made all the more treacherous by the fact that I was literally only just moving my belongings in." Robert Marsh reviewed this concert in the Chicago *Sun-Times*: "Staryk displayed a highly developed technique. Martinon and the Chicago orchestra are heirs to the great ensembles of the past, for here were Beecham's former concertmaster and Toscanini's principal cellist [Frank Miller] facing each other on our stage." The Chicago *Tribune*'s influential and volatile Claudia Cassidy wrote that "it was particularly interesting at this first concert because of the new players, notably the new concertmaster Steven Staryk. Mr. Staryk has ink-black hair, a kind of sturdy compact elegance, a beautiful tone and a strong style that instantly made itself felt."

A few months later, in February, Staryk made his first appearance as soloist, once again playing Tchaikovsky's Violin Concerto in D Major. The choice of the Tchaikovsky in Chicago, as in Amsterdam, was based on the following assessment by Staryk: "It is musically one of Tchaikovsky's best works, technically the most challenging in the repertoire, and unlike the Brahms or Beethoven, is less likely to engage the critics in matters of *interpretation*." Certainly the Tchaikovsky served him well in both cities. He recalls, "If one can look at one's own performance, I must say that when I played the Tchaikovsky in Chicago, it was one of the best performances I had ever given. I played up a storm. I even went to the lengths of borrowing a Strad that I knew and particularly wanted for that occasion."

The Chicago critics once again hailed Staryk: "Mr. Staryk had the high style, which was no surprise, just reassuring confirmation," wrote Claudia Cassidy. "He played the Tchaikovsky with elegance, fire, authority, and with a tone that had both song and bite. The audience saluted him as a visiting virtuoso while claiming him as our own."[40] Robert Marsh smugly noted that "we claim one of the best concertmasters in the business."

During his four-year tenure, Staryk appeared as soloist in the Tchaikovsky Concerto, the Mozart Sinfonia Concertante, the Mozart G Major Concerto, the Kurt Weill Concerto, the Brahms Double, Beethoven Triple, and Henk Badings Concerto for Two Violins, as well as the Bach Brandenburgs.[41] The Badings was performed with Samuel Magad in an effort on Staryk's part to reveal that violinist's abilities. Magad was later promoted to Co-Concertmaster on Staryk's recommendation.

Though he had firmly established himself as leader of the CSO strings and as a musician confident in the role of soloist, a certain sense of foreboding and an underlying tension haunted Staryk during his first two years with the CSO. His move to Chicago was the first return to the United States since the Symphony Six incident and he was mistrustful of the official word that his McCarthy Era troubles were past: "I took up this

73

position with a temporary visa and was 'cleared' two years later by the orchestra. There obviously wasn't that much to 'clear.' However, in getting the documentation together for the alien residence card, it was necessary to get police clearance from the RCMP [clearance that was refused twelve years earlier!]. The reversal of persecution in my own country and clearance by an American orchestra and the hypocrisy of the Canadians in this whole matter was quite extraordinary!" Despite his sense of impending doom, no problems emerged through official channels.

There was, however, an incident involving Staryk within the orchestra during this period that, even with all his previous experience, he could not have anticipated. "A young violinist, sitting near the back of the second violin section, had apparently been promised a promotion by Martinon," writes Setterfield. "However, by the rules of the contract it was necessary for the player in question to audition for his new position before a committee which included Staryk, and to compete against any other player who thought he or she was deserving of moving up. The audition was held and Martinon's choice was not the choice of the committee; he did not get the coveted position. His frustration simmered away all night, and at the rehearsal next morning, during one of the breaks, the disappointed violinist confronted Staryk, and, losing his temper, began to physically attack him: 'I remember that the only thing I was concerned about was protecting my fiddle. I wasn't worried about me. The guys were all looking on in amazement! Actually, he completely misunderstood the situation, thinking that I was personally responsible for stopping his move, but in fact he was quite wrong . . . I simply did not have that kind of influence. Fortunately this time it was not in my contract!

The orchestra, at Martinon's request, was experimenting with a fixed-position promotion system for seating section players. If an individual wished to better their position in the orchestra, they could voluntarily participate in auditions. The new system caused concern among older players who, by reputation, were excellent section players but who had not performed in a solo role for many years. The new system did not endear the troops to their conductor, and Staryk feels that a rotating system of seating, currently in use in most major orchestras, is the preferred method of keeping the greatest number of players content.

Staryk's position once again brought him into contact with renowned conductors. But it was the symphony's own associate conductor, Walter Hendl, who impressed Staryk with his ability to accompany a soloist: "I performed a Mozart Concerto with Hendl which was a joy, one of the most pleasurable experiences I have ever had as a solo player. The talent this man had as an orchestral accompanist was uncanny. There were two others in my career who possessed this incredible intuition: Walter Susskind and Andrew Davis."

However, Hendl was in decline when Staryk met him: "He had just about run out of orchestras and was drinking heavily, and the musicians in the orchestra were merciless in dealing with him.

"Hendl was a pianist as well as a conductor, and I'll never forget one performance in which Martinon, trying to gain popularity American style, conducted Gershwin's *Rhapsody in Blue*. Hendl played the solo piano part and it turned out to be a catastrophe, the likes of which I have seldom participated in on this level. Hendl, poor man, was all over the place, and of course Martinon, a poor accompanist at best, couldn't help him, so it became a total fiasco. Witnessing this concert, I realized that leaving the orchestra to those two must have been a frightening prospect for the knowledgeable Chicago music lover."

Two summers

Though his social contacts within the orchestra were few, Staryk formed a lasting friendship, based on mutual respect, with a man by the name of Richard Colburn: "I liked Dick very much; he was an understated person, an industrialist with his own major company, and possibly a frustrated fiddler. I really took to him. The story he told was that once he had wanted to try someone's Strad, but it was rudely taken away from him. He vowed that one day he would have one of his own. Colburn eventually acquired a most impressive collection. At the time I met him, Kenneth Warren, a Chicago dealer, was leading me toward a del Gesù. It was the "ex-Papini" of 1739, a great looking fiddle with a beautiful sound. I wanted it and Colburn helped me by putting up the money I needed to achieve the balance of the del Gesù's price after the sale of my Strad. He let me and Ida pay off the debt by playing quartets with him in Carmel and Los Angeles; two summers in California for a del Gesù!"

Winter of our discontent

If Staryk's acceptance by the Chicago Symphony, its audience and critics, was both immediate and lasting, Martinon's popularity quickly cooled. However, the debate surrounding Martinon (his choice of programming, the question of his competency), and the excesses enacted on all sides, is in itself a study in musical politics. What follows represents the chaos of the post-Reiner CSO.

Variety Magazine, April 26, 1967: "Conductor and musical director Jean Martinon is the latest victim of the Chicago Symphony Orchestra's tempestuous internal politicking. Martinon has resigned as of after the next season, reportedly at a time when the orchestra board was discussing his successor without consulting him."

In October of 1963, critic Peter P. Jacobi attended Martinon's inaugural concert: "M. Martinon flashed the word right off that this French conductor will be able to handle an orchestra of principally Germanic tradition, and bring to that orchestra not only the French stamp of color and romance, but the solid tone of central Germanic Europe."

Martinon was born in Lyon in 1910, and references to his nationality, with all its correlate associations, became a standard ingredient of reviews written by the Chicago and New York critics: "Martinon did not build the movement's structure with any particular logic. Still the sound was always appealing and textures crystal clear, resulting in an interpretation that I suppose would have to be labeled as French."[42]

Staryk confirms that "there was a certain lightness and transparency he brought to what was basically a heavyweight American German orchestra, though more brilliant than the Berlin. Martinon was able to get a much more sensitive sound in his recordings, which, unfortunately, were very few. Of course, this sensitivity was a necessary ingredient in the repertoire he was recording and did best. For the first two years I think it was a very good collaboration, a happy marriage."

Martinon had his own reasons to think so: "The Chicago Orchestra is the best that I ever had as musical director, both for the quality of the orchestra, which is marvelous, and for the fact that in the five years I was there I repeated only four pieces."

Martinon had entered, perhaps unknowingly, into a volatile political/cultural atmosphere. The Chicago critics were known for their biting diatribes against conductors, especially the *Tribune*'s acidic and influential Claudia Cassidy. Staryk goes so far as to claim that "Cassidy got rid of Kubelik, she got rid of Rodzinsky and some who came before. Conductors came and went. The board of directors was concerned that it would get to the point where no conductor would come to Chicago and the orchestra would be left without prestigious leadership."

But eager appreciation met Martinon's programming and a certain hope and enthusiasm characterized the reviews. "Bold and imaginative programming," declared one critic. "The city hasn't had such an up-to-date program from its orchestra for years. M. Martinon proved he would widen the repertoire, and that his audience would enjoy the adventure."

But Martinon's honeymoon with the critics soon came to an end. In September of 1964, Martinon took his orchestra on a tour which included a performance in Carnegie Hall. The reviews were mixed. In its November issue, *Musical America* reported the results of the first of the CSO's two performances: "Debussy's *La Mer* suffered seriously from this note-by-note examination of the music and there was not much to recommend the performance save its playing."

In 1966 *Musical America* promoted the inevitable comparison of Martinon to his renowned predecessor: "Though Reiner spent most of his Chicago years shallowly rooted in a hotel suite, and though his programs were far too conservative in repertory, he made music like a master and won himself a firm role in the affection and respect of his audience. Martinon can claim no comparable achievement, despite the undeniable loyalty of his admirers."

Another *Musical America* critic present at the CSO's second 1964 performance in Carnegie Hall noted a disparity of ability between players and conductor: "Beethoven's Symphony No. 5 was given a strange performance: the orchestra did not seem to know what was expected of it. The men were not able to follow Mr. Martinon's shifting tempos with any conviction, nor did they seem to play for themselves. These criticisms are not to imply that the concert was a horror, far from it, but for an orchestra so fine it was disappointing. One cannot help but feel that the conductor was a cut below his players." For their part, the players had to agree. First violinist Fred Spector recalls, "He tried to give the orchestra too many subdivisions of the beat, to the point where it restricted the playing ability of the orchestra."[43]

One result of these problems was reported by Robert Marsh in *Musical America,* in July 1965: "The Chicago Symphony thus faces its seventy-fifth season with the distinction of being the third oldest orchestra in the United States and the embarrassment of being without a recording contract while colleagues in other major cities continue to work regularly before the microphone." Staryk says that "it became very obvious that with Martinon there would be no musical fireworks and no recording contract."

Another problem came up later that summer. On August 21, 1965, Billboard reported that "The 1965-66 season of the Chicago Symphony Orchestra has been canceled. The action was taken by the orchestra's trustees after a breakdown in negotiations between them and Local 10-

208, American Federation of Musicians. Trustees of the Orchestral Association said they would develop a program without a symphony orchestra." The board of trustees eventually opted to include the orchestra in their program, granting the players an unprecedentedly high minimum and a contract that included an eleven-month season.

But by this time, Staryk had already begun to lose interest: "In the beginning Martinon was using all his best repertoire: Webern, Hindemith, other moderns, and a lot of French music. Some of the performances of Strauss and Stravinsky were also excellent. However, it was evident quite soon that this man was not the exceptional talent or personality that the orchestra needed; he was often referred to as the 'little French shopkeeper.' He was efficient, well-trained, but not as talented as a Monteux or a Munch."

Oboist Grover Schiltz observed that Martinon "tended to be very rigid. He also tended to be very much the professor. The men resented him from that standpoint — that no matter how you played a solo for the first time through, he always found something to complain about . . . Some of his ideas may have had validity, but by the time you got through his kind of — uh — egotistical French personality, you weren't ready to accept much of anything he said." "He was not a big enough man for this job, musically or intellectually," said percussionist Sam Denov.

But Robert C. Marsh, in a 1965 *Musical America* column devoted to the CSO, was adamant about the source of the CSO's troubles: "The real question about Martinon was not one of competency but of programming. In his first two seasons and in the preliminary announcement of the anniversary year ahead, Martinon was obviously interested in offering a certain number of new scores, but he still gave first emphasis to well-established works, many of which had been heard in recent seasons." Staryk clarifies the situation in this way: "After the first two seasons he began to run out of important contemporary works, and the audience was justifiably wanting to hear the bread and butter music: Bach, Beethoven, Brahms, Mozart, the traditional major works. Unfortunately for Martinon it was in these works that his limitations really showed."

On the occasion of a performance of Bach Brandenburgs, Martinon resurrected an old tradition: "He was acting the role of *Kapellmeister* and in the meantime ruining the performance," remembers Staryk. "He should never have picked up the fiddle and played but that is what he did and did badly. Even the Guadagnini violin loaned to him by Assistant Concertmaster Victor Aitay failed to improve his quality." Critic Roger Dettmer was in attendance: "Jean Martinon presided from a piano bench atop a two-step podium with bow in hand and fiddle under the chin which implied a camaraderie belied by the fleeting expressions of incredulity on the faces of the musicians."[44]

High Fidelity reported on another incident: "[The CSO] lost its principal oboe, Ray Still, by a disciplinary firing that will probably lead to arbitration." Setterfield reports that "Martinon began to complain about the oboist's facial expressions, accused him of reading in rehearsals, even of listening to a ball game between passages. In return, Still complained that Martinon deliberately snubbed him, refusing to give him the customary bow for a difficult solo well played. Martinon countered with the accusation that Still had deliberately left the stage in a fit of pique prior to the conductor's final bow, a breach of professional etiquette. . . .

Setterfield continues:

> Hearings opened on July 28, 1967, between the Orchestral Association of Chicago and the Chicago Federation of Musicians, Local 10-208. There were lawyers for the orchestra, lawyers for the union, and Still's personal attorney, all crowded into the modest office that was used for the hearing.
>
> Staryk's testimony turned out to be among the longest in the official record. . . .
>
> "Have the expressions on Mr. Still's face ever been upsetting to you?" was the question.
>
> "No."
>
> "Have they ever caused you to lose count?" he asked.
>
> Staryk wasn't sure he had heard correctly. "Lose count?" he asked.
>
> "Lose the count," repeated the lawyer.
>
> "Of what?"
>
> "Of the count." The lawyer was getting in deep, "say you were in a rest."
>
> "In a rest?"
>
> "Yes," said the lawyer, hoping he was near his target.
>
> "Of course not," said Staryk.
>
> The lawyer moved on to the question of conducting technique.
>
> "How does a conductor communicate his desires to an orchestra?" he wanted to know.
>
> "By means of his baton technique," Staryk said.

"I don't believe this witness is qualified to answer questions regarding conducting techniques," [the lawyer for the Orchestral Association] told the arbitrator.

The anxiously listening Still sat forward tensely in his chair. Staryk looked around the room, then reached down into a bag he was carrying and pulled out a record which he showed to those present.

"I released a recording in which I conducted," he said.

The lawyer couldn't believe it. "Did you conduct?" he asked.

"Yes."

"Then I withdraw the objection."[45]

"One would never imagine," Staryk now laughs in disbelief, "that there could be such simplicity in the law!"

"Here was an excellent orchestra," he continues, "that with a few alterations could have been exceptional. But Martinon was inconsistent, playing politics, surrounding himself with a group of the weaker elements who would support him at any cost to the orchestra. It was very discouraging from my vantage point, knowing what the potential was, and seeing it being dissipated by one man. In this respect I sympathized with Ray Still, who felt that if Martinon stayed, the orchestra would deteriorate, which one could already see was beginning to happen.

"I respected Ray as a musician. Perhaps he was an upstart, a character, and there were times when he did get Martinon's back up by aggravating him unnecessarily. But oboe players are a temperamental lot and Still was well within this tradition. In the RPO I witnessed a very similar type of player, extremely high strung and a tremendous artist. In a like manner, Mr. Still is an emotional artist and this is obvious in his music making. The man has a solo role and this comes out in his playing, in his general mannerisms. I have a completely opposite nature, I have been reprimanded for not showing enough emotion, *for not smiling.*

"It seemed petty, with the two of them picking at each other, and people in the orchestra taking sides, but for Ray it was a question of ideals and artistry. He had been in the Chicago Symphony for many years, it represented him and his ideals. I believed he was concerned about what was happening, not only for himself, but for the sake of the orchestra. In any case, Ray, at the time, was certainly a much more valuable and talented oboe player than Martinon was a conductor."

In Martinon's view, "There was a little game of destruction, and too many people played it."

"With Martinon," says Staryk, "it appeared to be a question of rules of the game. He was the Director and his authority was not to be questioned! It may have been that they were still doing it this way where he had come from. In minor league orchestras it may be necessary for the conductor to maintain more discipline. However, the major league orchestra, made up of the finest, generally, responds knowingly to each situation and the collaboration occurs at a higher level — somewhere beyond rules.

"In my opinion, it was a problem of insecurity. After all, Martinon landed a pretty big fish with the Chicago Symphony, bigger than anything he had had before, and he obviously did not know how to bring it in!"

"He wasn't a secure man inwardly," confided one orchestra member, confirming Staryk's view. "If you don't have that inner security, it comes across to the orchestra in three minutes. And sooner or later they will find out why you're not secure."

But Martinon felt he wasn't alone in this: "Many persons seemed insecure, and some wanted to make others insecure."

These problems aside, it may well be that Martinon was quite simply caught between a rock and a hard place. To satisfy his critics, he clearly needed to shift his focus away from the standards, in favor of more cutting-edge material. But the orchestral board felt he was putting too much emphasis on contemporary works, and not enough on the classics.

The various tensions caused by the situation were finally allowed to go on too long. "As everyone now knows," says Staryk, "Martinon's last couple of years were just delaying tactics by the board. In a very business-like manner typical of my association with that orchestra, I resigned at the end of the 1966-67 season and left Chicago."

ACT II
A Return to Toronto

"Readers of James Creighton's monumental *Discopaedia of the Violin* will quickly realize, perhaps to their surprise, that one of the most recorded violinists in the history of the instrument was born, lives and works in Toronto," chided the Toronto *Star* in the late 1960s. But in 1962, newly arrived from Amsterdam for his first extended visit in six years, the twenty-nine-year-old Toronto native expressed an opinion of his hometown that revealed little sentimental attachment. Staryk, quoted in *The Performing Arts in Canada*, said, "People in positions of musical power here are irresponsible and afraid to commit themselves . . . so in the end nothing is done. Toronto or Montreal should be on a par with any place in America. Cleveland is about the same size as Toronto, but in only 15 years Cleveland has molded one of the greatest orchestras in the world. What did it? One man; Dr. George Szell. Why shouldn't this happen in this town? The potential is here. The musicians are in many cases excellent; primarily through their own initiative.

"In retrospect," says Staryk in 1997, "the city certainly has become a major financial center, and it has been discovered in the United States as a result of an imported sports team, the Blue Jays! It can happen in sports, it can happen in business, but seems still unable to happen in the arts."

Staryk's reentry into Canadian musical life was a gradual process. In a review of a March 1967 performance, William Littler of the Toronto *Daily Star* remarked on Staryk's low visibility in Canada: "Although Steven Staryk numbers among Canada's foremost violinists, not many Canadians seem to be aware of the fact. The reason is simple enough. Staryk doesn't play all that often in Canada, even in his native Toronto." In between his work with the Royal Philharmonic and the Concertgebouw, Staryk, as the concertmaster of the CBC Orchestra, had recorded Stravinsky under the baton of the aging composer. After leaving Chicago, he led the CBC Symphony Orchestra in an eight-week centennial festival, performing as soloist in the series. This was followed by a solo recital at the

Canadian Pavilion at Expo '67, after which Staryk departed for Europe assisted by an Arts Grant from the Canada Council.

During 1968 and 1969 Staryk performed a number of concerts and broadcasts in Vancouver and Victoria: "At Sunday's Victoria Symphony concert," wrote Audrey Johnson for the Victoria *Daily Times* of October 7, 1968, "he swept through the most daunting passages with fluent confidence, surrounding sheer technique with effortless artistry and grace. The [Tchaikovsky Concerto] was played with the intensity of temperament such a work demands . . ." During this trip, negotiations began regarding teaching positions on the West Coast. In 1972 Staryk took up residence in Canada after sixteen years' absence, entering into positions as Head of the String Division at the Community Music School of Vancouver, visiting professor at Victoria University, and Artist-in-Residence at the Shawnigan Lake and Courtenay Youth Summer Schools. Staryk performed the Kurt Weill Concerto with Mario Bernardi and the National Arts Centre Orchestra (NACO) in May of 1972. He recorded *The A Major* Mozart concerto with the NACO under Bernardi, *The D Major* Prokofiev concerto with Akiyama and the Vancouver Symphony, and the Kenins Concerto with the Vancouver CBC Chamber Orchestra, as well as other concerts, broadcasts, and television appearances.

By 1974, Staryk had reestablished himself on the Canadian circuit. He returned to Toronto in 1975 as a visiting professor at the University of Ottawa, and as a founding member of Quartet Canada with Gerald Stanick, viola, Tsuyoshi Tsutsumi, cello, and Ronald Turini, piano. The Quartet was in residence at the University of Western Ontario in London. They toured Canada and the United States and embarked on a Pacific Rim tour in 1978, performing in Hawaii, Japan, and at the grand opening of the Arts Festival of the Seoul Sejong Cultural Center, Korea. Staryk eventually withdrew from the quartet because of its increasing commitments at the University of Western Ontario.

Staryk's return to Toronto represented the final twist in the trail of his orchestral career. "After other positions in the U.S. and in Canada, everything came full circle when, in 1982, I became the concertmaster of the Toronto Symphony Orchestra." But this return, too, was a gradual process, perhaps as difficult for Staryk as the process of forgetting the Symphony Six incident. The TSO had been under the directorship of Walter Susskind, Karel Ancerl, and Seiji Ozawa. At the time of Staryk's return, a young English conductor, Andrew Davis, was giving the orchestra the exposure it had been lacking: "Since 1974 Davis has toured Canada, appeared five times at Carnegie Hall, and signed recording contracts which have allowed the Toronto Symphony to break into the international record-ing market." In 1977 Davis took the TSO on tour to China. And the 60th anniversary season (1981-82) saw the opening of Roy Thomson Hall.

At about this time, Staryk was negotiating a contract with the TSO, but his next career step was in no way assured. He had already achieved a reputation for restlessness and no one anticipated a slowing of the pace. One interviewer caricatured Staryk on this point in 1979: "He nevertheless insists that he isn't subject to the three-year itch," wrote Littler in the Toronto *Star*. "His peregrinations have been a simple re-sponse to circumstances.

"His move from London to Amsterdam? 'After going as far as England, I had to go to the continent. The hard part was deciding between the Concertgebouw and the Berlin Philharmonic.'

"The move to Chicago? 'George Szell twisted my arm. I was still paying off one of the Strads so economic factors were involved.'

"Leaving the orchestra world for teaching at the prestigious Oberlin Conservatory? 'I'd had enough of orchestras and I wanted more time to do solo work.'

"Leaving Oberlin, Ohio, for Vancouver? 'The Kent State massacre happened just down the road. These were the Viet Nam years and we were raising a family.'

"Leaving Vancouver for Toronto? 'Vancouver was very nice but there just isn't enough happening there to use it as a base. I found myself on the plane all the time.'"

Even based in Toronto, the amount of time Staryk spent in airplanes did not significantly decrease. After three months of touring the Far East with Quartet Canada and Europe with the NACO, and a month in Moscow as jury member at the Tchaikovsky Violin Competition, Staryk perhaps felt the need to slow down, and entered into negotiations with the TSO to take up the familiar responsibilities of concertmaster. The negotiations, however, did not at first produce a satisfactory arrangement and Staryk continued his freelance existence in Toronto. As he told the *Toronto Star* in October 1979, "I like a mixture of activities. Teaching is as close to creating as you can get. And in chamber music you have the chance of a real collaboration. I want it all."

1982 may have been the year that Staryk got it all. Following further negotiations Staryk signed an agreement with the TSO. "This was at a time when I had left the orchestra scene for many years. Not needing the job in any way whatsoever, I returned, in a strange twist of fate, to lead the orchestra in which I had once lost my job. I wonder now if it was vengeance or an attempt to vindicate myself. I had refused the job in the late sixties when invited by Seiji Ozawa and I had built up a reputation as concertmaster, refusing more positions than I had attained." Staryk accepted the TSO position after receiving and turning down a repeat invitation to lead the Royal Philharmonic under Rudolph Kempe and other first offers from the Berlin Philharmonic, also from Kempe; the Philadelphia under Eugene Ormandy; and the Los Angeles Philharmonic, on the recommendation of Arthur Fiedler. Staryk later received a repeat invitation from the Royal Concertgebouw Orchestra while occupying the concertmaster's chair in Toronto.

"Fortunately," says Staryk, "by the time I returned to the TSO, it was an entirely different organization, from management, to board, to conductor and union. The tours during this period were so much more significant. Instead of Ann Arbor, Michigan, there was New York, then London, Paris, Amsterdam, Vienna, Prague: major cities in Europe."

The Strad reported that "currently Staryk is on the music faculties of both the University of Toronto and the Royal Conservatory of Toronto. And after a 15-year hiatus in orchestral work, Staryk this year accepted the position of concertmaster with the Toronto Symphony. This appointment came as a surprise . . . By his own admission it is an attractive contract, one which ties him down to subscription series concerts only."[46] Indeed, Staryk's contract freed him from responsibility for the Pops and Children's concerts, the summer season, and most of the concerto accompaniments. Aside from the draw of such a contract, Staryk allied himself with Toronto and its symphony for personal reasons: his elderly parents lived in the city and his eleven year-old daughter, Natalie, was enrolled in Havergal College. Staryk told an interviewer at the time, "I didn't want to leave my parents at this point and I was thinking of my child. I have schlepped around the world enough to feel a need to settle. It's mere coincidence that it happens to be Canada."[47]

The musicians of the Symphony warmly welcomed Staryk's return as Concertmaster. A Symphony publication confided that "when Steven Staryk was named the new Concertmaster of The Toronto Symphony there was a collective sigh of appreciation. Appreciation first and foremost from the orchestra's musicians who promptly dispatched a letter to TS conductor Andrew Davis stating that Staryk's appointment 'means much to the orchestra in many ways.'"

From 1971 through July of the year of his appointment, Staryk had played eight solo performances with the TSO: Mendelssohn's Violin Concerto twice, *The Four Seasons*, the North American premiere of the

Tippett Triple Concerto with Rivka Golani, viola and Daniel Domb, cello, J.S. Bach's Violin Concerto in E, the world premiere of Klein's *Paganini Collage for Violin and Orchestra*, the Walton Concerto, and Prokofiev's Violin Concerto in D.

When his former conservatory mate, pianist, Glenn Gould, died of a stroke on October 4, 1982, ten days after his fiftieth birthday, Staryk was asked to perform at the memorial service. He joined contralto Maureen Forrester in one of the most poignant outpourings of religious feeling in the canon, an aria from Bach's St. Matthew Passion, *Erbarme dich, mein Gott,* "Have mercy on me, O Lord."

In the summer of 1983, with Staryk now at the helm, the Toronto Symphony embarked on a tour of sixteen European cities, including concerts in London, Paris, Amsterdam, Zurich, Vienna, and Prague. Norman Lebrecht, writing for the London *Times,* remarked that "a young English conductor and Sir Thomas Beecham's former concertmaster — respectively, Andrew Davis and Steven Staryk — have galvanized the Toronto Symphony Orchestra into believing it can match the best in North America . . . Six months ago, [Davis] was joined by Staryk, who interrupted an international career as a soloist to help bring the Toronto orchestra up to world standard."

As part of the tour, the TSO gave a concert in Amsterdam's Concertgebouw, performing Mahler's Fifth Symphony. Staryk was able to warm up in the spot under the stage that sheltered him twenty years earlier, and found the warm reception of his old colleagues and the Amsterdam crowd gratifying.

Back in Toronto, at the end of September 1983, Staryk performed the Shostakovitch Violin Concerto Op. 99 to critical acclaim. A month later, reflecting on the costs of his career, Staryk took a moment to speak with the Calgary *Herald:* "I thought that being in one place for about 25 weeks of the year would give me more time with my family. That was one of the main reasons I took the job — that and a sense of obligation to the musicians in the TSO who invited me to join. But I am so busy with all kinds of solo, orchestral, and chamber work that I seem to be spending more time preparing it all than ever before. I even had to cut out some of my teaching, because my schedule was becoming impossibly cramped. I really don't have time for anything. Even some of those activities which I value and would like to invest time in have been cut; life is a compromise from cradle to grave . . ." There are the occasional rewards: of the September Shostakovitch performance, the Toronto *Star* had written: "Concertmaster Steven Staryk's performance was assured, almost understated, and the epitome of musicianship. He's a classy player, one who commands your attention without idiosyncrasy, even in the third movement's difficult cadenza."[48]

"Life," Staryk affirms, "is a compromise from cradle to grave — except for my music."[49]

The Toronto Symphony's 1984-85 season opened with a performance of the Brandenburg Concerto No. 5 featuring Staryk, Jean Baxstresser (now principal with the New York Philharmonic), and Davis. In May of 1984, the TSO with Davis and the Mendelssohn Choir traveled to Carnegie Hall, a venue in which the Choir hadn't sung for thirty years; Elmer Iseler, conductor of the choir, explained that "we have not been invited." The New York *Times* critic responded well to the performance of Elgar's *The Kingdom*, a score with a substantial violin solo, giving "kudos especially to concertmaster Steven Staryk." In September and October, Staryk played the first of the Brandenburgs and the Schumann Violin Concerto.

Bach, Beethoven (the Triple Concerto), and Mozart — both the Sinfonia Concertante and the Violin Concerto No. 3 — were scheduled for Staryk in 1985. A recording session for the CBC of Strauss's *Ein Heldenleben* and the Shostakovitch Violin Concerto with Andrew Davis and the TSO was followed by a live performance of the *Heldenleben* in Roy Thomson Hall. In a later performance of the Shostakovitch in Windsor, Staryk expressed his view that the Concerto in A Minor, Op. 99 "is one of the major violin concertos, but I think the cause of its lack of popularity is that it isn't exposed enough."

The CBC, as it turns out, has not done its part to improve this situation. There were a number of difficulties with the cover notes for Staryk's recording of the Shostakovitch, many dates were in error, and Staryk sent a letter with corrections to Allen Schechtman, Manager of productions and recordings. However, on the recording's reissue in compact disc format many years later, the problems in the cover notes were corrected by packaging and issuing the work not as the Shostakovitch Violin Concerto, but as Richard Strauss's *Ein Heldenleben*. This development was discovered in 1997 when a former student of Staryk's purchased what appeared to be a copy of Strauss's work on CD; the cover advertises Andrew Davis and the Toronto Symphony with Steven Staryk, solo violin. The conductor, orchestra, and soloist are correct but, upon listening to the disc, the work clearly is not. Staryk good-naturedly hopes that "not too many are listening to Strauss as Shostakovitch and Shostakovitch as Strauss."

"The first thing I do is pull out the record, read the label, and count the bands," reports the experienced and wary record producer Andrew Kazdin. "And even if it says 'Scheherazade,' I'll play it to make sure I don't have Blood, Sweat and Tears instead of Boulez and the Philharmonic."[50]

In December of 1994 a search was made of the CBC's recording archives for masters of Staryk and John Perry's complete Beethoven Sonatas for Violin and Piano, originally recorded in three periods between February 1980 and May 1982. It was discovered that all the digital and some of the backup monolog masters were misplaced or lost. Through the next year and a half, in a series of encounters not unlike those depicted in Kafka's *Trial*, all the missing sonatas were eventually found, primarily because of a single, efficient, and responsible person, Barbara Brown. Staryk believes that "whatever means corporations undertake to increase efficiency — merging, downsizing, moving corporate headquarters to Eastern European or third world locations — the responsible and efficiently functioning *individual* will always be the key to the company's survival or demise. Like an orchestra, a corporation is only as strong as its weakest link." Staryk wonders why there are so many uninformed and irresponsible people in the Canadian Broadcasting Corporation, possibly the only organization that could act as an effective advocate of Canadian culture, and feels that if he isn't completely forgotten in Canada, then he has at least lost any lobbying clout he once enjoyed.

Considering the frailty of the Canadian recording industry, Staryk counts himself fortunate to have recorded in Canada at all. In 1970, critic John Kraglund summarized the situation in an article entitled "At last, a Canadian Recording for Violinist Staryk," published in the January 14 Toronto *Globe and Mail*: "For years, two of the most frequent, perhaps most justified complaints of Canadian concert artists have concerned the difficulties of getting recordings on domestic labels and getting engagements with major Canadian orchestras. As most of our domestic recording companies are merely tentacles of U. S. or European companies, the likelihood of major changes in the recorded music field seems slight, despite improved recording facilities . . . Among the artists who have most frequently voiced complaints is Toronto violinist Steven Staryk . . . whose numerous recordings have been on a variety of fringe labels, imported into Canada and consequently poorly circulated."

André Perrault, Canadian entrepreneur and distributor of classical recordings, commented on the peripheral status of Canada's recording industry: "There is room for Canadian records, but I don't think Canada is big enough on its own. All record manufacturers are international. If we make Canadian records, they must be represented outside. Unfortunately, the major record companies in Canada are just branches so they don't make the big decisions. It's very difficult for them to introduce Canadian products on the market internationally. So we must rely on contact with the major manufacturers; which means New York."[51] Even if there were increased circulation of the works of Canadian artists, classical recordings lack an audience in Canada. A 1981 report noted: "The market for classical music records is growing around the world, but Canada lags behind most Western countries . . . Classical records had only 2.8 per cent of the Canadian record market in 1979. The range was between five and 10 per cent in other countries . . . Since the record companies, needing to operate at a profit, are unlikely to take the initiative and make any changes in their policy towards Canadian classical records, the onus is on the arts councils, music organizations and other public agencies to bring about any change."[52]

Andrew Lipchak, Director of the Arts branch of the Ministry of Citizenship and Culture for the Province of Ontario, wrote in 1983 that: "The arts in Canada are the products of a nation that is still very young. Canada as a political entity is only 115 years old. Its arts reflect traditional, largely European forms of expression alongside attempts to develop unique voices reflecting the here and now of our own Canadian experience. The absence of its own long-standing cultural tradition has therefore meant that while appreciation of a variety of arts has grown, the arts are still often seen by society as a luxury or frill. Compared with the hundreds of years of artistic tradition and achievement in older countries, Canada is still developing its own artistic roots."

Staryk notes "a serious lack of concern and respect for the arts. There are problems with the recognition of the Canadian artist. The fact that Canada itself is insignificant musically on an international stage makes it difficult to be a Canadian musician unless you somehow hit the jackpot, as Glenn Gould did. There is no record company of any significance, and the existing concert and broadcast organizations seem incapable of giving Canadian artists a high profile. Other countries, where classical music is a more important matter, promote their artists, even a little country like Holland. But then, it is one of the older Western cultures." Says Andrew Lipchak: "Canada's regional character has been at the same time a strength as well as an obstacle to the emergence of a Canadian national cultural image and identity." Staryk is less generous: "Canada is primarily still a hockey culture."

The result is a deadening complacency in the musical life of the country. Jacob Siskind addressed the issue from Ottawa after witnessing a CBC Radio Talent Competition: "Gilbert, Aitken, Staryk and Turini all got their basic training in this country but had to go elsewhere to have it sustained and developed . . . [The CBC] must find a way of probing more deeply into the musical consciousness of the Canadian scene if it is to find new talents of their caliber and help them to develop comparably."

Staryk has invested heavily in the development of Canadian talent. In the 1980s he was teaching at the University of Toronto and at the Royal Conservatory, where he was on the Advisory Board to the President. He was involved in the Suzuki program at the Conservatory, working with Erica Davidson to assist students in the transition from Suzuki to traditional methods and acting as the Honorary Head of the program. Staryk also participated in the school's orchestral training program for advanced students and young professionals not yet employed. In addition, he was performing and recording for the CBC. The Complete Beethoven Sonatas for Violin and Piano were recorded at this time, as well as the Shostakovitch and Strauss recordings made with Andrew Davis and the TSO, and the complete Bach Brandenburgs.

But with his overloaded schedule of teaching and performing, Staryk's existence allowed little or no margin for any problems that might arise.

ACT III
The Pressure of Circumstance

"Mr. Staryk has been troubled this season by what he describes as an occupational hazard," wrote the OCSM *Newsletter* in January of 1988: "neck and shoulder pains apparently caused by a pinched nerve. He suffered a severe attack during the Beethoven series last fall. To counteract this trouble he is following the Alexander Technique."

Staryk's troubles began in 1986: "I had three rear-end collisions in a thirteen-month period, one after another; it was shortly after that that the tendonitis started to develop." The *Globe and Mail* reported: "Therapy for the condition included physiotherapy, tensors of various types, anti-inflammatory medication, and exercises. In retrospect, Staryk feels this regimen only masked the pain and finally did more harm than good."[53]

"It was a shock for me," Staryk says. "You take for granted that after so many years there are not likely to be any problems." He took the summer months off, then eased back into playing with the Tchaikovsky and Mendelssohn concertos in performances with regional symphonies in the Fall. A performance of the third movement of the Tchaikovsky *Concerto* for the Royal Conservatory's 100th anniversary concert elicited admiring remarks from the local critics. William Littler wrote for the *Toronto Star* of February 11, 1987: "And then there was the question mark of that star Conservatory pedagogue, Steven Staryk, the TS's concertmaster, who has been away from his chair for months recovering from tendonitis. Would he be up to the fiendish demands of the finale of the Tchaikovsky Violin Concerto? We needn't have worried." And from *The Financial Post* "Steven Staryk put his soreness aside and dazzled . . ."[54]. Staryk donated his CBC honorarium for this concert to the Royal Conservatory.

Though bursitis-tendonitis may only have slowed his professional life for the moment, Staryk was living with the slow death by cancer of his mother.

Still the "unknown" Canadian violinist, Staryk was faced with a complacent public in Toronto: "That he coped equally well with selections from the major violin repertoire was no surprise to those familiar with his numerous recordings," wrote John Kraglund of the *Globe and Mail*. "Nor was it a surprise that he drew only a half-capacity audience, for Toronto audiences have not revealed overwhelming interest in violinists during the past few seasons. And Staryk has the further disadvantage of being reluctant to cater to the popular taste." On another occasion, Kraglund wrote: "More was the pity when Simon Fraser University played host to Steven Staryk, one of the world's best violinists, and drew only an approximate one-fifth capacity audience. Nevertheless, the show went on, and Staryk, true to form, made it very much a show of the first-class fiddling that has earned him international praise. His solo concert provided an effective forum to show up the exceptional quality of his playing — the cool, unerring sense of purpose to his style; a big technique of such purity and strength that it imparts almost a feeling of vertigo."

Despite the Canadian public's apparent disinterest in his work onstage, Staryk has been an active supporter of Canadian culture in all of its musical manifestations. "As an Arts Award winner from the Canada Council," wrote Keith MacMillan in *Musicanada*, "and at one time the concertmaster of the CBC Symphony, Steven Staryk has always maintained creative musical connections with Canada and has honorably fulfilled the requirement of every right-thinking Canadian artist: to play Canadian works, and, as a teacher, to encourage others to do so." Staryk discussed his involvement with new Canadian music at the time: "I've had five premieres in the last two years: violin concertos by Glick, Hoffert, Kenins, Fiala, and a duo by Harry Freedman. [All these works are dedicated to Staryk.] Robert Farnon's *Rhapsody for Violin and Orchestra*, Harry Somer's Sonata No. 2, *Trois Caprices* by Jean Papineau-Couture, Andre Prevost's *Sonate pour violin et piano* and many more are in my repertoire." (As far back as 1971, Staryk had premiered Lothar Klein's *Paganini Collage for Violin and Orchestra* with Karel Ancerl and the Toronto Symphony.) On June 13, 1981, the *Windsor Star* described his performance of the Kenins Violin Concerto in Detroit: "Staryk played it as if he were born to it, in a performance in which he mastered the technical difficulties so completely one forgot about them, setting free the soaring spirit of the work to take off unimpeded."

Staryk's commitment to the performance of new music by Canadian composers has received only limited recognition. "With all the Canadian works I've performed and recorded, you'd think by now somebody would at least say 'thank you.' Take the case of the CBC record of

Kenin's Violin Concerto. The work was commissioned for me and I premiered and recorded it, and the cover of the record doesn't even mention that I play! And then the disc won the Canadian Music Council prize, and no one ever notified me!" At points along the way, Staryk has attempted to bring his activities to the attention of people occupying official positions in Canadian cultural life. In 1969, Staryk received a request from *Musicanada* for information on his performances of Canadian works. Having recently performed Canadian works in Dublin, London, Amsterdam, and Berlin, he obliged the magazine and Keith MacMillan, its editor, and, in turn, received this public response: "The Editor has received, from a celebrated Canadian violinist currently living in the United States, a letter of gentle but unmistakable reproof. Steven Staryk points out that, although he keeps us well supplied with lists of his performances of Canadian works, *Musicanada* so far has not mentioned these in print. . . . (Steve, you should now be reassured of our genuine interest, even though we may not always express it adequately. Thanks.)"[55] Thanks has also occasionally come to Staryk from private sources. One admirer wrote in 1987: "As a Canadian I am indebted to artists like yourself who have subsidized Canadian culture for too long. This will and must change and you will receive your reward."

The rewards were too few and too late for Staryk. Pushed into a corner by circumstances and needing a release from the pressures of his Toronto existence, Staryk left the TSO. In a news release dated April 13, 1987, Toronto Symphony President H. Thomas Beck announced that "Steven Staryk will be resigning his position as Concertmaster at the end of the current 1986/87 concert season in June." For Staryk, the TSO is a microcosm of the enigma of the arts in Canada: "Why hasn't this orchestra achieved the recognition, recording contracts, etc., that it deserves?" And this from a very objective point of view: "I am obviously not waving the patriotic flag; I have simply played in enough orchestras to have experienced the differences and heard enough to compare."

President Beck continued: "While on leave of absence this past season due to some previous injuries, Mr. Staryk received a number of major teaching offers from universities in the USA." Said Staryk: "After seriously considering all aspects of my career, I've accepted a Professorship at the University of Washington in Seattle, effective September of this year. The TSO will always be a part of me."

Staryk later described the impetus for his decision to Murray Ginsberg of *International Musician*: "I've been concertmastering, teaching, soloing, and playing chamber music for so long that it's become an impossible task as a career. I'm leaving the orchestral world and will be concentrating on teaching."[56]

Before leaving Toronto, Staryk undertook a final project for the CBC, starring in a two-hour film on the life of Vivaldi. Staryk the actor? "Well, not exactly an actor," he told Ginsberg. "When they phoned to ask whether I was interested, I told them that I would do it, providing I just play and do what I always do. I said they could dress me up in a costume, put a wig on my head, but I can't be anyone but Steve Staryk.

"The movie was shot in Montreal. When I got there, my God, I had no idea there would be so much to do. The next thing I knew I was learning Italian. I had speaking parts, all kinds of prompting, conducting and new kinds of pressure. And it was wall to wall playing after a week of filming, by which time I had forgotten how to play. I had segments of three and four minute shots, either playing the fiddle or conducting, and these took all day. I did about eighteen movements of Vivaldi concerti and whatever, often playing works with which I wasn't at all familiar and reading from faint copies of copies (without my glasses, which I customarily wear when I play). That's a hell of a lot of playing for a two-hour show, even though a couple of other violinists contributed the odd movement."

Later, Staryk told the OCSM *Newsletter*: "Auspiciously, the CBC film about Vivaldi seems to have been my swan song, though I don't think too highly of this production. The movie ends, or rather it *should* end, with Vivaldi leaving Venice, the city that had so much to do with his career. By coincidence, I was leaving Canada. I will be visiting as guest soloist and teacher and trust the professional relationship between Canada and myself will never be totally severed."

Exit, stage right

"Steven Staryk is probably the most accomplished violinist this country has produced," wrote Eric McLean of the Montreal *Star*. "His career began in Toronto where he played with the orchestra, and I first heard him in a stunning performance of the big solo part of Mozart's D Major Divertimento with Boyd Neel's orchestra in the 1956 Stratford Festival."[57]

Whether or not Canada "produced" Staryk is open to debate. His mother responded to the promise of a better life in Canada and left her native Ukraine. She raised her son in Toronto and educated him in Canadian institutions. But as a young man, Staryk left Canada (and a cultural atmosphere that he felt restricted his further development), and gained recognition elsewhere, finally returning in his maturity, only to leave once again, dissatisfied and ill at ease. Retiring in the United States, Staryk is aware that he has never received the kind of recognition from his own country that an international reputation among colleagues, conductors, and critics indicates he deserves.

When asked in 1978 whether talented musicians could build a career in Canada, Staryk answered: "Yes, but the individual will have to do it himself, and it will be limited. If he depends on Canada to launch his career through official channels, he'll find that, internationally, Canada has absolutely no influence."[58]

There is some evidence to suggest that, from a social viewpoint, Staryk did not fit well into the Canadian power structure. After Staryk had already made his move to Seattle, he received a communication from the Acting Principal of the Royal Conservatory, asking if he wished to remain on the Advisory Board to the President and informing him that in light of his being "removed by such a great distance it might be wiser if you tendered your resignation." Apparently a matter of Conservatory housekeeping had been overlooked, but Staryk feels that it is odd he was never offered a comparable position, at the Royal Conservatory or at other major Canadian schools, to the ones he was offered in the United States. There is an informality in the States that seemed to take no exception to his background. Staryk did not develop within the sheltered, WASP, upper middle class, and was ill at ease within the starched-shirt culture and politics of Canada. The company Staryk kept, seemingly the wrong company - Robert Dodson, former Principal of the Conservatory, and Robert Creech, former Acting Principal - left Canada. Though on the street level Toronto has become the "most culturally diverse city in the world,"[59] the power structure maintains a conservative orientation.

Asked if he had any regrets surrounding his departure from Canada once more, Staryk gave tribute to the CBC: "Of course there are regrets. We are all to a greater or lesser degree subjective. Canada has given me something, particularly the CBC which had so much to do with my career in this country. To me as an artist, and I feel very strongly about this, the CBC has been the most important organization in Canada for the majority of performers, and for all Canadians." However, the forces working *against* the Canadian artist are equally great: "Canada's cultural check-writers have not, traditionally, recognized local or home-grown talent. Looking at this now from an independent position, I've come to the conclusion that the majority — certainly in the past, and still too many at present — are either afraid to commit themselves, lest they expose their ignorance, or they are simply not aware of major contributors unless, like the proverbial squeaky wheel, they are making a lot of noise. And so it continues, various positions are held by unqualified and irresponsible people muddling along, awarding their local prizes to each other, while at the same time, deaf to the wheels that are well-oiled and do not squeak, until those wheels leave for more receptive places."

In the 1970s, Gwenlyn Setterfield wrote about Staryk's work for the CBC: "The CBC recordings (with the exception of the international ones which are not available in Canada at all) must be ordered from a central distributing center in Toronto. Whatever the reasons, perhaps union contracts or the pressure not to infringe on private business, this CBC policy of hiding their recorded output from public view is certainly a deterrent to most buyers and reduces the performer's chances of becoming well-known in his or her own country, since the CBC catalogue is the only one of significant size in Canada." In 1997, Staryk discovered that the sum of his solo recordings had been deleted from the CBC catalogue. "The CBC was an important outlet for recording and performance, but 'the hand that giveth, also taketh away.' At least the CBC *did* give before taking away."

In the end, the politics involved melt away, leaving only the lingering dissatisfaction that achievements have come undone and are forgotten.

RECORDINGS: THE SPLICE OF LIFE

"Some sound better, others worse, depending on the manner in which one plays and the manner in which one is recorded. I'm speaking of range of dynamics, color, inflections, subtleties, not the splicing of right notes for wrong ones." Staryk pauses in his second floor studio at the University of Washington's School of Music. "Without a good engineer and good acoustics, you can walk in with a Strad and wind up having it sound like something from Woolworth's." Open on the desk beside him is a violin case holding his "Barrere" Strad and four exotic-looking bows. One wall of the studio is decorated with record jackets, placed there by a former Teacher's Assistant. "Mikes are set up so that the soloist is heard at all times, every note, and quite often then some." The weather outside is rainy and Staryk, leaning back in his swivel chair with a smile creeping across his face, has a glint in his eye. "A well-known anecdote puts the situation in a nutshell: two of today's top concert violinists were joking with each other after listening to a recording made by one of them. The one who didn't record took a friendly stab at the other: 'Don't you wish *you* could play that well?'"

Staryk has been released on many minor labels: Orion, Saga, Baroque, Monitor, Masters of the Bow, Everest, Virtuoso, Disque Select. But his work has also been found on Telefunken, Philips, HMV-EMI, Imperial-EMI, RCA, Columbia, and the CBC's SM and SM 5000 series. Among the 190 compositions he's recorded are sixteen premieres, ten of which are works by Canadian composers.

Staryk's recording career began in earnest during his stay in London. As leader of the RPO, he found himself often recording difficult cadenzas with little or no preparation: "I once walked in for a Beecham session which, as it turned out, was devoted to Haydn's Drum Roll Symphony No. 103, without my Strad. It was on consignment to be sold in Berlin." Staryk quickly looked back through his section to see who had a decent instrument, spotted a colleague, Michael Rennie, with a Rugieri, traded the Vuillaume which he came with and recorded the solo in the second movement.

When the music demanded concise *tutti* playing, Staryk rallied his players around a set of bowings and a unified concept of phrasing, sometimes again, on a moment's notice. "It was often a scramble," he says. "For instance, we went over to Paris on one occasion to record Haydn's Solomon Symphonies. There was hardly time to think about bowings, phrasing or anything. It turned into a sight reading session, and, as usual, was recorded and released. We did an average of one symphony per three-hour session. These were, of course, reviewed later and described as no less than the definitive versions!"

Another recording which occurred under abnormal circumstances was Bartok's *Two Portraits*, recorded for HMV with Rafael Kubelik. "The session was squeezed between a morning rehearsal and an evening performance at Glyndebourne," Staryk remembers. "I was transported from Lewes, Sussex to the Abbey Road studio in London and back again, *grande prix* style, in the car of a colleague, Andrew Babynchuk." The results were disappointing: "In my opinion, the *Two Portraits* was done very badly. There was no time to listen and make suggestions about anything. The engineer was a man named Andre, a flute player of little distinction, and although he rose to an important position at EMI, engineering was not one of his talents either."

If the music to be recorded was particularly demanding and he had the time, Staryk would not only bow but also finger the passagework for his section. Such was the case in Bartok's Concerto for Orchestra, and many other recordings displaying brilliant violin section-playing.

The RPO was doing up to one hundred recording sessions per year with Beecham, Boult, Kubelik, Kletski, Rodzinski, Sargent, and others. "The recording of some works kept popping up over and over," recalls Staryk. "These were usually the works that Beecham was not at home with, like the Brahms and Beethoven symphonies, works which he took forever to complete."

Apart from *Scheherazade*, which was a Golden Record, selling over a million copies, the recording which brought Staryk the most attention at the time, and even forty years later, was Richard Strauss's *Ein Heldenleben*. Prior to the recording session, Beecham had words of advice for his young concertmaster on the characterization of Mrs. Strauss. Staryk recalls, "The coaching, if it could be called that, consisted of my playing the passages for Tommy just before the recording session, and him telling me stories and anecdotes about Strauss's wife, whom the solo portrays. I had done my homework, as I always have; besides being prepared to play, I had heard in great detail every recorded version of the piece more than once."

Heldenleben was assembled piecemeal after Beecham's death in the Spring of 1961 and released as a memorial farewell and tribute to the conductor. "As far as I was aware," Staryk says, "it was never really and properly completed as a recording. I ultimately sat down with Victor Olof of EMI in order to salvage what was acceptable from the few takes. The record which was finally released was not ideal, and, in fact, I have a tape of an actual performance given shortly after the recording sessions which is infinitely better than the commercial record."

"The cadenza is brilliantly played by Steven Staryk," wrote Neville Cardus in *Gramophone Record Review*, "though I could have wished for a more pointed characterization and a more pungent tone." In response to Cardus's qualification, Staryk explains that "they didn't have mikes set up for either pointed or pungent." Charles Reid, impatient critic of the *Daily Mail*, found that "Steven Staryk's playing of the over-long solo violin part is as sweet and supple as I have heard it." Considering that Staryk and Beecham did not separate on good terms, Staryk finds it ironic that he figures so prominently in Beecham's swansong. Although the album continues to be reissued, it receives no mention in Beecham's biographies.

Between his time with the Royal Philharmonic and the Concertgebouw, Staryk recorded many of Stravinsky's works as concertmaster of the CBC Symphony. "He was either seventy-five or eighty," recalls Staryk, "and the CBC, I believe in collaboration with Columbia, were producing a Birthday issue. Robert Craft rehearsed the orchestra, but it was Stravinsky who was on the podium conducting when we actually made the recordings. I had a further association with him when I was in the Chicago Symphony. A money problem developed (which was serious business with Stravinsky) and the contract with the orchestra and recording company was broken off."

During his Amsterdam period, Staryk recalls that the Concertgebouw recorded *Swan Lake*, Mahler's Fourth, *Til Eulenspiegel*, *Don Juan*, *Petroushka* and numerous violin concerti with Grumiaux.

The Chicago, under Martinon, recorded Bizet, Massenet, Roussel, and other French music. But Martinon was without a recording contract, and with the Orchestra Association subsidizing the orchestra's studio time, there was a need for maximum efficiency. "We would go in and knock off an album in two hours, including intermission. Usually it was a matter of playing twice through and that was it, and because mistakes were embarrassing and expensive, they were scarce, but the tension was tangible; this was excellent training for many low-budget solo recordings I was to make."

The cost of cutting a solo album for an orchestra in the mid 70s was a reported $50,000. Andrew Kazdin, Audio Consultant to the New York Philharmonic, explains: "A full orchestra in the studio costs over two dollars per second. If the conductor says, 'We'll start at letter G,' and a violist asks, 'Where?' he's just bought lunch!"[60] The pressure under which today's orchestral players perform has created its own musical aesthetic. "Equalized tensions," wrote Virgil Thomson in 1947, "the basis of streamlining and of all those other surface unifications that in art, as in engineering, make a work recognizable as belonging to our time and to no other."[61] Though the aesthetic is undeniably "modern," and our own, we probably cannot take any more credit for our unconscious efficiency than the Romantics could for their excess. And, as with every pendulum swing of stylistic taste, there are drawbacks to the modern sound. As Staryk says, "There was fantastic efficiency and everyone was careful; however, it wasn't always very beautiful."

Our modern penchant for seamless perfection in the recording room doesn't necessarily effect the beauty of recordings, but it has an incalculable effect on the way we play and what we expect to hear through the headphones and from the stage. We have created an image of ourselves on disc that is extremely difficult to live up to in reality. The technological force behind the construction of this image is the splice.

Actually, the term "splice" is antiquated; it harkens back to the days of the stopwatch, razor blade, and tape. Today's recording engineers view soundwaves produced on the screen of a computer and "edit" with the click and slide of a mouse. But the result is the same: a note-perfect performance patched together from multiple takes. Perfect performances make nice aural statuary. Gordon Epperson, Professor Emeritus of Cello at the University of Arizona, writes: "The wish to go back and do it again, to eliminate errors but, most of all, to realize an ideal concept of a piece, is surely universal among musicians. [But] our concepts change and evolve. To settle everything definitively, even if it were possible, would be death. A recording may occasionally preserve a great performance, but it remains only one possible rendition, and after a time its utter predictability is likely to pall."

Much has been accomplished in the history of the music business through sleight-of-hand, but splicing has introduced an element of pure deception. The engineer can produce material in the studio that moves beyond what the performer is capable of producing on stage. "Audiences are less dazzled than they once were by soloists," Staryk points out, "even though they dare not say so. Even the professional musicians still do not freely say so. A great deal of this is due to recordings. Audiences are accustomed to hearing soloists portrayed ideally, unaffected by an occasional inability to project, by obvious technical imperfections, or by acoustics. In fact, they hear soloists play on recordings like seldom in reality."

If the recording is a calling card of the performer, then the performer has misrepresented him or herself to the audience, promising more than can be delivered. Though it may sell records, this inflation fattens the artist for the knife of stage work. While the artist is under great pressure to live up to recorded material and produce, for the audience, a performance that resembles the recording, he or she is not necessarily able to impress an audience with the sound of live playing. We once had a more holistic view of the music and a grasp on why we were performing and what we wanted to communicate; today we hear a more technically oriented performance style which can, at times, be more finicky than profound.

Epperson points out that "the recordings of Casals, Kreisler, and Paderewski belong to that era [before splicing had made its appearance, when we got a reasonable facsimile of how an artist really played.] The entire side of a wax disc might be done over many times during the actual recording, but there were several minutes on each final take during which nothing could be faked."[62] Beecham once remarked on his collaboration with Szigeti for a recording of the Prokofiev Concerto Op. 19: "My dear boy," clucked Beecham to Staryk, "I shall never forget the Opus 19: we recorded the *Scherzo* 19 times." In Szigeti's defense Staryk explains that "splicing without today's technology was much more difficult, and ultimately the performer had to get through at least five minutes without mishap!

"As most record collectors know by now, the process of recording direct-to-disc is very similar to the first recordings ever made, in that the music is cut directly on the lacquer with no tape or other paraphernalia coming between. Hence the fidelity of sound."[63]

Accustomed to working under pressure, Staryk prefers the honesty and intensity of recording direct-to-disc (next to live concerts and broadcasts[64]); recordings made in this way approximate the immediacy of live performance. He has made two direct-to-disc recordings, the Bach E Major Concerto with Boyd Neel and *Concerto for Contemporary Violin* by Paul Hoffert, written for, and dedicated to, Staryk. Stravinsky's *L'Histoire du Soldat* is on the reverse side. The discs were made in a space better suited to commercial recordings (which rely on the use of echo chambers), and there were many problems with mike placement. During the Bach recording session, Staryk first sat in the middle of the orchestra, but couldn't hear himself. Then he was moved apart from the orchestra and surrounded with sound barriers to achieve some separation; many hours were spent on a variety of arrangements but nothing worked well. "They gave me copies of the takes, and when I listened to them all, I found that the one which was released was certainly not the best. Because it was the last, we assumed it was best, but not so. You can feel the last movement's tempo getting faster — a combination of boredom from repetition and excitement from sheer stress! And because the studio was air-conditioned and getting colder, the pitch was going up. There it is, and that is the one that went on the market. I have no idea which takes they used for the Hoffert/Stravinsky recording. I forget how many we did. I listened to some and just said, 'Use whichever you want.'"

Staryk's direct-to-disc recordings were made in 1979, but as with his orchestral recordings, his first solo output on vinyl dates back to his Beecham years.

Staryk was at a Glyndebourne opera party when contacts leading to his first commercial recording were made. Part of the post-production tradition at Glyndebourne was for members of the cast or orchestra to take turns performing party tricks for each other. When it came to be the orchestra's turn to provide the entertainment, Staryk organized a gypsy band which he then prompted and led. His colleagues were delighted to find this hidden talent in their Leader and word reached Denis Preston, owner of an independent record company, RSL. Preston had successfully marketed jazz and pop music, but wished to branch into other areas, including the classical field. Staryk, with his fiddling and prestigious position, seemed an obvious cross-over point. Preston spoke with Staryk and plans for an album were made: "Having played so much straight classical music (with some film music and jingles now and then), I really felt the need to play some folk music. After all, it was part of my background; I had grown up with it, and I missed it. In London, there was really nowhere to hear such music, although later in Holland I found the gypsies and went to hear them as I used to in New York."

There were difficulties in assembling a gypsy orchestra in the London of Staryk's time: "I hand-picked the players myself, and they were a high-powered lot, mostly from the Royal Philharmonic. Jack Brymer played clarinet, Frederick Riddle was the violist, Simenaur the cellist, and the violinists were Scherman and Pievsky." The native talent felt their way awkwardly through the music with the bemused coaching and encouragement of the ethnics: "It really was very humorous. I brought along some old records of authentic gypsies so they could at least hear what it sounded like. Somehow they just looked out of place when they tried to reproduce it, because the cultural differences were so great. They didn't understand in the same way as people you can find in Toronto, who come from different ethnic backgrounds and hold on to their musical traditions.

"I remember that we searched and searched for a cymbalum player, and finally located one, who turned out to be barely passable. On a later recording we didn't even bother, we simply doctored the piano by sticking paper between the strings to get something of a cymbalum sound. But not on the first album; there we did it right. A composer and arranger from the RPO, Leonard Salsedo, copied most of what could be copied of this type of music from old authentic recordings: "It was important to get just the right sound and inflection, aspects of style which could not be written in traditional notation. I must say, in this respect, Denis was very patient. We would book x amount of time but if it still wasn't right he would book more and pay for it." The resulting collection of Hungarian, Rumanian, Bulgarian, and Russian folk tunes, *Gypsy Campfires, with Primas Stefan and the 'Royal Tziganes,'* was released on Imperial (EMI-Holland) originally, then in 1964 on EMI's World Record Club.

For their second collaboration, Staryk proposed to Preston a recording of the Wieniawski Caprices for Two Violins, Opus 18. The work had never been recorded and so was attractive from a market standpoint, and the notion that Staryk would play both violin lines was an added draw that would echo Heifetz's redoubled efforts on the Bach Double Concerto. Preston, a great-nephew of Wieniawski, readily endorsed the project. The 1719 "Wieniawski" Strad, one of the concert instruments of the composer, was borrowed from Staryk's collector friend, and a Polish pianist, Adela Kotowska, was engaged to accompany the other works on the album: Wieniawski's Polonaise in D Major, a Mazurka, Legende, and Scherzo-Tarantelle. Kotowska's accompanying experience was extensive; she performed for Carl Flesch's masterclasses and had accompanied Szeryng, Goldberg, Hendl, and Odnoposoff. Staryk says, "The Wieniawski was recorded in the summer of 1960, in London, just after I had moved to Amsterdam. It was all done with severe budget restrictions (the Royal Tziganes had not produced a penny yet). We did our sessions late at night when the studio was free and went into the wee hours of the morning. The technician was young and inexperienced, a relative whom Denis was breaking in, so he didn't cost much. The supervisor of the sessions, David Katz, was a violinist and 'fixer' (a London expression for the contractor) who had great admiration for me. He was talented and had excellent ears, but was very hyper and excitable; both he and his wife were very "up" people. They also had a very hyper poodle. David's wife would come to pick him up, and since we were never sure how long we would go on, she and the poodle often sat in on the sessions, and if I wasn't anxious at the beginning, I would be then.

"It seemed that this recording was jinxed from the start. For instance, there was the problem of tuning. Because there was no accompaniment for the Caprices I would walk in, tune up, which was fine for each individual part, but the A could vary from one session to the next, and when it came to dubbing in the second part, I had no common reference point. I had forgotten to record an A or to use the piano A for reference. It drove me crazy; however, there was nothing to do but suffer." Additional problems arose with Staryk's instrument: "The whole recording was meant to have been played on the "Wieniawski" Strad, but after I had used it for only a matter of weeks it became clear to me that there were problems with it. It was not a healthy fiddle, it tired. I prepared for the recording with it only to find that after the practicing was done, so was the fiddle. I had to switch to my own Strad after recording only the Mazurka and Legende, thus instigating more tuning troubles."

Further mishaps surfaced when the tapes were edited for the final pressing. "As a result of bad cataloguing, or mis-filing, or other mischances," writes Setterfield, "some of the tapes were mixed up, so that, although the Wieniawski has been released on several different labels, not one is as it should be according to the actual choice of final takes made at the time of recording."

"There were rejects on all of them," Staryk confirms. "There is not one release of the Wieniawski on five labels which is totally correct."

In a letter to Preston in 1968, Staryk enumerated the problems: "Having listened to the EMI copy of the Wieniawski, I really don't know *what the hell is going on!* I hear the *corrected* version of the Polonaise which was *not* the same version released by either Imperial in Holland or Virtuoso-Everest in the USA — somebody sent the *wrong* version to Holland and America — and the Polonaise was re-recorded *at your request and insistence!* On the other side of the EMI copy I hear the *not-corrected* version of Caprice No. 3, which, however, is the *correct* version in the U.S. release. Somebody sent the *wrong version* to EMI. Sorry Denis, but life is too short and I don't need assistance in making mistakes!"

Aside from production difficulties, there were difficulties in distribution, especially in arranging a deal with EMI for the album's release. Although recorded in 1960, the Wieniawski album was not released until 1964, through EMI's Imperial label based in Holland, and still later in the United States on the independent Virtuoso label. Eventually, in 1968, the album found its way to EMI proper, and was released along with Staryk's *Every Violinist's Guide*. Eight years after its inception, the reviewers latched on to the recording: "Staryk, in this sort of music anyway, is among the great ones," wrote *Gramophone* in May 1968. "He is fully romantic, yet has superb rhythm, and his *mezzo voce* soft tone is lovely. A program that should reawaken an appreciation of what solo violin playing meant to a generation ago." And there was more: "He has tremendous experience, a wide knowledge of schools and styles, an impeccable technique, immense faith in the public, and the guidance of an impresario of near-genius."

"Hype," scoffs Staryk.

"A dazzling double header" counters Claudia Cassidy of the Chicago *Tribune*. "Mr. Staryk plays superbly, with a dark and glittering amplitude of technique, temperament, and style. This is the same Staryk of almost oriental impassivity, who doesn't even encourage applause on his entrance [to the Chicago Symphony stage]. Believe the music, not the facade."[65]

The review from *Records and Recordings*, a British publication, opened with the pronouncement: "Staryk's performances on this disc clearly demonstrate that he is one of the great virtuoso violinists of our day."

Meanwhile, Preston had ideas for more recordings on EMI's prestigious HMV label. He felt that Staryk was close to a breakthrough. "I really think 1965 could be Steven Staryk Year," wrote Preston enthusiastically in 1964. But in 1965, Preston tempered his high spirits and wrote to Staryk in a more guarded tone: "A long-term contract might be in the offing but these things move slowly." Staryk considers the situation: "It is very difficult to know just what was going on, or to what extent Preston's own efforts and ambitions were stopped at EMI. He was not a man to gossip or say much about what went on behind the scenes, perhaps because he didn't want to discourage me. I do know that he was anxious to break into the classical field.

"Later I became aware that there was a major problem at EMI for violinists. One of the very senior men there was married to Giaconda De Vito, an Italian violinist of moderate ability, and it was said that with the exception of Menuhin, who had a lifetime contract with the company, few others could get a serious look-in. Somebody (for example, Alberto Lysy, who was brought in by Menuhin) would do a couple of records and then be gone. Others would find an entrance, generally have a brief stay, and join the deleted from the catalog."

In 1967 Staryk undertook a project with a Canadian composer living in England, Robert Farnon, to record Farnon's *Rhapsody for Violin and Orchestra*. Since the album was to feature Staryk, it was decided that the second side would include Saint-Saens's *Introduction and Rondo Capriccioso* and Sarasate's *Zigeunerweisen*. However, there were difficulties: "We were booked for one session, at which we were to record both these works, but Douglas Gamley, while an adequate pianist, was not so good with the stick, and things did not go well. Furthermore, the 'session' turned out not to be that at all. By the time we had a balanced sound, the inadequate budget allowed enough time for a once-through, and that was that." In January 1968, Staryk wrote to Farnon's agent in London: "I am in agreement that the Rhapsody be coupled *with any work you choose*, with the exception of the *Rondo Capriccioso* and *Zigeunerweisen*." In February, the agent wrote back, announcing: "I have located the Three Track Master Tape of *Zigeunerweisen* and *Introduction and Rondo Capriccioso*. Please let me know what you think of it." Staryk didn't think twice: "Would like to remind you that I have told you what I think of *Zigeunerweisen* and *Intro and Rondo Capriccioso* very recently!" he wrote back. "I hope you weren't thinking of coupling it with the Rhapsody!" The Rhapsody was eventually paired with Farnon's *Prelude and Dance for Harmonica*, hitting the market on the Polydor label ten years after Staryk's original session.

Every Violinist's Guide, an album in which Staryk performs etudes by Kreutzer, Dancla, Rode, Fiorillo, Kayser, Dont, and Wieniawski, was another Preston project. The sessions for the album took place in London: "The hall had been booked at extra cost as I would no longer do serious recordings in Preston's studio at Lansdowne House, which was dead as a door-nail acoustically. But at Bishop's Gate we were recording in between the thunder of a printing press in the next building, which we hadn't been aware of. It was a question of hoping for a long enough silence to 'get it in the can' through one take for each caprice, which fortunately were short and, in most cases, fast." The album was released on the Imperial label, then re-released in Chicago on the Virtuoso label. Ed Harris, Virtuoso's owner, hoped to link Staryk's album to several others in a series of educational recordings. Both Janos Starker and Julius

Baker recorded material to this end, but the project and Staryk's contract with Virtuoso disintegrated in 1970 when Staryk asked for information touching on his royalties: namely, why he hadn't received any. Harris and Staryk went their separate ways, but thanks to Preston, the *Guide* was brought to life again at EMI and released on their HQM label. On the cover were endorsements from some of Staryk's more renowned colleagues: "Steven Staryk has made a decisive and everlasting contribution to heighten pedagogic standards of today and of tomorrow! With sincere congratulations from Henryk Szeryng." David Oistrakh offered "Congratulations for this valuable idea and recording of pedagogical repertoire." "To Steven Staryk with my greatest admiration for his masterful playing of these beautiful Caprices. Very cordially, Zino Francescatti." Francescatti, on one of his return engagements in Chicago, asked Staryk to please replace his copy of the album, as he had given it to his mother!

This album was later reissued, along with several other Staryk recordings, in a six-disc compendium entitled *Four Hundred Years of the Violin: An Anthology of the Art of Violin Playing.* For the majority of critics, this extensive solo album was an introduction to Staryk and his work. "The man's control is demonic," wrote George Jellinek for *HiFi/Stereo Review* when the album was chosen as that publication's Best of the Month. "The transparency and absolute ease of his playing are boundless . . . His playing is often reminiscent of that of Heifetz in its unruffled security. In vain did I wait in this lengthy program for a reassuring sign of normal human failing, at least one instance of impure tone or inelegant phrasing, for it was not forthcoming. That this virtuoso fiddler could have remained undiscovered by the major labels when artists far less gifted are given ample recorded representation is a minor miracle."[66]

American String Teacher agreed. "Why it took so long for the Planet Staryk to reach Earth will always remain a mystery . . . The present [six record] set is simply stupendous from any angle. His playing brings to mind the young Heifetz for its complete span of the entire virtuoso *panache*, coupled with a finely stylized and musicianly approach to the larger works."[67]

"The irony is that critics keep insisting Staryk has everything but the name," wrote William Littler in the Toronto *Star.* "Steven Staryk has played in many countries and made many records, but he has never had a Sol Hurok [a well-known impresario] to promote him."[68] For Staryk, the fact that it took a six record set to bring him the widespread attention he had long deserved only "proved what I had always believed: it is quantity, not quality, that impresses people."

A recording impresario, Giveon Cornfield, is credited with the six-pack packaging idea. Cornfield operated a Canadian label, Baroque, which specialized in the more rarefied classical repertoire and which later merged with Everest Enterprises in Los Angeles. When Cornfield asked Staryk to record with him in Montreal, Staryk agreed. The recordings took place in the summertime, during Staryk's break from duties with the Chicago Symphony, and produced three albums. The first, a disc of Italian sonatas, contained two authentic items, the Corelli Op. 5 No. 2 and the Locatelli G Minor of 1732, and two arrangements, Nardini's D Major and Veracini's E Minor. Of the arrangements, Staryk comments wryly, "None of the reviewers seemed to notice." The second album included Bach's BWV 1021, BWV 1023, and the F Major and G Minor sonatas which bear no distinguishing numbers, both of which were recorded with the eminent harpsichordist and scholar Kenneth Gilbert. The third featured the first recording of the Pisendel Sonata for Violin sans Basso continuo, a premiere of Papineau-Couture's *Aria for Solo Violin*, as well as works by Geminiani, Hindemith, Stamitz, and Prokofiev.

"I was staying in a house on Peel Street where it was so hot and humid that it was unbearable," Staryk remembers. "Giveon used an old church in the downtown area to do his recording. We scheduled the sessions very late at night so that there would be less danger of traffic noise intruding and to escape the debilitating heat. Of course, when night came, the air cooled down, but then the bats came out which was a bit disconcerting. Also, I got tired around one o'clock in the morning! Nevertheless, Giveon was knowledgeable, and the sound was good, so I did three albums with him and the bats."

The recordings became part of the six-pack and were issued on Everest: "The *400 Years* project was the only recording endeavor to which I have ever contributed any money," says Staryk. "In this case, $400 for 400 years, which was really an insignificant amount. But despite the fact that it was the album which created the greatest visibility and exposure, I never received one penny from it."

In 1969, Staryk worked with Cornfield's new company, Orion, to produce *The Art of Steven Staryk*, which combined a recital program originally recorded for broadcast with WFMT Chicago of virtuoso pieces, sonatas by Haydn and Leclair, and the scorned *Introduction and Rondo Capriccioso* and *Ziguenerweisen* from his London sessions. "When I saw some of the stuff that was coming out, early suspicions were confirmed. Quantity was obviously most important, and I felt that these pieces might as well be on the market with the rest of the stuff. They weren't half as bad as some of the things I was hearing." One of many recordings Staryk feels represents him well, as mentioned previously, is a stunning 1969 live radio performance of Paganini's Concerto No. 1 with the Norddeutsche Rundfunk, Hamburg's Radio Orchestra, coupled with eight *Caprices* and released through James Creighton's Historic Recording Society as part of a series called "Masters of the Bow."

Cornfield also wanted to record Paganini. "I was to have done the complete twenty-four Paganini Caprices," says Staryk, "but we never could come to an agreement over expenses. He wanted me to go to Los Angeles to record, but instead I did them in the summer of 1969 in an old church (which had been set up as a studio) in Dundas, Ontario. It has burned down since; obviously, Paganini's the wrong composer to record in church. The engineer was Don di Novo, who was a real pro in the business, an excellent technician as well as a musician himself. He understood the instrument and knew how to get the right sound and perspective. We recorded twelve Caprices and I scrapped plans for the rest, being uncertain of a release. Four of the Locatelli were done at the same time."

The Caprices were eventually released in the United States by the Musical Heritage Society and in Canada by Disque Select. Once again, Staryk's work was awarded "Best of the Month" honors by *Stereo Review*. Murray Adaskin reviewed the recording: "Listening to Staryk's performance on this superb disc, one comes away with a feeling of awe and wonder at the sheer mastery. Here is violinistic wizardry."[69] The radio station of the New York *Times*, WQXR, aired the recording along with another release of the Caprices played by Paul Zukofsky. A panel of critics was in the studio to give a comparative critical response. The critics included Irving Kolodin, Edward Downes, and Martin Bookspan; George Jellinek acted the part of moderator. The first unidentified selections played by Jellinek were Staryk's versions of the Fifth and Ninth *Caprices*: "As the needle was lifted from the record, Messrs. Kolodin and Downes proclaimed such superlatives as 'phenomenal . . . absolutely extraordinary . . . breathtakingly virtuosic . . . an eye popping recording . . .' while Mr. Bookspan hastened to declare that he had a distinct advantage over his colleagues. He had 'been in the Vanguard Studio when the editing of this particular recording was taking place,' he said. Barely pausing to take a breath, he hurried on to tell his fellow-panelists, and their listeners, how much the recording had impressed him, and how surprised he was to find this particular violinist doing this repertory since he was more well-known for his performances of contemporary music.

After several minutes of this, Mr. Bookspan was interrupted by one of his colleagues, demanding to be let in on the secret of who this miraculous violinist was.

"'Paul Zukofsky,' he affirmed.

"A silence followed; then came Mr. Bookspan's surprised exclamation on being told that he was mistaken.

"'It's Steven Staryk,' the moderator informed the panel.

"'I'll be darned,' replied Mr. Bookspan."[70]

George Jellinek completed his own "Best of the Month" review of the Paganini with some more head-scratching: "I have already expressed in these pages my virtually boundless admiration for Staryk's playing. In spite of his outstanding track record as a former concertmaster of the Royal Philharmonic, the Concertgebouw, and the Chicago Symphony, he is still not sufficiently known."

Many of Staryk's tapes sat on dusty shelves in London and elsewhere, unreleased for years. Such was the fate of *Concerto for Violin and Jazz Orchestra*, by William Russo. Staryk recalls, "This work, originally titled the *English Concerto*, was commissioned by Lord Astor for Yehudi Menuhin, who premiered it at the Bath Festival. Russo discussed it with Menuhin, showing him the jazz inflections and the style. Jazz musicians don't seem to be intimidated by 'names,' they just hear what they hear. Menuhin indicated that he understood, but it came out in his, Menuhin's, way, not in the jazz style Russo wanted, so he decided not to record with Menuhin, although if he had, it would have been released immediately. Russo approached Preston for suggestions about who might record the work and that is when I got into the picture. We recorded with a group called the London Jazz Orchestra, consisting of the best jazz men Russo could find in England.

"Of course, the matter of the release of the jazz concerto dragged on and on as usual. EMI wasn't interested because of their tie with Menuhin, and eventually I just got tired of it all, as did Russo, I expect. We did perform the work in Chicago at a concert in which Gerry Mulligan was also soloist; quite a remarkable evening, I remember. It was eventually released in 1991 on CD by GM recordings, having endured the longest incubation period of any of my recordings."

"Bach's D Minor Partita is another one that never reached the turntable, due to my request not to issue. Another stop order grounded four *Ave Marias* which I just couldn't bring myself to release, no matter what it would have done for my career, on earth or in heaven. It was just a bit too unsophisticated! I did agree to four Tchaikovsky pieces, as part of the same 'popularization project' in Holland, on the little 45 rpm recordings much like they sold with the latest rock tunes."

Another project which didn't make it from the studio to production was a recording of the Teleman Concerto for Four Violins with Staryk playing all four parts. This was to be part of an album, the contents of which he cannot even recall; the tapes were left in London with Denis Preston.

At one point in his career, Staryk felt that he was close to a major breakthrough with EMI. Staryk had recorded the two Prokofiev Sonatas with Mario Bernardi for Preston, who was under contract with EMI, and plans had been made for two further albums, one featuring the Walton Sonata coupled with the Vaughan Williams *Concerto Academico*, with Bernardi as pianist in one and conductor in the other. (Mario Bernardi was conductor of the Sadlers Wells in London at this time and the two Canadians were very visible on the London scene.) The other album was to include the two popular concerti by Bruch and Mendelssohn. Staryk was wined and dined by EMI representatives after a 1968 performance of the Mendelssohn with the RPO in Festival Hall, and recognition on a large scale finally seemed a possibility. But time passed with no announcement of a release. Staryk moved to America and still no word of the release date. Finally, Bernardi met with Preston and found that although Preston was still under contractual obligation to supply three classical recordings, he was withholding the Prokofiev tapes because if he were to submit them to EMI, his investment in the venture would be too great: "Unless it's good for Denis, you can forget it, chum," concluded Bernardi in a letter to Staryk. Preston suggested the possibility of deals with other companies, the meeting spiraled to a close, and Bernardi left Preston with his chief consolation: "Down went another glass of Scotch and I out the door."

"The actual recordings of the Prokofiev Sonatas were very good," Staryk adds, "and eventually were released on a bad pressing by London Records (Canada) and on a much better one by the Musical Heritage Society in the United States. As for the other plans of that time, Preston passed away and all is forgotten. EMI had Oistrakh, Kogan, Rostropovitch, all names on which they could capitalize with minimum strings attached and guaranteed sales. That's what the record business, or any other business is all about. Royalties used to come in from the European releases, but not a penny from the others, except the CBC — and most of my CBC recordings were done on a fee basis. As for releases, deletions, whatever, I have very little information regarding what is happening."

Aside from the two live releases, Staryk's pick of his own recordings might include a CBC Kreisler album, the Shostakovitch Concerto and *Heldenleben* recorded with Andrew Davis and the TSO,[71] the Prokofiev Concerto with Akiyama and the Vancouver Symphony, the Walton Sonata with Helena Bowkun, the Paganini Caprices, and the biggest project of them all, the complete Beethoven Sonatas for Violin and Piano.[72]

The latter was recorded for the CBC with pianist John Perry, an artist with whom Staryk has logged years of enjoyable collaborative work. The two met in Oberlin and have concertized together for many years as the Staryk-Perry Duo. "There is a quality of rapport between these two artists which makes their joint recitals an unusually stimulating experience," said *The Strad* magazine.[73] The Montreal *Star* went further:" Theirs is a particularly polished collaboration that has developed beyond a conscious combination of violin and piano to become an exercise in intuition." When the CBC misplaced the Duo's Beethoven recordings, Staryk phoned Perry with the news and Perry delivered a jibe: "Well, should we record them again?" Staryk shot back, "Are you kidding!?" "Just checking your sanity," replied Perry. The missing masters were eventually found.

"Occasionally a student or colleague from somewhere brings me news of releases and/or deletions," says Staryk. "Just recently a call from Chicago informed me of a release on CD from Munich of the old Orion production, *The Art of Steven Staryk*. Bad news. Not what I would ever want reissued. News arrives of the deletion of both *Heldenleben* and Shostakovitch on CD; good recordings disappear while the bad reappear! With what is presently available of my recordings on CD it would be preferable to have nothing, and at the rate it is going, this should not take long. Then I could pretend to shop for those invisible recordings and exclaim as did Mischa Elman, **"There you are — sold out!!"** The human mind is fortified with escapes and delusion. At least with the CD accompanying this publication there is a glimpse of what I've recorded. This CD comes closer to the original masters than any previous pressings on any labels, and it is released with my approval."

Evening has settled over Seattle and a silence fills the studio. Leaning forward in his chair, Staryk removes his glasses and rubs his eyes. As we prepare to leave, he wraps the "Barrere" in a silk cloth, closes his case, and shrugs into overcoat and cap to protect himself from the rain.

At age three or four, with a loving pragmatic non-stage mother
who endured a turbulent life. (Circa, 1935-36.) (Staryk Collection)

"Plucking away" in the first orchestra at age 10, with first violin teacher and conductor John Moskalyk. John's son Myron was later to become one of Staryk's pupils. (June, 1942.) (Photo by J. Novik)

In "Quasi-Ethnic" concert dress for the "Soloist." (Circa, 1943-44.)
(Staryk collection)

Employee

UNEMPLOYMENT INSURANCE COMMISSION

**CERTIFICATE OF EXCEPTED
EMPLOYMENT**

issued under Section 7 of the Contribution Regulations

Certificate Number 505--10504

174 Spadina Ave.,
Local Office at Toronto 2B, Ont.,

Date November 20, 19 45.

THIS IS TO CERTIFY THAT Mr. Steve Staryk

residing at 350 Crawford Street, Toronto, Ontario.

is excepted from the provisions of the Unemployment Insurance Act, 1940 in respect of his employ-
(his or her)

ment as Violinist
(Occupation)

by The Canadian Broadcasting Corporation
(Employer's Name)

354 Jarvis Street, Toronto, Ontario.
(Employer's Address)

while the conditions of this employment as specified in the application dated November 16 19 45.

remain unchanged, but is not excepted beyond May 20, 19 46.

for G. S. Collins,
Manager.

N.B.—It is important that any change in the hours of work which would disentitle the employee to exception under this Regulation
be notified to the above Local Office immediately.

UIC. 457-1—10M—8-45

Permission granted by a government agency for employment of "minors." The first
CBC recital at age 13. (Toronto, November, 1945.) (Staryk Collection)

With Duke Ellington (guest star) at the St. Regis Hotel. Staryk at right.
Dance music (drinking permitted) every night for 13 "illegal" months at age 17.
(Circa, 1948-49.) (Staryk Collection)

A performance of "Ode to Napoleon" by Arnold Schoenberg and String Quartet by
Glenn Gould, with Glen Gould at the Stratford Festival. (Left to right, Rowland
Pack, Jack Nielsen, Glenn Gould, Steven Staryk, Hyman Goodman.)
Time Magazine (Circa, 1955-56.)

Boyd Neel and the The Hart House Orchestra. Staryk alternated between assistant Concertmaster and Concertmaster. (Circa, 1954-55.) (Staryk Collection)

Particpating in one of many chamber groups between 1950 and 1956. A Piano Quintet with Ernesto Barbini (Left to right, Staryk, Stanley Kolt, Ernesto Barbini, Donald Whitton, Leslie Malowany) (Staryk Collection)

Departing for Europe at Toronto's "Malton" airport. (Left to right, Staryk, Myroslav Biniowsky, Staryk's mother, John Dembeck, Robert Spergel, Staryk's step father. (September 1956.) (Staryk Collection)

Sir Thomas Beecham conducting, Steven Staryk leading the Royal Philharmonic Orchestra at Royal Festival Hall. Michael Rennie at 2nd desk. (London, Circa, 1957-58.) (Staryk collection).

Ludwig van Beethoven Sinfonie Nr. 6 in F-dur „Pastorale" op. 68

Allegro ma non troppo (Erwachen heiterer Gefühle bei der Ankunft auf dem Lande)

Andante molto Mosso (Szene am Bach)

Allegro (Lustiges Zusammensein der Landsleute)

Allegro (Sturm)

Allegretto (Frohe, dankbare Gefühle nach dem Sturm)

Pause

Peter I. Tschaikowsky Violin-Konzert in D-dur op. 35

Allegro moderato
Canzonetta (Andante)
Finale (Allegro vivacissimo)

Frederick Delius Walk to the Paradise Garden

Georg Friedr. Händel Ballett-Suite „Love in Bath" arr. Sir Thomas Beecham

KLUBHAUS KONZERT

Tonhalle Grosser und kleiner Saal Mittwoch, 23. Oktober 1957, 20.15 Uhr

1. ABONNEMENTS-KONZERT

Royal Philharmonic Orchestra London

SOLIST Steven Staryk VIOLINE

LEITUNG Sir Thomas Beecham BART. C.H.

'Dangerous Comparisons' there are times when the best review is a liability. (refer to the review on page 52. (Zurich, October 24, 1957.) (Staryk Collection)

122

Ex "Lord Coke" Guarneri Del Gesù 1744. The first 'Big One' comes with the first major appointment. (London, 1956.) (Staryk collection)

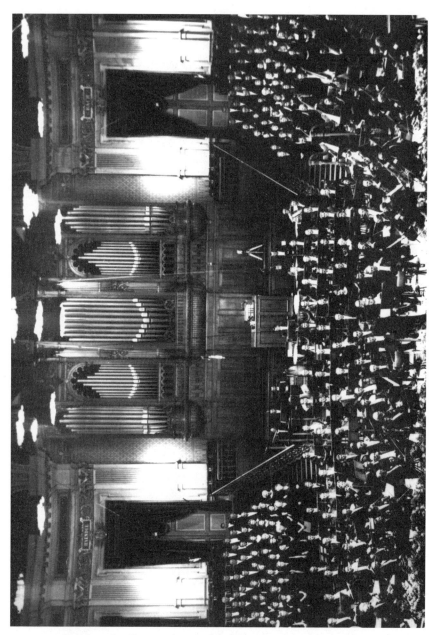

Staryk as 1st Concertmaster of the Concertgebouw Orchestra of
Amsterdam with assistant conductor Peter Erös who joined Staryk
29 years later at the University of Washington. (Courtesy Peter Erös)

One of Staryk's on going 'trades,' the ex "Hochstein" Stradivarius 1715. A most strikingly beautiful example of the golden period. (Staryk Collection)

Ida Busch, "The beautiful blonde of the Concertgebouw" whom Staryk busily courted through North America, Europe and Japan and married prior to their departure for Chicago. (Amsterdam, Circa, 1960-61.) (Staryk collection)

Recording Farnon's Rhapsody in Lodon with Robert Farnon conducting.
(London, Circa, 1963 or 1967-68.) (Staryk collection)

Chicago Symphony Orchestra at Orchestra Hall (Chicago, 1963-64.)
(Courtesy Chicago Symphony)

At an official social function of the Chicago Symphony. (Back row left to right-Edward R. McDougal Vice President of the Orchestral Association, Mrs. W. Newton Burdick President of the Women's Board, Jean Martinon music director, Steven Staryk Concermaster, frontrow seated Mrs. Ida Staryk, Mrs. Nery Martinon). (Circa, 1965). (Courtesy Chicago Symphony).

'Splicing and setting standards for 'live' performances!
(CBC Vancouver, Circa, 1973-74.) (Staryk collection)

With the 'ideal' duo partner John Perry at the Courtenay (B.C.) summer
festival (Circa, 1973-74 or 75.) (Staryk collection)

'Coaching' a very talented 6 or 7 year old daughter Natalie, who fortunately (in Father's opinion) pursued more practical interests in Veterinary studies at Tuft's University. (Toronto, Circa, 1976-77.) (Photo Myron Boyko)

Staryk to be awarded the Shevchenko medal at the Premiere of the Fialla Concerto dedicated to him. (Left to right, official of the Ukrainian national committee, George Fialla, Piero Gamba, Steven Staryk) (Winnipeg, October 13, 1974.) (Staryk collection)

Touring Amsterdam's Canals on vacation with family. (Left to right, Ida, Steven, Natalie) (Amsterdam, July, 1978.) (Staryk collection)

Admiring Mr. Eto's Strad in Tokyo during the 2nd tour to Japan (on this occassion with Quartet Canada). (Tokyo, May, 1978.) (Staryk collection)

The fiddler's "variety and spice of life." Examining and playing Strads, Dei Gesù and Bergonzi at the home of Mr. Lam. (New Jersey, 1979.) (Staryk collection).

The "formal" formation of Quartet Canada in Courtenay B.C. 1975 or 1976. (Left to right Tsuyoshi Tsutsumi, Ronald Turini, Gerald Stanick, Steven Staryk) (Staryk Collection)

From " Jingles to Juries." The reality of today's musical games for those
who can play them. (Top) Staryk in a Toronto studio recording commer-
cials (1981), (bottom) with Valery Klimov on the Tschaikovsky competition
jury. (Moscow, 1982.) (Staryk Collection)

Closing the circle of orchestral life with the Toronto Symphony, Roy Thomson Hall. (Toronto, 1982- 87.) (Courtesy Toronto Symphony)

D *I* ⌣
-E

Wednesday, May 28th, 1986.

Mr. Allen Shechtman,
Manager Productions/Recordings,
C.B.C. Enterprises,
P. O. Box 500, Station 'A',
Toronto, Ontario.
M5W 1E6

Dear Allen:

Further to our conversation last Monday [May 26th], the
following is a list of errors on the back cover of the
Shostakovich [SM 5037] which you asked me to send you .....
I did not proofread, or see anything prior to this.

In the first paragraph in English, the correct date is given,
1948, re the completion of the writing of the concerto. It
is also correct in the French, but in the German translation
it became 1958, which is not correct.

In the second column, second paragraph, 1965 is not the
year Staryk was chosen by Sir Thomas Beecham, as Beecham
was dead, and Staryk was in Chicago. The French and German
translations got the right year, 1956! In the same column,
same paragraph, Staryk was not appointed concertmaster of
The Toronto Symphony in 1962, as he was already occupied
in this post in Amsterdam with the Concertgebouw. This
time, perfect score, the French and German got it wrong
as well. The Toronto Symphony date is 1982.

That's all I could find; hope it won't be too much trouble
to correct. If it is, I suggest we use it on a quiz show:
how many wrong dates can you find? The prize could be the
album!

Hope to hear from you soon.

Sincerely,

Steven Staryk

SS:g

C.C.   Mr. Harold Redekopp,
          Area Head of Radio Music.

A sample of 'Trials and Tribulations' with unqualified personnel. "Some receive an
unfair share of ineffeciency." (Toronto, 1986.) (Staryk Collection)

138

The usual expression that comes with any questionable performance "it may have been terific, but it wasn't good." (Stratford, 1981). (Photo Barbara McDougall)

As was customary in Staryk's career, he was the 'first Canadian' invited to participate on the jury of the Tschaikovsky competion. (Moscow, 1982.) (Photo Emil First)

In the role of Vivaldi with Vittorio Negri. A CBC-TV production.
(Montreal, 1986.) (Staryk Collection).

'Don Antonio' in his Swan Song before departing for Seattle.
(CBC-TV Montreal, 1986.) (Photo Fred Phipps, Producer Richard Bocking)

THE WESTIN HOTEL
Winnipeg

Dear Steve:

Charles Dobias who is here assistant Concertm.
in the Orchestra gave me your Newspaper
Interview & we talked a lot about you during
good food & Wine. Well you have done enough
in your life!!! & I have also continued to work
as you do. Well I am Conducting the Orchestra
Tonight Dvorak String Serenade, Mendelssohn Violin
Concerto Dubeau Soloist, Haydn Symph. No 90 & the
Kaiser Waltz of Strauss. Since I will be Conducting
in Seattle next month, I hope we get together
for food & Wine! I have good Old friends
there as I have been Teaching University
Orchestra. about 40-45 Years ago !!!
Well, the Progr. in Seattle is as I remember
Vivaldi without you!
I still play the fiddle mostly out of Tune!
Schmoeckedoves mostly very well!
I Eat & Drink always very well!
    All my best to you, remember

Two Lombard Place, Winnipeg, Manitoba, Canada R3B 0Y3 (204) 957-1350 Telex 07-587624

(Staryk Collection)

Dear Steve:

Charles Dobias who is here assistant Concertmaster in the orchestra gave me your newspaper interview and we talked a lot about you during good food and wine. Well you have done enough in your life!!! I have also continued to work as you do. Well I am conducting the Orchestra tonight Dvorak String Serenade, Mendelssohn Violin Concerto Dubeau Soloist, Haydn Symphony no. 90 and the Kaiser Waltz of Strauss. Since I will be conducting in Seattle next month, I hope we get together for food and wine! I have good old friends there as I have been teaching University Orchestra about 40-45 years ago!!! Well, the program in Seattle is as I remember Vivaldi without you!

I still play the fiddle mostly out of tune! Schmockedores mostly very well! I eat and drink always very well!

All my best to You, remember Sasha

   Schneider was to conduct an all Vivaldi program in Seattle and therefore the reference to the concert without Staryk as Vivaldi. 'Schmockedores' was a code word in his closer circles for making love. (Winnipeg, 1987.)

One of five feature articles in the Strad covering Staryk's career. The first
appeared in 1957. This cover story, 1994. (The Strad, London, 1994.)
(Photo Barbara McDougall).

Accepting the first Distinguished Teacher Award received by a faculty member of the School of Music in the history of the University of Washington. (Seattle, 1995.) (Staryk collection.)

Ex "Barrere" Stradivarius 1727. The end of a long search for the 'ideal'.
(Photo - Emil Herrmann) (Staryk Collection)

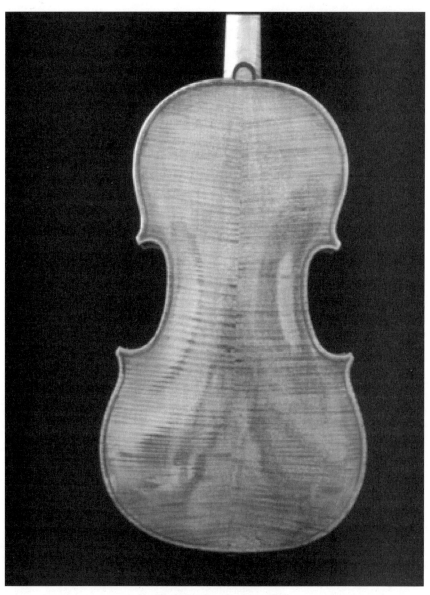

Ex "Barrere" Stradivarius 1727
(Photo - Emil Herrmann) (Staryk Collection)

"Demontration and explanation in the greatest of detail. (Seattle, 1997.)
(Photo Nachum Erlich)

"However after all is said and done, continue to ponder the words of
Geroges Enesco: "Music has a higher function than just to occupy one's
spare time."I sincerely hope so!   (Photo Nachum Erlich)

147

COMPETITIONS, CAREERS, AND ALL THAT CROCK

The fame of great men ought always to be estimated by the means used to acquire it.

- Francois de la Rochefoucauld

"When I was young and foolish," Staryk remembers, "without cares except for practicing, naturally the concert stage was an attraction. Even making trips, no matter where, was exciting. The desire for a solo career came gradually, with many influences from the outside reinforcing inward impulses. Like a racehorse wanting to get out and run, there was a desire within me to leap out of the gates and onto the track."

London promised to give him the chance.

A career in a nutshell

During his Royal Philharmonic years, Staryk made many solo appearances while simultaneously upholding the responsibilities of the orchestra's leadership. His first important engagement was on December 1, 1957, with Jascha Horenstein and the RPO in Royal Festival Hall, performing Paganini's Concerto No. 1. Staryk then paired with pianist Gerald Moore for a Wigmore Hall recital on May 4, 1958 — a career move at the same level of significance as an American recital debut in Carnegie Hall in New York.

On the evening of the 4th, a large audience filled Wigmore Hall, perhaps drawn by Staryk's position in Beecham's orchestra. After a successful first half, Staryk walked onto stage following intermission, ready to tackle Paganini's Caprice No. 5 using the difficult original bowing. As he acknowledged the applause, Staryk spotted Ruggiero Ricci, "the only exponent of this and every other Paganini trick at that time." Ricci's presence would have been unnerving in any event, but Staryk's decision to use a bowing that only a handful of the world's virtuosi had mastered made it even worse. "Luckily I didn't know he would be there," he says now with a laugh.

Staryk performed in every major city in Great Britain, playing the concerti of Mozart, Brahms, Paganini, Tchaikovsky, Sibelius, and Glazunov with conductors Beecham, Horenstein, Pritchard, Dorati, Silvestri, and the Royal Philharmonic, London Symphony, BBC, Hallé, Scottish National, and Royal Liverpool orchestras. Just prior to his departure for Amsterdam, Staryk performed the London premiere of Kurt Weill's Violin Concerto.

In spite of his extensive concertizing, gaining access to certain microphones at the BBC studios proved difficult for Staryk. The BBC required their players to undergo an audition. "There is a well-known story about violinist Szymon Goldberg, whose recordings were played on the BBC for years," writes Setterfield. "Finally he came to do an actual on-air recital and of course had to go through the official audition. Much to everyone's chagrin, he was rejected."[74]

Staryk underwent a similar experience: "I auditioned with Celia Arielli, the wife of Eric Gruenberg. They were a sonata team until they split and Eric decided to play concertos. There was a type-casting system at the time in Great Britain and if you played sonatas you didn't play concertos and vice versa. I had given some public recitals with Celia and found her excellent, but I was apparently still a concerto player in the eyes of those in Broadcasting House. We auditioned, but were rejected. The BBC was not very flexible at that time."

Displaying a distinctly 20th Century bias, the BBC sought out specialists to fill holes in the programming. "For a while," says Staryk, "my appearances on the BBC were mostly in Russian concertos, perhaps because of my Ukrainian background. They wanted the Tchaikovsky, the Glazunov, and that was all. Eventually I did break out of Imperial Russia, and played sonatas, normal mixed programs, and recitals, in addition to continuing concerti performances with the BBC Symphony (London), and the BBC Northern (Manchester). I hadn't re-auditioned for any category so maybe they were just getting short of fiddlers!"

After moving to the Netherlands and taking up responsibilities at the Concertgebouw, Staryk returned several times to Canada. He performed a CBC-TV recital in Montreal, then played the first Bach and Prokofiev concerti in Toronto, followed by the Sibelius in Winnipeg. He concertmastered a variety of programs, including a televised CBC performance of Bach's Fifth Brandenburg with Glenn Gould, Oscar Shumsky, and Julius Baker.

It wasn't until 1967, however, that Staryk dropped other commitments to place his solo career at the forefront of his activities. Prior to this, Staryk had attempted to gain exposure largely through recordings: "The frustrating thing about the recording business is that I basically used it as a compromise outlet for solo performances, accepting the problems and disappointments, and telling myself that 'at least this is where they can occasionally hear me alone.' The only alternative was to keep to the somewhat more serious, sane, and stable side of the business, playing in orchestras and teaching.

"But someone would always come along, get excited about the recordings, write great reviews, promise an exciting breakthrough on disc, and wind me up again. And I went round and round, since, as they say, as long as there is life, there is hope."

Armed with hope and a grant from the Canada Council, Staryk resigned from the Chicago Symphony and left once more for Europe. "I just felt it was time to reorganize my career," he said at the time. "I want to return to Europe to re-establish my contacts there in the solo concert and recording field." Of course, as this door opened, others shut: "Last year I turned down the concertmaster post with the Philadelphia Orchestra," he told an interviewer, "and in January I refused a similar offer from London's New Philharmonia Orchestra, conducted by Otto Klemperer."

And so, returning to the milieu of his first successes, Staryk performed his second Wigmore Hall recital with Mario Bernardi on October 16th, 1967, playing on the "ex-Papini," "ex-Duc de Camposelice" del Gesù in a program of Beethoven, Brahms, Debussy, Papineau-Couture, and Prokofiev.[75] The remainder of the concert year was spent recording in London and performing in England, Holland, Germany, and Switzerland, primarily on state radio.

But Staryk's return to London did little to calm his restlessness or satisfy his desires. He came to realize during this period (which included the EMI experience), that "solo careers are not unlike political campaigns for election," and, convinced that this was not his "cup of tea," he began to search out a steady current for his life.

Staryk entered into negotiations with U.S. schools to secure a teaching position for the 1968-1969 school year. Earlier inquiries sent to Canadian institutions and individuals had turned up nothing: "The Canada Council is very anxious to see you remain in Canada in 1968-69 and we would be quite ready to help in some way or another," wrote an assistant to the Associate Director of the council. "However, at this point, I have no idea of how it could be done, but I would appreciate it if you would maybe let us know the outcome of some of the discussions you had with other people."

Hopping deftly from this sinking ship to the land of the Mayflower, Staryk moved his base of operations to Ohio in the Autumn of 1968, accepting a full professorship at the Oberlin Conservatory. At the age of thirty-six, he was the youngest Full Professor in the school's history.

A rogues' gallery

Staryk's position as concertmaster inevitably put him in contact with that limited group of musicians who tour and give concerts. His recollections of these individuals portray vivid personalities and exciting collaborations, and in listening to Staryk's anecdotes, one senses that he was in contact with a golden age of musicians and musicianship.

"Giorgi Chiffra was one of those nineteenth-century style pianists with a stunning technique, and a very dynamic approach," Staryk recalls. "He was a Liszt specialist, and although he was young, his playing was really from another era, like something you read about. It was a memorable experience to hear him."

Another virtuoso pianist, Arturo Benedetti Michelangeli, was famous for canceling his engagements at the last moment and for his generally eccentric and difficult personality. "Through his repeated cancellations he created an incredible aura around himself," says Staryk, "but to my taste, it was a bit like a circus. I don't know whether he traveled with his own piano, or how it was arranged, but the legs were not the normal height and the registration, or the hammer heads or whatever, were adjusted so that the instrument had a ring that was quite different from the usual. For Scarlatti and similar music, it was quite effective, but not for everything."

When Michelangeli failed to fulfill a 1970 engagement with Karel Ancerl and the Toronto Symphony, Glenn Gould was brought in to play Beethoven's Emperor Concerto on a day's notice. Ancerl, reportedly dismayed, remarked to a Czechoslovakian CBC employee in Czech: "Michelangeli? Gould? Where do you people get such kooks?"[76]

As concertmaster, Staryk worked with a number of other pianists, including Artur Rubinstein, Leon Fleischer, Rudolf Serkin, Alfred Brendel, Hans Richter-Haaser, Wilhelm Kempf, Moura Lympany, Clifford Curzon, and Emil Gilels. He recalls that Gilels "would be having a conversation below stage with the piano tuner, who, by coincidence, was from the same area in Russia. They would be talking, then the call would come and Gilels would go up onstage, play the concerto, then come right back down and continue his conversation as if nothing had intervened. Of course, for Gilels it probably would have been about the sixth time through the piece that day because he was one who constantly played.

"One pianist, Benno Moiseiewich, seemed to have the same eyes, the same face as Rachmaninoff, only he was very small and had more hair. He was of the old romantic Russian school and played many concerts in England, but I don't know if he ever went outside that country. I do remember that he was known for his Rachmaninoff. At rehearsals he smoked cigarettes non-stop, putting them down beside him where they would burn holes in the Steinway. He also gambled away his fees for future concerts long in advance. Another romantic I met in Chicago was Paul Stassevitch, who was known both as a violinist and pianist."

Russia, at this point, was producing the majority of the world's great instrumentalists, especially violinists. Probably the most beloved Russian violinist was David Oistrakh. Staryk recalls a number of performances with Oistrakh. Among them was a Chicago Symphony performance that paired Oistrakh with his son, Igor. Together they played the Bach Double Concerto, after which the senior Oistrakh, who was also conducting, performed Mozart's A Major Violin Concerto. "It was an exceptionally good concert," says Staryk. "Stylistically it was questionable, but David Oistrakh was a gifted musician and his conducting was like his violin playing, musical and naturally intelligent. He got the orchestra to sound and there were no problems; even when he was playing the violin at the same time and just making the odd gesture, it still came together."

As Leader of the RPO, Staryk participated in the first major recordings made in the West by Mstislav Rostropovitch. On top of his concertmaster duties, Staryk fulfilled the role of interpreter for the cellist. He recalls a session spent recording the Dvorak Cello Concerto with Sir Adrian Boult: "Rostropovitch had a system that he used in which he divided the work into sections. He knew where all the obvious places for splicing were, so he never even attempted to play the entire piece right through, he simply did it in sections, playing one part through six or seven times, then moving on to the next. He would stop at each prearranged place, regardless of whether it had been better or worse."

The orchestra didn't understand the cellist's method, and no explanation was offered to them. During a session for Prokofiev's Symphonia Concertante with Sir Malcolm Sargent, Rostropovitch repeatedly stopped just before playing the last few bars of the piece. "This really turned everyone hyper," says Staryk with a smile. "They just didn't know what was going on and Rostropovitch wasn't concerned. The coda is extremely difficult, right at the top of the instrument, like a fiddle, and he had carefully calculated not to expend any more energy or take any more chances than necessary. He got everything else out of the way, leaving only this very last little bit, then away he went, hell for leather, over and over until there were enough takes to cover any misses, then said, 'Thank you very much, we are done.'

"I remember we had gone overtime and there were jokes and comparisons about unions in the U.K. and U.S.S.R. Much, of course, was overlooked on an occasion such as this, especially since Rostropovitch was cleverly using the (supposed) language barrier to his advantage!"

While acknowledging his abilities, Staryk found Rostropovitch's stage mannerisms distracting: "There is no doubt that he is a great instrumentalist and showman. There are all kinds of gestures — kissing, embracing, bowing — it's all part of the hype for this man. I remember when I first heard him in Toronto, in concert as well as on recordings. Some of the classic repertoire he played, Haydn or Bach for instance, was questionable to say the least. But the Dvorak was legitimate: beautiful and honest playing, the piece had become his 'song.'

"His stylistic choices aside, there was an undeniable commercial orientation to Rostropovitch's thinking. Upon arriving in Australia for a tour, his first statement was reportedly, 'I played more concerts and made more money than David Oistrakh last year.'"

Staryk grew up with working-class ethics and a working-class sense of propriety. He reached centerstage by way of the section violins and plays music honestly — reaching for the essence of a composition, and portraying it free of excess. Staryk is impatient with performers who wrap the music in layers of personality or performers whose egos corrupt their faculty of self-criticism. He remembers going with Paul Scherman to observe Mischa Elman's rehearsal for a return London recital after many years' absence. Staryk went grudgingly to appease Scherman, who was a friend of Elman, and wasn't impressed with what he heard. The day after Elman's recital, Scherman received a phone call: "How are you, Mischa?" asked Scherman. Came Elman's response: "Did you read the critics? Scherman, culture in Europe is dead."

Fritz Kreisler was another famous performer who didn't immediately impress. "I failed to get the message from old fiddlers like Kreisler," says Staryk. "At that time I was certainly not a sentimentalist! I listened to the historic broadcasts and went to hear him play on two occasions, but by that time Kreisler was practically deaf and playing badly. Kreisler was supposed to be one of the great interpretive masters, but to me he was only interpretively great in his own salon music, which suited his particular personality, and not in the other repertoire. It may have been that his style was, for me, already *passé*. In my opinion, Szigeti was closer to an ideal interpreter."

Staryk worked with Yehudi Menuhin on numerous occasions. As a boy prodigy, Menuhin had signed a lifetime recording contract with EMI. In his later years, after the unconscious mechanism of his youthful playing inexplicably disintegrated, this requirement became a burden: "I remember with Menuhin some extremely difficult times," says Staryk. "In particular, there were the many sessions to record the Tchaikovsky Concerto, which added up to perhaps twelve hours of studio time, but brought us no nearer to completion. Despite every effort — yoga, meditation, standing on his head — the recording was never released. There were many hours of tape that Menuhin, with his schedule, was not likely to edit, so it was suggested that this version be issued as a 'do-it-yourself-kit,' something I'm surprised the industry hasn't yet capitalized on."

The relatively unknown Zino Francescatti is held in very high regard by Staryk: "To me he was one of the most marvelous human beings. He was an honest, sincere, and unpretentious man, uninvolved in either state or corporate politics. He didn't try to be a musical ambassador, build empires, or push this or that fad, political opinion, diet, or exercise regimen, as some of his colleagues did. Their lip service becomes more convincing than their musical service, while Francescatti's consistent playing gave, for me, an honest message."

And there were many others whose paths Staryk crossed — the magical Igor Bezrodny; the unorthodox Tossy Spivakovsky; that towering Sevcikian edifice, Leonid Kogan; Michael Rabin, the "genius of tomorrow" whose life was cut short at thirty-five; the affable virtuoso Ruggiero Ricci; "Humble Henry" Szeryng who was chauffeured around London in a Rolls Royce; Nathan "The Wise" Milstein; and the refined Belgian, Arthur Grumiaux, who was once so thoroughly dismayed by the unruliness of the Netherlanders during a Concertgebouw recording session that he complained to Staryk: "The next thing you know, they'll be dancing!"

A polished musician of great taste and natural talent, Grumiaux was short on stamina: "If there were two sessions booked for one day," recalls Staryk, "he would complain about being tired, and yet the sessions were not long and there was a lot of time spent sitting and listening to the tapes. But Grumiaux was not accustomed to long periods of work; he was not a person to practice an extraordinary amount, keeping the fiddle up for a long time was hard on him.

"Grumiaux did a couple of tours in North America, but he, and his best repertoire, were too subtle to create the superficial impact that is required here. His style and repertoire project better on recordings. He also hated traveling, particularly flying."

The French violinist Christian Ferras involuntarily inspired a fear of flying in Staryk. Ferras was a favorite of Herbert von Karajan and recorded frequently for Deutsche Grammophon with the Berlin Philharmonic. Although a gifted violinist with a beautifully refined sound and a successful career, Ferras suffered depressions and ate and drank heavily. Staryk recalls an incident involving Ferras in Victoria, British Columbia: "While in Victoria, he suffered a heart attack and was hospitalized for several days, including that of his scheduled concerts with the Victoria Symphony and Laszlo Gati." On the day of the first performance, an anxious Gati phoned Staryk, who was living in Vancouver, to ask him to fulfill the engagement on Ferras's behalf. Staryk agreed and arrangements were made to fly him across the harbor by seaplane in time for the matinee performance. Staryk arrived at the dock that drizzly morning, met his pilot, and jumped into the waiting plane with three hours to spare before the start of the concert on the other side of the water. Inside the two-seater, Staryk had the Mendelssohn Concerto open across his knees, but found himself losing the line of the music as the pilot flew underneath the low-hanging clouds along the coast line, seemingly just above the masts of the boats appearing out of the mists. Staryk repeatedly assured the pilot that there "really is no need to arrive at the destination if there is the least hint of danger!"

The concert was enthusiastically received. Staryk relates that expectations generally placed on the soloist are perhaps lowered on such occasions, so that if one performs well under the difficult circumstances, it often creates a sensation with the public: "Francescatti began his career in such a way. He was sitting in the violin section of a French orchestra when he was called on at the last moment to replace a scheduled performer; a career was suddenly created. The riskiness of these situations appeals to the audience and the critics. It also can lower one's anxiety, as just doing it at a moment's notice is already a partial victory."

Life in flight

"I've traveled around the world and seen the airports and hotels, which is all you see when you concertize. You arrive at the airport, get your room, go to the concert hall, and then you're off to the next place. You look at the list. What's next? Kalamazoo? You hope that you will be able to get out of the town, that you will not be snowed in. The amount of enjoyment is minimal. The only reward is to play with good orchestras, good chamber groups, good pianists, and there aren't all that many of those."

Zino Francescatti shared a similar view of traveling: "Francescatti told me once, as we were standing together backstage at the Concertgebouw before a performance, 'At this hour, I would wish to be in my living room sitting in front of the fireplace reading a book. When I was young and wanted to play more, there was less. Now I am old and I am tired and I wish to be at home.'"

Staryk was drained by the rigors of traveling and concertizing while simultaneously holding down a teaching position, or an orchestra job, or both. "I suppose if one was traveling with an entourage, or, like Szeryng with his diplomatic passport, staying at the Savoy, being chauffeured here and there, everything very first class, traveling would not be so bad."

But few artists can afford to travel in this manner. Staryk recalls that "Szigeti used to cut corners by looking for moderately-priced hotels, things of that sort, right up to the end of his career, because he had become accustomed to doing that from the beginning."

Less fortunate violinists have been known to circumvent the costly hotel stay altogether. "There was an early Galamian student," says Staryk, "an excellent fiddler who had one or two appearances with the Concertgebouw, even did the whole Beethoven Sonata cycle in Salzburg, and was playing around in Europe, not the top dates but the minor circuit. He lived in Amsterdam and drove around to many of his concerts in his little Simca. In order to save money, he would pack his sandwiches and sit out in his car eating them, waiting for concert time. If the engagement was close enough to Amsterdam, he would not book a hotel room. He would change his clothes in the dressing-room, warm up, do the concert, jump into the Simca and drive all night back to Amsterdam. He was an example of a man who played very well. Perhaps not the most magical playing, but good. He certainly deserved more than he got. In my view it was a very sad situation; however, he may have been quite happy in 'following his bliss,' as Joseph Campbell advises."

Even for those with sufficient pocket cash, existence on the road is a grueling series of obstacles and physically uncomfortable situations: "If you are doing it the usual way, taking care of your own bags, struggling through customs, fighting with the airlines about taking a fiddle on the plane with you, then putting it under the seat so there's nowhere left for your feet, getting rooms that are adequate but not great, killing time alone in strange cities, eating grease, salt, and sugar because there is no time or alternative, cutting corners, it is simply not so glamorous. Then there is always the abnormal family life; perhaps the wife can do her own thing, but what of the children?"

More subtle than baggage-claim skirmishes, yet equally disturbing in the life of the concert artist, are the post-concert intricacies. "Often the party is more taxing than the job itself!" says Staryk. "Most are simply a bore. You are very tired in the first place, and often encounter the so-called experts who begin telling you all about music, or those who haven't a clue: they just came for the party. Then there are the hosts who have invited their friends who all know each other; they sit around and discuss the local gossip and you wind up being a wallflower, standing in the corner wondering 'What the hell am I here for?'" A Kreisler story is very telling in this respect: "My fee is $1,000 for the concert," he would say, "$3,000 if it includes a party."

"There are occasions," Staryk admits, "when the conversation is interesting and skirts around the topic of music, and the food is good. If the atmosphere is congenial, I forget that I am tired and simply have a late evening out. But usually I try to put in just as much time as is necessary so as not to appear rude, and then I excuse myself and leave; the plane, after such occasions, always leaves very early in the morning!

"There was very little I found glamorous, except for the music — if it was good. Undoubtedly there are romantic episodes for some. (After all, the whole story of the performer, on any instrument, concerns virtuosi and their swooning fans.) My most memorable romantic episode occurred with my wife Ida, who collaborated in a concert with me in Montreal. As I recall, all our performances were excellent — pre-concert, concert, and post-concert — and we stayed at the Ritz Carlton Hotel!"

Some artists would occasionally avoid the scene altogether. "I remember watching Milstein make his escape at intermission after playing his concerto with the Chicago Symphony," says Staryk. "The orchestra was still trickling off the stage as he was heading out the door, so you know how quickly he packed up. I asked him, 'Aren't you waiting for your fans?'

"'No,' he said, pointing to his watch, 'there's a good movie on TV tonight and I'm not going to miss it.'

"There is a common conception that great things are happening at a concert, magical moments, that something significant is occurring in which everyone is taking part. In the meantime you, the soloist, could be looking down thinking, 'I need a new pair of shoes,' or, 'I forgot to press my pants.' Somebody in front is yawning, that woman in the third row is knitting, and everybody is wrapped in their private world."

"One can too easily become enamored of the glamour, which I think is nonexistent," wrote Staryk's fellow Torontonian and Royal Conservatory-mate, Glenn Gould.[77] Gould quit the stage only a few years after attaining international star status; he despised traveling and playing before live audiences. To avoid this, he channeled the remainder of his pianistic output entirely through a studio microphone. "Performing in the arena had no attraction for me," said Gould. "Even from what little I then knew of the politics of the business, it was apparent that a career as a solo pianist involved a competition which I felt much too grand ever to consider facing."

Of course, the young and famous Gould had already faced the gladiators. He performed a recital in New York, at Town Hall, to an audience which included David Oppenheim of Columbia Records. A contract and *The Goldberg Variations* followed and Gould's career was underway, conspicuously without the events considered by some to be the prerequisite of a concert career.

Competitions

"There has lately developed in *la province* a disconcertingly continental tradition of *musique sportive et combative*," wrote Glenn Gould for *High Fidelity* in December 1966, following a Montreal violin competition. "The festival was a particularly alarming event upon the Canadian musical scene because until recently, such international tournaments have been virtually unknown in this country. In the English-speaking provinces such events are discouraged through both a tacit understanding of the futility of musical jousts and an entirely credible concern with the showing of the home team."

Canadian violinist Jane Charles (now living in Ireland), a former student of Erica Davidson, attended Staryk's Toronto masterclasses. When she placed in the Canadian Music Competition provincial finals, she notified Staryk by letter. Charles was ten years old and competing with musicians as old as twenty-four. There were three jury members present: a violinist, a singer, and an oboist. "Thank you so much for your letter, and BRAVO! on your competition placement," the opening of Staryk's reply read. "Sixth out of thirty-three in a category which could include contestants twice your age with a mixed-bag jury is quite an accomplishment. With this success, I would seriously advise, no more competitions for awhile!

"Music competitions are very dangerous," he explains, "especially at an early age. Making music should not be placed on a level with athletics. What comes through in a competition ultimately is more horse-power than anything else. The jury members sit there, hearing one after another, and the subtleties get lost. The more subtle, the more it's bound to lull the jury to sleep (especially at the end of the day). Competitions are political gatherings, and the politics depend a great deal on where the competition is being held."

"The time has passed when a win at an international competition could bring top managers to an artist's door," reported *Newsweek* in February of 1986. "There are so many competitions, so many former winners with prematurely fizzled careers that a big win has lost most of its buying power."

"Also, it is a matter of lean years and fat years," continues Staryk. "That first prize winner can be a mediocre talent who is rated the same as a great talent who appeared in a previous year; they both hold the same prize, but the former is only the best of a meager talent crop while the latter is truly worth taking note of. The juries sometimes withhold first prizes for good reasons, but just as often for bad."

Though Staryk himself competed as a teenager in Toronto, and later in London and Geneva, he feels that the impact of a win has changed with the times. "It appeared for awhile that international competitions would bring back some sanity to the performer seeking a solo career," says Staryk. "To a point they have, but between the political machinations behind the scenes and the rash of new competitions, it is no wonder that their influence is diminished. My experiences have been frustrating. Since I take these responsibilities very seriously, I could not continue on the jury circuit. Playing God in too flippant a manner can harm more than an individual's career."

The problem is not just the huge number of competitions, but the meager returns harvested by the winning competitors. Prizes rarely cover the costs of entry fees, travel, and hotel bills, not to mention the financially unprofitable hours spent in preparation. Not all competitions command universal respect, nor will they necessarily finance a start on the recital circuit and/or management fees: "The stakes in Montreal were high," relating to the Tchaikovsky competition, wrote Gould, "as the Carling Cup relates to the British Open — a bit short on prestige, perhaps, but distinctly long on cash."[78] And to top it off, in the smaller, less prestigious competitions, there is no guarantee that the jurists will be well-suited to their task, or even agreeably disposed toward the more talented competitors.

Gould, again for *High Fidelity*, wrote: "In certain European competitions (the Tchaikovsky and the Queen Elizabeth of Belgium among them) the jury is empaneled from a list of stellar performers of the day — artists who, because of the security of their own worldly success, are often as not astonishingly liberal in the dispensation of their judgments." For the most part however, continued Gould in the Canadian publication, *Music Magazine*, jurists "are generally very conservative and not exactly on the ascendancy of their careers. They rarely vote for real originality, but recognize a certain kind of performer, a certain mean of ability and stylistic approach."[79] Staryk, himself once a Tchaikovsky Competition juror, adds that "Jurists, in general, are obligated to select efficiency over musicality. They consist of less-than-phenomenal performers and are now largely the same group, moving from one place to another."

Of course there are often extra-musical biases affecting the choices of the jury. David Oistrakh received second place at the Wieniawski Competition in 1935. Two years later, at the age of 28, a decisive first-place victory in Brussels launched his career. Of the Warsaw loss, a former Oistrakh student confided: "[Oistrakh] hinted more than once (in his closest circle, of course), and with visible bitterness, at the anti-Semitic tint of the Warsaw jury's verdict, and added that many of the judges (in his words) 'had reserved their opinion . . .'"[80]

Sometimes jury members simply cannot agree. "My instinct is I would like to give the prize to all of them," concluded jury member Mieczyslaw Horzowski after listening to five finalists perform in Carnegie Hall for the 1976 Leaventritt Piano Competition. William Steinberg, also on the jury, felt differently: "I am the only person here who does not play the piano, and I would have refused to conduct these people," said Steinberg. Mitsuko Uchida was one of the five.

For some, competitions do more to limit than expand their career: "I understand very well that competitions seem like the only way out for many performers," said Gould. "They provide a Good Housekeeping Seal of Approval. The tendency, though, for certain winners of competitions has been to hone that handful of pieces that they have played since they were sixteen. That is a very sad situation."[81] Sad, but it is not difficult to understand why this approach has evolved. Lydia Artymiw competed in the Leaventritt Competition: "In a concert, if you miss a note, you don't worry," she said. "Here you immediately feel that it's fifty points against you."[82]

The vast majority of First Prize winners of important competitions are quickly forgotten unless their musical and extra-musical skills are promoted through extensive managerial follow-through and publicity or by some external factor that impresses the win on the mind of the public. Such an impressive win was Van Cliburn's 1958 Tchaikovsky Competition victory. Van Cliburn was the first American to capture the top prize at that competition and the timing of the event, occurring as it did during the Soviet/American Cold War, gave the victory a political spin. For the American public it was clear proof of the ascendancy of Democracy over Communism and was capitalized upon by RCA and Van Cliburn's promoters. Staryk comments that "because of the political interests involved, the Van Cliburn victory turned into the perennial Van Cliburn Competition, even though Van Cliburn the performer is essentially a one-concerto pianist whose career soon petered out. Beryl Senofsky, winner of the Queen Elizabeth Competition, is largely forgotten, even though he broke the same Soviet domination in the violin world. Eric Friedman, who to some extent was concertizing and recording with RCA, was ill advised to boost his career by entering the Tchaikovsky Competition; not winning did him more harm than good."

Examples of others who slipped out of the limelight encircling the world's handful of top performers after winning a major competition include Igor Bezrodny, who won the Tchaikovsky Competition, Sidney Harth, first prize winner in the Wieniawski Competition, and Miriam Fried, who placed first in the Queen Elizabeth.

Staryk formulates a possible response to the enigma of these player's limited post-competition success: "There may have been ingredients, necessary for the role of superstar, which were missing." Rudolf Serkin's cryptic explanation of why the jurists of the 29th Leaventritt failed to award a First Prize mirrors Staryk's assessment: "Each of the finalists is absolutely equipped to perform in public and the booing of the audience was perhaps justified," he said. "But we felt that none of the finalists was quite ready for this prize, that each one had something but not one had everything."[83] "Nonetheless," continues Staryk, "in the past there were some well-known stars who lacked one or more of the ingredients of today's consummate artist: the personality, the social facility of the world ambassador, the omniscience of the divine giver, and who yet played the fiddle amazingly well.

"Take the case of the more private and austere Heifetz, for instance; who knows if he would have achieved the fame today that he enjoyed earlier in the century? His was a time when socializing and politicking were not as necessary as presently. It appears that simply doing it better than the competition will no longer suffice."

Careers

High-profile music careers in this age do not happen of their own accord in response to purely musical catalysts; they must be cultivated through aggressive marketing. Often the selling point will be an aspect of the player's personality: physical appearance, temperament, vivacity. Sometimes the traits are ones normally considered liabilities: fickleness, physical disability, and even mental instability, as in the case of medicated pianist David Helfgott, made famous by the movie *Shine*. "All of it was shapeless and utterly incoherent," wrote Richard Dyer in the Boston *Globe* after Helfgott's March 1997 recital, "entirely in the present, without memory of what has happened in the past or movement toward fulfillment. It was without phrasing, form, harmonic understanding, differentiation of style, and often basic accuracy; worst of all it was without emotional content."[84]

In a musical utopia, the development of an artist would be a matter involving only the artist and his or her mentors, colleagues, and students, in combination with blind luck or fate — or, for some, a practiced and vigilant awareness: "Luck can be assisted, it is not all chance with the wise," as Baltasar Gracian once wrote — and that chief whetstone, the audience. Ivan Galamian, for one, didn't believe in the business of careers, advising Ani Kavafian to "play your violin well and hope for the best."[85] The somewhat disingenuous Isaac Stern asserts that "there is no way that you can create a career for someone without talent and no way to stop a career of someone with talent."[86] (Staryk calls on Napoleon for a different viewpoint: "Ability is nothing without opportunity.") Yet Stern represents to many the quintessential networking, politicking superviolinist, separating the sheep from the goats in the violin world. He is certainly the most powerful of the career-makers. Stern protégé Yo-Yo Ma recommends, perhaps with the optimism engendered by Stern's advocacy and his own early success, that aspiring musicians avoid competitions and play in local venues to build their careers.

At least part of the game of creating a name for oneself in music lies in making and nurturing contacts, in learning how the circuit operates, in politicking. If an individual is unwilling or unable to operate on a political level, the services of an agent can be purchased. This agent or manager is expected to make the phone calls, act as press agent, and do whatever money or influence can to manufacture a star. He or she must be chief critic, advisor, and psychologist to the performer.

Discovering, early in his career, that it is impossible to sell oneself alone, Staryk solicited the help of an agent in London by the name of Wilfrid Van Wyck. Van Wyck managed some of the high profile artists of the time; among his clientele were Rubinstein, Szeryng, and Milstein. Staryk found his relations with this manager agreeable, always straight-forward and businesslike: "In the first place, Mr. Van Wyck himself was a gentleman, pleasant to deal with, always completely honest about the situation. I was never under an exclusive contract with him, which meant I was free to do work apart from that which he lined up. He simply took his percentage, a standard ten percent out of any fee I re-ceived for engagements which he arranged."

In the Netherlands, Staryk tried a number of managers, including Beek and Koning, who represented the Columbia circuit operating out of New York's 57th Street. He ultimately chose De Freese in Amsterdam, "who, like Van Wyck," writes Setterfield, "handled foreign artists but functioned outside of the major international culture cartels."[87]

Management in Europe worked more efficiently with fewer mate-rial resources to find performance venues for their clients and, when an engagement was secured, they took a smaller piece of the pie: "The busi-ness arrangement was, again, simply a ten percent commission on the fee," recalls Staryk, "with no charge for the expenses of mailing, phoning, etc. You supplied your own brochures, photographs and reviews, and, if available, recordings. De Freese, for example, booked a tour of German and Swiss State Radios, in one mailing, with just this material.

"There is very little chance (in fact none at all) of a concertmaster of a major U.S. orchestra getting a similar deal from even a one-man operation on 57th Street. But suppose you decide to play the game and go for one of the bigger managers. You have the same bagful of reviews, brochures, etc., and he agrees to accept you *for a retainer*. This means that you are on his list, and perhaps he gets you a few dates on his B or C circuit if he has one. *You* pay for all the publicity flyers, promotion, telephone calls, postage stamps, meals, travel, and hotels; *he* takes twenty per cent of your concert fee, and you keep paying the retainer on top of everything else!

"Finally, of course, all your money is used up (or if you are lucky, all the sponsor's money is used up). So after a bit of splash with the commu-nity concert series in the boondocks, provided that you continue paying the retainer, your name will remain in his books (but not on the posters). If you are naive enough to believe that good reviews and favorable audience response to what comes out of the instrument are enough, you will be very disappointed when fame and fortune don't materialize."

The lack of fortune is most immediately felt: "It's not a big money-making business, being a concert soloist, unless you happen to be one of the handful at the very top, the big attractions,"[88] says Ronald Turini, former Quartet Canada member and current professor of piano at Western University, London, Ontario. *Newsweek* reported on that top handful who are (or were) shamelessly in the money: "If closely guarded figures can be believed, there may be as few as half a dozen singers (Kathleen Battle, Jessye Norman, Kiri Te Kanawa, Montserrat Caballè, Placido Domingo and, of course, Pavarotti), a handful of pianists (Rudolf Serkin, Vladimir Ashkenazy, Vladimir Horowitz) and a couple of violinists (Isaac Stern, Itzhak Perlman) who command top dollar. Music's current heavyweight champ, Pavarotti, impeccably groomed for the title by manager Herbert Breslin, gets a reported $100,000 for two hours on a concert stage."[89] And that was in 1986. Norman Lebrecht recently placed Luciano's yearly income at between sixteen and eighteen million dollars.[90]

Stereo Review critic George Jellinek wrote to Staryk in 1969 advising him to contact Herbert Breslin, mastermind of the extensive machinery supporting, in addition to Pavarotti, Joan Sutherland, Alicia de Larrocha, and Marilyn Horne. Jellinek warned Staryk: "The way Breslin puts it, it is more or less impossible to build a name without a considerable financial sacrifice on the part of the artist. Of course all managers tell you that, but Breslin may be more honest about the situation." Staryk wrote back to say that asking for assistance was "going against the grain for me," and that "my colleagues and I have been exploited and continue to be exploited by agents, managers, and public relations people of one sort or another."[91]

However, Staryk admits to the limited possibility of arrangements made outside the 57th street circuit. "There are some things you can do yourself. If you are a concertmaster, for example, you can cultivate contacts with conductors. This is sometimes based purely on the musical collaboration; other times, the conductor may believe that he/she has something to benefit from the relationship as well. You might get some solo appearances, but only up to a point, because the conductors themselves are controlled by the big agencies.

"The management companies working out of New York control or have much influence in the entire business on a global scale. The days of the latest talent appearing in salons are gone. Now it is practically all orchestrated from Manhattan." Within this scheme, there is some room for advancement through luck or good timing. Staryk quotes Berlioz: "'The luck of having talent is not enough, one must also have a talent for luck.' There are a lot of things that have to come together, and money alone won't necessarily do it, nor will talent alone. Of course, there's always the unfortunate who finds himself at the wrong place at the wrong time, like the player who carefully scheduled his debut in advance only to find on the day of the concert that the special, previously unannounced concert by David Oistrakh would hit town that very same night."

Many musicians attempt to garner support through the foundation and grant systems. This often will involve dealing directly with individual donors, not always a pleasant task. "Take egotism out," wrote Ralph Waldo Emerson, "and you would castrate the benefactors." Staryk is skeptical about the possibilities of even locating these moneyed persons: "There are fewer and fewer of those people around with that kind of money and willingness to spend it on some unknown or even relatively unknown violinist or pianist. The expenses are horrendous for a violin soloist; for example, aside from all the other requirements, the violinist will ideally need a Strad, a del Gesù, or at least a Guadagnini, in order to even begin the race with an acceptably competitive vehicle. Then, even with a sponsor, the competition is tremendous and the internal politics among the major New York managers ever fickle. There is never more than a very small group concertizing. Once, when asked about this, Sol Hurok is said to have replied: 'Why should I invest x amount of dollars and speculate when I only have to post STERN on the billboards and sell out?'"

The crock: isolated observations

Drama is a legitimate element of the voice recital and Jessye Norman captivates her audiences with it, entering fully, at times frighteningly, into whatever role the music and text demand. Her largesse absolutely envelopes those watching her; with expressive hands and face, she determines when, and even if, there will be applause. But for Ms. Norman, the drama begins backstage with her treatment of the stage hands and supporting staff who, when they fail to meet her demands, are treated to rages and insults. Seymour Bernstein's words of criticism for a tyrannical conductor could apply to any musician at her level of influence: "In reality," he writes, "all this amounts to using music as it was never meant to be — as a weapon for power — and, what is worse, as a divider of the person from his own humanity. For nothing — and least of all, music — entitles anyone to behave cruelly to others."[92]

"He was rough, rude, and conceited, and once told me he was going to have a career even if it meant walking over dead bodies," reported violinist Cecilia Arzewski of Pinchas Zukerman.[93] (Arzewski was a fellow Galamian student and a member of that group of violinists sent to the U.S. from the Tel Aviv Conservatory with scholarships from the American-Israel Cultural Foundation. Others in the group included Zukerman, Miriam Fried, and Itzhak Perlman.)

Perlman displays amazing facility and naturalness on the violin and the audience reciprocates his charisma onstage with true adoration. But there is a strong underlying element of showmanship to his performances that can at times force the music into a secondary role. For his encores, Mr. Perlman has a six-inch stack of music brought onto the stage for him, from the middle of which he ostentatiously extracts one or two pieces, like a magician with his cards.

Pavarotti, employing his own sleight of hand, spent nearly as much time receiving adulation as singing during a 1997 Key Arena concert in Seattle. His promoter padded the concert's program with unannounced guest artists — a machination that left the audience holding expensive ticket stubs, but cheapened memories of the artist.

The tickets for *Shine* pianist David Helfgott's performance in Boston were $50 apiece. "One's disappointment should not be directed at Helfgott," concluded critic Richard Dyer in his Boston *Globe* review. "Instead one feels anger at a film that created a myth so powerful that no individual could possibly live up to it. And even more anger should be directed at the exploitative market forces that are now pushing the real Helfgott to deliver something only the film Helfgott could to a public that will pay for whatever it gets."[94]

Those same market forces are continuously at work to exploit the virtues of the female body; the image of a woman in varying stages of undress selling a product is so common a sight that we rarely give it a second thought. Until recently, the classical scene had managed to keep itself somewhat unsullied. Ironically, a Canadian violinist, Lara St. John, among others, is helping to bring the industry up to date. On the cover of her debut release through Well-Tempered Productions, the youthful Lara St. John stands before the public eye wearing only a violin. The image is somewhat artful, but we are clearly buying more than just Bach.

"There are people who want to keep our sex instinct inflamed in order to make money out of us," wrote C.S. Lewis in *Mere Christianity*. "Because, of course, a man with an obsession is a man who has very little sales-resistance."

Vanessa-Mae's 1995 recording, *The Violin Player*, sports a photograph of the violinist frolicking with her instrument in the surf. With her befunked renditions of Bach, Vanessa-Mae is enjoyed by the mainstream and is not specifically addressing her work to the admirers of art music. However, when her recordings have crossed into the serious repertoire, she has attracted trouble from the critics. "There are actually two Vanessa-Maes," wrote Henry Roth in his *Strad* review of one of Mae's recent recordings for Angel. "One is a fetching, scantily clad teenager who saws away cleanly and ecstatically on an electric fiddle, with no serious artistic purpose . . . The other Vanessa-Mae is a conscientious student of modest talent who deigns to record major works previously recorded by such superstars as Heifetz, Oistrakh, Milstein, Perlman and a veritable legion of formidable artists. The result is performances characterized by a pleasant but thin tone propelled by a slowish vibrato, and a sound which seldom communicates more than one color. Vanessa-Mae's intonation is reasonably on target, her facility adequate and her training good, but it would be easy to name 20 or 30 violinists of her generation who are far more accomplished ["200 to 300 violinists," Staryk contends and adds that "perhaps Vanessa-Mae's recording should have appeared on the label Totally Unnecessary Productions,[95] rather than Angel."] . . . Vanessa-Mae is essentially a vaudeville-type performer and would be wise to remain in that field. ["This is another example of what is presently called **'classical crossover.'** Diluting serious music to sell to that segment of the public who are unable to swallow the original."]

Perhaps we need not be alarmed by these new currents in classical music; after all, there is historical precedence for glam. "The lack of any serious musical endeavour is such that even Sir Thomas is reduced to peddling Tchaikovsky around the suburban cinemas," wrote a London journalist of Sir Thomas Beecham in 1940. "When, by some means or other, a fair audience is attracted to a good concert, their reaction soon betrays that it is a case of casting pearls before swine. A sign of our musical ill-health is the increasing vulgarity of musical announcements. One of our more notorious pianists now adorns her bills with a portrait in colours."

Then again, there is an unnerving element of reverse evolution to the changes we are witnessing. Vladimir Spivakov, a violinist whom we had come to take seriously, appeared in full color but something much less than full concert dress on the cover of a recent Russian publication.[96]

Outstripping her shivering colleague Lara St. John, violinist Linda Brava, a former pupil of one of Staryk's colleagues, displayed herself in simple, natural hues for *Playboy*'s April 1998 Sex and Music issue. The accompanying article, "Brahms Bombshell," drew comparisons between the euphoric experience of sex and that of listening to Mozart and Beethoven. "There must be," says Staryk, "for the sake of sanity, some boundary between *Playboy*'s sex and Bach's Passions!" And succinctly capturing the spirit of the times, an inset from the *Sunday Times*, in this same issue of *Playboy*, reads: "Playing Dirty, the Latest Babe to Sell Us Bach."

"We have to promote classical music for both the wrong and the right reasons just to survive," Nadja Salerno-Sonnenberg told *Strings* in a May 1994 interview. "The days when you could let the music sell itself are gone . . . If the cover said *It Ain't Necessarily So and Other Encores by Nadja Salerno-Sonnenberg* and had a picture of a tree, it wouldn't sell."[97] Salerno-Sonnenberg's solution to this commercial concern was to present a moody image of herself on her CD cover wearing a tight black skirt and stiletto heels. According to the violinist, the cover was intended to elucidate the character of the pieces selected.

Despite her evident talent, and in keeping with the marketing strategy described above, the fabric of Salerno-Sonnenberg's reputation was spun out of her personality and stage mannerisms. Her smoking, laughing, gyrating, baseball-loving self wins admirers and fills concert halls. However, the doors are open to the critics as well as the adoring public and each gobbles her up in their own way. When the chief critic of the New York *Times* caught her act, he labeled Salerno-Sonnenberg "moderately gifted."[98]

"Her stage mannerisms were out of control," wrote Seattle *Post Intelligencer* critic R. M. Campbell after a May 1997 performance. "She often bounced up and down, side to side. Sometimes her legs, dressed in black toreador pants, were so far apart it would appear she was riding a quarter horse. She made faces — smiles and grimaces — an ingénue in a silent film showing trepidation, excitement, happiness. She shook her hands before playing in an exaggerated fashion, twisting her shoulders." Campbell went on to complain about Salerno-Sonnenberg's activities during the orchestral *tuttis* and her violation of the tacit understanding among musicians that what is most difficult in the practice room should be made to look easy on the stage. "Of course," concluded Campbell, "the concert stage has a long history of eccentrics. But she outdoes them all, and on Monday her art was not sufficient compensation."[99]

Why didn't Steven Staryk have a major solo career?

"His body remains immobile as he plays slow movements, his face impassive — as if he were looking down at a display case in a department store instead of at the keyboard," wrote Helen Epstein of Vladimir Horowitz. "When he plays fast movements, the pianist of necessity moves more, but there is rarely a flicker of recognizable emotion across his face. The emotion goes into his fingers."[100]

Staryk exhibits a similar reserve onstage. There is even something reminiscent of the daguerreotype in his presence, in the aura of dignity and purpose he projects. He is not a manufactured product or a legendary figure who is able to counter the current trend of exaggerated exhibitionism or offer the alternative of impassivity. Staryk was caught between eras, between periods of performance style, between Horowitz and Heifetz on one side and Perlman and Salerno-Sonnenberg on the other.

"Steve's an honest person, straight ahead, no tricks, no phony interpretations in his playing," says Victor Feldbrill. Whereas "Stern leans over the stage, sending messages to the audience, . . . Steve is more like Heifetz, reserved, serious; it's efficient, straight playing . . . He doesn't try to sell himself."[101] Pianist John Perry adds this description, born of close collaboration: "Some musicians take a piece of music and fit it to their strengths, avoiding what shows their weaknesses, evolving a style that supersedes the style of the music. Steve is conscious of any such self-imposed boundaries, making any sacrifices to do what the music intends. There are no cute little gimmicks, no holding the note an extra long time for effect. Steve's music-making flows with the line of the music, it is full of temperament, feeling, passion." Despite having earned the respect of colleagues, Staryk, like Salerno-Sonnenberg, has been criticized for his performing personality. Unlike Salerno-Sonnenberg, Staryk's reserve has been at the center of the debate.

This matter of stage presence is a crucial issue for him, and one which ties directly into the problem of recognition as it relates to his career. Staryk's was a fame spread not by the publicity machine or by dollars, but by word of mouth, almost clandestinely. But his fame has been limited to colleagues and students and to the concert-going public of the cities in which he has lived. In terms of widespread recognition, Staryk's career path failed to reach the elevation of "superstar." Why?

William Littler, in a review for the Toronto *Star*, made the following observation: "The warmest applause for his performance came from the stage, from his fellow musicians, from professionals who react to the way the notes are actually played, more than to glamour and fame." But Littler felt that more was due the public: "They want emotion, they want to observe the performing temperament at work. . . [Staryk] projects no aura of glamour, and he conveys no impression of surmounting obstacles. He just stands there and plays, then retreats diffidently into the wings."[102] Wilfred Van Wyck, Staryk's London manager, says "He was, and no doubt still is, a musician's musician, rather than a performer for the general public."

There is an emotional detachment, or a perception of detachment, that Staryk's critics have time and again pointed out. Walking onstage he is graceful and self-contained, and when acknowledging applause, slightly aloof and proud in appearance. With his old-world decorum and his reticence in behaving familiarly toward his listeners, Staryk is slightly out of place in an age of Perlmanesque informality. Staryk does nothing extramusical to endear himself to audiences.

There is a cord-like tenacity to Staryk's tone, and a conception of line and phrasing in his musical thought, that forms a silvery, sustained spinning-out of sound. The current trend in modern-instrument playing runs counter to this Apollonian aesthetic, leaning toward thickness in the sound, drama in its portrayal, and a degree, more or less, of sentiment.

The lack of these elements in Staryk's playing may have kept the major record companies at a respectful distance. A New York assessor for RCA wrote: "After listening to this tape and the Everest recording, my impression is that Staryk has absolute command of the violin. His playing is exemplary from an instrumental standpoint. His musicianship is sophisticated as evidenced by his knowledge of the various styles most appropriate for each composition. . . . He does not, as in the case of many more famous musicians, apply a strict set of personal mannerisms to whatever music comes to hand. But I am not overwhelmed by his powers of communication. As an instrumentalist, he need take a back seat to no one; but when listening to him, I am more aware of virtuosity than emotional involvement."[103]

The Calgary *Herald*, on March 30, 1981, wrote that "although Staryk's playing has all the elements common to every great violinist — superb technique, impeccable intonation, and brilliance of tone — there is also a certain quality to his playing that for some people is thoroughly compelling and for others is rather off-putting. Staryk is not a particularly gushy or flashy performer. Often he gives the impression of being somewhat aloof or intellectual, even cold, but for me his concert Saturday evening was none of these things. I found Staryk's concert to be an outstanding musical event by an artist of profound musical insight and depth." In agreement and yet fundamentally at variance is this New York *Times* review: " . . . of even greater importance is the impressive collaboration of Staryk and Perry in the complete sonatas for violin and piano by Beethoven. These two artists have developed a sensitivity . . . clean-lined crystalline-textured playing many intellectual listeners prefer . . . their set is highly competitive and is especially recommended."

The range of responses to Staryk's playing is revealing: "The concert opened with a solid, workmanlike performance of the Leclair Sonata No. 3 and the Beethoven Sonata in A Minor, op. 23 — both of which were played in a straightforward fashion. I would have preferred a little more nuance in the tone . . . but one cannot fault the sheer accuracy and consistency of the playing."

"Staryk showed scarce interest in what he was playing," wrote another critic. "[The music] came out notably unshaded and unsmiling."

"The virtuoso writing [in the Walton concerto] is naturally attractive to superior technicians and in Steven Staryk we indeed had a superior technician. His is a no-fuss, almost cool virtuosity, a deceptive veneer of ease overlaying an astounding fingering command. The appeal is more directly aural than emotional."

Victor Feldbrill admits that, "in some ways, he is more interesting when you aren't watching."[104]

While one critic wrote that "the unruffled serenity of his playing mated particularly well with the cool lyricism of Hindemith's E flat Major Sonata," another felt that, precisely because "the Hindemith Sonata is from that early period when the composer was still concerned with emotional appeal in his writing . . . it may not have been an ideal choice for Staryk, who tends to avoid emotional involvement in his interpretations."[105]

William Littler wrote in the Toronto *Star* that "the same self assurance which makes him an effective performer seems to keep him from being a profound interpreter. His playing had more confidence and ease than insight and stylistic differentiation." But in contrast, the Winnipeg *Tribune* reported on another occasion that "Mr. Staryk gave a penetrating, deep and beautiful interpretation of Mozart's rare genius, which truly had spiritual greatness and quality. The concerto was played with strength and emotion but kept in classic simplicity." Written on different occasions about changing sets of circumstances, any one of the above reviews might have captured some truth about Staryk. Now they coexist, alternately agreeing with and contradicting each other in silent debate.

Critics

"A few conjectures, a supply of admonitions, many acute isolated observations, some brilliant guesses, much oratory and applied poetry, inexhaustible confusion, a sufficiency of dogma, no small stock of prejudice, a profusion of mysticism, a little genuine speculation, sundry stray inspirations, pregnant hints and random apercus; of such as these, it may be said without exaggeration, is extant critical theory composed."[106]

"In my own case, as far as reviews go," says Staryk, "I've been very lucky: the grade point average has been very high and it hasn't always been justified. There have been good reviews of performances which I would just as soon forget, and there were bad ones about performances that I thought were more than just good." The most truly devastating review was written by Peter Mose, a special to the Toronto *Star*. Mose reviewed Staryk's performance of a Mozart concerto with the Toronto Symphony in 1986: "About Steven Staryk's rendering of Mozart's G Major Violin Concerto," he wrote, "the less said the better. His playing was forced and uninteresting, often both ill-sculpted and only approximately in tune." ("No matter how well you perform," commented Sir Laurence Olivier, "there is always somebody of intelligent opinion who thinks it's lousy.") Luckily for Staryk, a critic for the *Examiner*, Paul Stein, heard things quite differently "Only rarely have I heard a better performance. He must have a particular affinity for the Mozart style, playing with sweetness, clarity and just the right volume . . . Staryk's technique was flawless . . . He excelled particularly in a sparkling rendition of the cadenza in the first movement; his phrasing of the two little folk tunes concluding the concerto was delightful."

The critics unleashed an equally masterful volley of journalistic counterpoint during a 1977 Brahms Festival in Toronto's St. Lawrence Centre Town Hall. John Kraglund, writing for the *Globe and Mail* on Quartet Canada's playing of the G Minor Piano Quartet, said, "I found myself more conscious of the individual parts than of the whole," while William Littler wrote in the *Star* that "Quartet Canada has developed from a collection of soloists into a real ensemble, and in all three pieces the players functioned as one." Kraglund found Staryk's Adagio "schmaltzy," while Littler wrote, "His very restraint saved the Adagio movement from the sentimentality sometimes visited upon it."

It was again, miraculously, both four balls and three strikes for German critics writing about Staryk's April 1978 performance of the Mendelssohn Concerto. He was traveling with Ottawa's National Arts Center Orchestra on a tour of Europe, when the *Bonner Rundschau* wrote, "[Staryk] proved to be an extraordinarily well-versed and skillful interpreter [but] he played with vibrato befitting the first violinist of a gypsy band, too broad and too slow. Although it carries the tone, it makes him restless." The critic of a rival paper, the *General Anzeiger*, reviewing the same concert, found that "although he played with great technical brilliance, his rendition of the subsidiary phrases of the lyric-elegiac first movement, and the cantilena of the Andante, were rendered in a super-cooled timbre, without even the hint of a romantic vibrato. . . ."[107]

Staryk offers some insight into the confusion: "How can one individual critic give a definitive assessment of a performance? The players themselves cannot even agree! For example, in a duo, many times I have come off the stage with a colleague after a performance to find that his/her reactions were completely different from mine. In orchestras it is even more interesting. I have rarely walked off the stage after an orchestral performance where everyone, even the best players, felt the same way. To some it was the greatest thing that ever happened, while the others were so bored, they were counting the cracks in the floor! Aside from personal tastes and varied backgrounds, memory is ever fickle and can immediately turn off!"

The matter of individual perceptions aside, Staryk feels that critics generally do not do their homework. "Just as he expects conductors and recording engineers and managers to work as hard as he does in pursuit of the highest possible standards," writes Setterfield, "Staryk sees no reason why public discussion of the musical product cannot aspire to the same level of excellence. It is quality he is looking for, not adulation."

Or, if they do their homework, they thereby inevitably extend themselves beyond their capacity. "A critic," he says, "deals with the entire art, from renaissance to modern, from chamber music to opera. No one can specialize to that extent and be that well informed on all of it, and yet in their reviews they pretend to be very specific, sometimes even attempting criticism in depth."

General complaints

Staryk scans today's music scene through the trade magazines, over the radio, in concert, and occasionally on television, and compares it to what he has known. With the insight of experience, he stacks the choices made in his own career against those made by the newer generations of violinists. He observes their playing styles and stage manner, and is saddened by what he sees as a regression into superficiality. "Music is first and foremost to be heard. Except in certain specifically theatrical forms, like opera, the focus is not meant to be visual. Yet, in spite of this, classical musicians today seem to be mimicking the stage antics of their rock music counterparts.

"Within its historical context this is not surprising. The stars in every period of music history have set trends, and at present the trend is definitely to sway and sweat! These perfomers usually attract an audience with similar tastes, since, as a Latin proverb tells us, 'To captivate the masses is to ensnare the vulgar.'

"The terms of the purely entertaining aspect of the art are simple: we are back to the circus in classical music. Each new product must either be younger, sexier, or handier with a gimmick than the last."

Stravinsky was critical of the excesses of performers in his own time, displaying the composer's natural concern for trueness to the intentions of the creator (as far as they can be discerned through notation and an understanding of musical idiom).

> These are just so many practices dear to superficial minds forever avid for, and satisfied with, an immediate and facile success that flatters the vanity of the person who obtains it and perverts the taste of those who applaud it. How many remunerative careers have been launched by such practices! . . . Exceptions, you may say. Bad interpreters should not make us forget the good ones. I agree — noting, however, that the bad ones are in the majority and the virtuosos who serve music faithfully and loyally are much rarer than those who, in order to get settled in the comfortable berth of a career, make music serve them.[108]

We are inundated with mediocre representations of art, watered down so as to be palatable to the largest number. Staryk points out that "our present method of communication relies ever more on the tube, and the lowly quality that emanates from it. It is inevitable that most have been mentally conditioned to stare blindly, listen with deaf ears, and tragically believe almost anything!

Even the art music we buy of our own volition is sold to us today as entertainment through the promotional methods of big business: flash, sex, larger-than-life images. Image sells, and, like children, we are tricked by fancy packaging. But for some reason, we are hungry for the things we are buying and the images we cling to. A need, perhaps a spiritual one, is asserting itself.

Fortunately, there are traditional remedies available to us: the path to immediacy, reality, and substance is the age-old path of the artist. The artist's way is nothing out of the ordinary, in fact it is very ordinary; it simply requires a different way of seeing things.

Alternatives

There is a sense in which music from the hands of master artists is saying, "Look, here is what mankind can do." And, as an aside, "What have you created?" In responding to this prick of conscience, to the perhaps discomforting realization of the extent of our unrealized potential, it doesn't matter what we create — poems, musical compositions, office buildings, consensus, secure children — as long as we engage ourselves. Through life lived as art, or by the precepts of an art, we step into the cycle of putting out and taking in, of giving and receiving.

There is satisfaction to be found within this new orientation and an odd sensation of both fulfilling and turning away from one's self-interest. "To divert interest from the poet to the poetry is a laudable aim," wrote T.S. Eliot in his essay "Tradition and the Individual Talent." "The emotion of art is impersonal. And the poet cannot reach this impersonality without surrendering himself wholly to the work to be done."[109]

"The situation is the same for me always," Horowitz once said. "I am the medium between the composer and the public. I must achieve the right spirit and emotions of the composer. *That* concentration gives the aura to the artist. *That* concentration produces the electricity."[110] T.S. Eliot explains further: "What happens is a continual surrender of [the poet] as he is at the moment to something which is more valuable. The progress of an artist is a continual self-sacrifice, a continual extinction of personality." Taking up the thread, David Oistrakh adds that "the best performances of Prokofiev's music, or of any other good music for that matter, is one in which the personality of the performer does not obtrude in any way. That is precisely what one could say of Prokofiev's playing."[111]

The artist is first a product of tradition and takes a place within it, upholding and furthering, to the best of his or her ability, what has been passed along and giving old material an inevitably personal spin. This is necessarily an internal process; how an artist then moves out into the world is a matter of individual conscience and principle.

Looking ahead, looking back

Staryk's forecast for the future of classical music is not optimistic: "It's like what they say about reaching middle age and beyond, about being over the hill: you pick up speed descending on the reverse slope."

"If I had to do it over again," he adds, "I would go the route of early music. The performances of early music artists are less distorted, there is less interference from ego. The pure tone and minimal vibrato seems to force a focus on inflection and phrasing and intonation: basics of good musicianship are emphasized and the music itself is still treated with dignity. An honest approach to research and investigation keeps the performances both valid and vigorous. Take for instance my favorite recording of the *Vivaldi Four Seasons*: a disc by Harnoncourt's group with Alice Harnoncourt performing the solo part, a combination of virtuosity and *Werktreue* that is outstanding."

The Early Music movement may be pointing a way out of our predicament, but perhaps we can facilitate greater change by looking back in a different way. There have been periods in our past during which classical music seemed to thrive. Roger Sessions told of a 1930s Berlin in which musicians lived a healthy, balanced, and respectable existence: "The professional life of German musicians is a very special thing — the result partly of the fact that they love music, partly of the fact that music in Germany is such a necessity . . . The general level of musicianship is extraordinarily high, thanks to the fact that there is a tradition and culture still very much alive, and because there is so much competition and opportunity . . . the listening public is enormous and diverse — there is variety without equal in the other countries I know."[112]

Maybe by studying the context of this musical or social phenomenon we can learn to create it again at will, minus the fascism. Perhaps we can catalyze the evolution of a society which promotes truth and substance over appearance, a love of beauty over money and power — a society where, from an early age, children are taught the arts and languages alongside the sciences and commerce in a balanced formula. Andrew Lipchak, Director of the Arts Branch of the Ministry of Citizenship and Culture for the province of Ontario writes of the importance of such a restructuring of emphasis:

> Our fate as a culture depends more on our access to the visions of our artists than it does on our international balance-of-trade accounts. For our artists help to define our identity, voice our aspirations, and instill pride in ourselves as a people.
>
> What underlie the arts are values on which a humane and healthy society is based: self-pride, a respect for others and a desire to communicate and share experiences. The arts foster a caring attitude and a questioning spirit. They teach discipline and an appreciation of excellence.
>
> Such values are crucial to the healthy development of young people. Unless children are stimulated and challenged intellectually and encouraged to develop and express their ideas and emotions, they are likely to grow into adults who have difficulty coping in this complex and quickly changing world.
>
> We need our artists, for it is they who can help us to understand that the highest art is that which speaks directly to us out of our own experience, and speaks universally as well.

PEDAGOGY

*To be good is noble, but to teach others how to be good is
nobler - and less trouble.*

- Mark Twain

In 1968, as a young professor at Oberlin, Steven Staryk addressed the
issue of the shortage of quality string players in North America and Western Europe in an article in the school's newsletter. "History and experience have made apparent the ethnic, social, economic, and cultural conditions most often necessary for the successful production of violinists,"
he wrote. "The violin requires infinite patience, maximum talent, either
an emotional, economic, or social need of one sort or another, and eventually the best teaching (sooner preferably than later).

"Talent is plentiful on both continents, though each has particular
strengths and weaknesses. Western Europe, with substantial state support
of the arts, and traditions, certainly has a sympathetic cultural environment. North America, on the other hand, does not. Both continents
have passable to excellent teaching for those who seek it out.

"The major causes of a shortage of professional quality string players are the highly developed economic climates and very high living
standards found on both continents. There are infinite choices of profession, many of which require only a fraction of the effort and time the
violin demands, while offering greater material rewards. There is a lack of
patience for the process of development.

"Far too much emphasis is placed on the participation of beginners
in groups within our current educational system. Start-up groups reach
greater numbers, but on the basis of lower standards that, in the end,
frighten away sensitive ears and potential recruits. The approach to the
string family cannot entirely duplicate that of the winds and brass; to
begin with, strings don't fit into a marching band. An average string
talent, after eight to ten years of study, is not even remotely close to the
level of his colleague in the wind, brass, or piano disciplines. The violin
takes much more time.

"The only partially successful group method of violin teaching thus
far, that I know of has been that of Shinichi Suzuki, and that only to a

primitive level. The primary contribution of this system has been the tapping of a new source of potential violin talent in Japan. Its success is due largely to the social, economic, and cultural environment of the Orient — an environment that resembles that found in Eastern Europe from the late 19th to the middle of the current century."

Isaac Stern corroborated this view in the Los Angeles *Times* of September 1984: "As Stern looks back on recent history, he acknowledges that Jews came to the violin as 'their passport from the ghetto.' It wasn't by accident that so many *Tevyes* fiddled on the roof in eastern European *shtetls*. Thus, the Israeli connection and the violinist's avid recruitment of protégés from his adopted country. Similarly, he sees Asians now as 'potential members of this top group.'"[113]

"The Jewish mama has been replaced by the Far Eastern mama," confirms Yfrah Neaman. "The Far East is fighting a battle for prestige, with the violin as its principle weapon."[114]

"Whether by heritage or by necessity," says Staryk, "the people of Japan, Korea, and other Far East nations share a seriousness of character, determination, and racial qualities (including physical aptitudes) sympathetic to the violin. Unfortunately, this new generation of violinists from the Orient is largely unaware of Western Europe's traditions of music, and is naively seeking superstar status with the help of super stage mothers.

"Another entry into the cultural mainstream is the Eastern European block, with players who are to some extent aware of the Western traditions but who are still largely products of yet another culture which had competed in and dominated international competitions, and who therefore assume that their interpretations and style could not be wrong! This globilization ultimately works itself out as dilution of traditional Western styles and is further complicated by the fact that very few mainstream pedagogues, either in the private or public realm, exist to carry on the traditions.

"The usual crass commercial focus of the industry encourages the newcomers to strive for material success and further distracts this generation from the necessity of understanding, absorbing, and ultimately passing along Western-European cultural traditions.

"This mixed new generation will eventually realize that there can only be so many superstars, only *three tenors* at any one time. 'The world is like a big orchestra conducted by God, and everybody plays second fiddle,' according to Yirme Verbenikov; but God must certainly be cringing on the podium since there is hardly anyone qualified to teach the second violins the orchestral repertoire.

"I strongly recommend that we discourage quantity and encourage quality. Only good violin playing, not bad, should be heard publicly at any level to encourage and attract newcomers to its infinite beauties. Even in cases of amateur and student orchestras or groups, effort, enthusiasm, and zeal do not replace knowledge, discipline, talent, and experience. Mediocre performances are a serious threat to recruiting a potential public as well as students to serious music. Amateur and questionable student performances should be confined to relatives, teachers, and friends. I expect more than mediocrity, but perhaps Beecham was right when he commented to me, 'My boy, we are entering the age of mediocrity.'"

Genesis of a teacher

Staryk has continually found himself in the role of diagnosing and treating the musical problems of organizations and individuals. The foundation of his teaching necessarily lies in his own student years, and the groundwork of technique and musicianship that he built. Staryk has winnowed the most valuable information from the traditions of the violin and synthesized this knowledge with his playing to create a coherent and translatable art. Add to this a solid core of personal integrity, high standards, and the years of experience, and one begins to understand why he has become a teacher of such formidable stature.

One prerequisite of learning how to teach well is first learning how to *learn* well. Jaak Liivoja-Lorius, writing for *The Strad* in March 1983, summarized Staryk's catholic approach to learning:

> Although Steven Staryk is the epitome of the well-schooled violinist, no one teacher stands out as more important than another in his development during his student years. Indeed, Staryk has often said that it would be unfair to single out names since he studied with or observed virtually anyone he felt had something to offer. Obviously a much safer, albeit more conservative, approach would have been to have persisted with a smaller number of teachers and to have remained with one for longer periods of time. At least this is the traditional way, a process of learning which eventually allows the player to be categorized as an Auer, Rostal, or Galamian student.

In Staryk's case, such categorization is impossible. Within the most organized sense of the term, Staryk really should be considered a self-made violinist. This is not to say that he has done it completely unaided — far from it — but it is no small credit to him that he succeeded in assembling a technical mastery over the violin and bow, widely recognized as one of the most assured of our time, by combining the many diverse influences into one superbly functioning entity. And, since Staryk was the architect of his own technical apparatus, he has gained immense insight into the practical relationship between technique and music making.

A unique style of learning emerged as a method of teaching for Staryk, each informing the other in the evolution of his musicianship. "Teaching and being taught are a reciprocal process," he says. "From my early days as a developing violinist, I was studying, learning wherever I could, and others were coming to learn from me."

On teaching and teachers

"The study of music may be divided into two general categories: that which is treated scientifically, and that which is treated intuitively," writes Parke G. Burgess Jr., a doctoral student in conducting at the University of Washington. "This division characterizes the differences that have long separated academics from performers." Staryk adds that "the intuitive performer should strive to acquire the knowledge of the academic."

"One place," continues Burgess, "where the analytical mind and the intuitive genius not only meet but are forced to verbalize their relation [is in] the teaching studios and rehearsal halls of the performance world. The teacher of performance is forced by his circumstances to describe and demonstrate the workings of his own mind so that the student may better understand him. He uses whatever means are at his disposal: he speaks scientifically, he uses metaphor, he employs gestures, he plays or sings — showing the student his meaning."

Another such means is, surprisingly, silence. "Four-fifths of all meaningful instruction," writes Samuel R. Delany, "is the attentive silence teacher must proffer student, during which silence, among his or her own fumblings, the student actually learns — a silence in which teacherly attention must all be on which mistakes *not* to correct."[115]

Teaching is a strenuous and creative activity when done well and, given our current social climate, one which requires not only courage, but a lead jacket. "Mark Twain's remark on teaching at the head of this chapter probably has more to do with morality than skill," says Staryk, "but perhaps it's applicable to both, and either way, I don't agree: in our present society, teaching anything has become more than just a challenge. In today's academic jungle, the possibility of getting shot for administering a low grade renders the teacher's trade not only troublesome, but downright dangerous. Luckily, direct violence against teachers is not common in the violin world. Many of my colleagues have spoken to me of their preference for not taking on the responsibility of another person's progress on the instrument; they feel it is best to just play and take care of their own problems without this added burden.

"Those who place themselves in the yoke of the instrument find that the violin is totally absorbing and that it makes one practically self-sufficient. On the other hand, it's a social undertaking that allows one to collaborate in everything from duos to opera! If a person has the desire and talent, then the rewards are great, not necessarily financially, but personally, socially, and emotionally. The only demand in return is constant attention. Those not prepared to serve the 'King of Instruments' are best advised to participate as a discriminating audience.

"The instrument itself and the sensation of playing it defy scientific explanation. At its inception, study of the violin requires patience and dedication, requirements that encompass the entire family of the student. For most families there will be struggles over motivating the child to practice, and the family must plan to continue their involvement with the performer well into the later years."

For parents frustrated by our society's lack of concern for excellence, or for those in despair over their child's lack of motivation or enthusiasm for work, this letter from David Oistrakh to his son Igor may encourage:

"Dear Garinka," he wrote. "I am glad that you are now learning harder, as mummy tells me. You realize that nothing makes mummy and me sadder than your laziness and naughtiness. If you would realize how important it is for your future independent life to acquire as much knowledge as possible now in your childhood, in your youth, where everything that you read, see, and hear is absorbed by your memory consciously as by a sponge and then stored forever, then you would take mum's, dad's, and your teacher's admonitions more seriously. They have already trodden the road which you are only just starting to walk . . ."

"In between those early and late years," Staryk continues, "you must have either the luck of the Irish, or, more practically, an intelligent, inquisitive, open, and well-informed mind in order to find the right teacher, in order to uncover who teaches what, how, and why, and in order to minimize the pitfalls! Young talent must beware of the aggressive and insecure teachers out to solicit students without any real concern for, or ability to promote, their development.

"Through my experience of teaching at ten different schools in the United States, Canada, and Europe, I have found great disparity between the weakest and the strongest players in my classes. In the mixed bag of a given studio of violinists, there are those at an intermediate level and those at a generally acceptable professional level. I have seen that it is impossible for many on the lower end of the scale to benefit from all that goes on. Those individuals would have to attend all of their peer group's lessons and come to all the masterclasses, and even then, depending on their level and background, they might not totally comprehend what is going on, even though I explain in the greatest of detail and demonstrate. Only those at the most advanced level technically and with a sophisticated musical background can experience and recognize intellectually, emotionally, and physically what, on that higher plateau, the fussing is all about. In this respect, I agree with those who argue that you can't explain everything.

"Orchestral and chamber music should be extensively and seriously taught as preparation for those talented enough, though perhaps not lucky enough, to eventually earn their livings from solo careers. A violinist should learn not to perceive all music through the F holes of a fiddle; the focus should be on the entire repertoire. We should discuss music that involves the violin but is meaningful also when heard within an operatic, orchestral, or chamber context. It was by playing with orchestras, with excellent colleagues and conductors, through all the discussion and hairsplitting, that I began to understand music in a total sense.

"Students who are less talented should be sensitively made aware of their lack of talent and/or aptitude. One can be talented musically but not have the aptitude for a particular instrument; if playing the violin feels awkward and difficult at the beginning of a career, and 'orthopedic teaching' has not helped, you can be sure it will be crippling long before the end. If they insist on continuing, these students should be guided and assisted with great care, for occasionally a late bloomer, whose potential is not immediately apparent, enters the studio. For those who clearly shouldn't be pursuing this career, one must convince them that music is best enjoyed as a hobby. If I were to start over, I might do many specific things differently, make other decisions, but I would play the Baroque fiddle, as I mentioned before, *on a professional level, as a hobby!*

"I am not a proponent of the 'have nothing, know nothing, but I've got the future' philosophy, and I find it difficult to know where to draw the line between encouragement and reality. I was told at the University of Washington when failing an auditioner that 'you are not Heifetz and this isn't Juilliard,' and that I would one day see the candidate's name in lights. The candidate, in my opinion, not only was too old ever to catch up, but also lacked basic information. Heifetz's teaching was questionable, and Juilliard is far from being at its zenith, and both, despite their formidable reputations, were and are only superficial and formulaic responses to two questions: 'Do I know what I am looking for in a teacher?' and 'Am I as realistically informed as I should be?' All of which reminds me of an anecdote told by Oscar Shumsky regarding a lesson with the aging Leopold Auer: "Finally, about fifteen minutes into the lesson, a comment from Auer, 'Don't scratch.' Ten minutes later, 'Don't scratch.' Five minutes later a more emphatic 'Don't scratch.' The lesson ended with a memorable, 'Alright, scratch!'"

From stage to studio

"There are famous performers," Staryk points out, "who, aware of the shortcomings of their golden age, become famous teachers overnight. These individuals rarely have their authority questioned or their methods criticized, despite the fact that there is often no connection between the ability to perform at a high level and the ability to teach sympathetically and with insight; thus the Emperor struts in his new clothes while the majority of mere mortals stand quietly by. There was a case of a well-known string player who was imported by a well-known university some years ago. After a few weeks had passed he approached a colleague on the faculty and inquired what he was supposed to be doing:

"'Well, teaching of course.'

"'But how can I teach,' he replied, 'when they can't play?'

"I can empathize to a certain extent; it would be ideal to only teach those who already can play, to help them play better. But then, those who can't have to be taught *somehow*, at least to manage passably. Only the very talented are selected to study with elite teachers or at elite institutions, and they often leave the teacher or school playing much the same as they did at the start of their studies. But whether they benefit much or little becomes secondary to the advantages of gold-plating their *curriculum vitae.*

"It seems to be the nature of violin students, with an occasional notable exception, to blindly follow the course set for them by a teacher, especially if the teacher is famous. This complacency grows out of the overwhelming technical or physical difficulties involved in mastering the instrument itself. Hobbled by this preoccupation, students of the violin are probably not aware of their anachronistic adherence to the master-slave dynamic of a century ago. This mode of relating works most disastrously against the student if the teaching is simplistic, as, for example, when the teacher advises repeating the passage ten times over, and if that doesn't work, another ninety, and if this still doesn't solve the problem, concludes that the student obviously lacks talent, a conclusion often precipitated by an overflowing studio.

"The student is too often told 'this is how the illustrious [so and so] taught me; it worked for me and should be good enough for you; take these fingerings and bowings and practice.' Without the solicitude of a responsible teacher, the vulnerable and young beginning or intermediate student rarely feels in a position to object and will wither and fall away both musically and in terms of self-esteem.

"But where does one look today for good teaching? Institutional teaching is driven by economics and plagued by the insecurity of individuals. Name teachers are purchased by the big schools and conservatories to attract the numbers that will allow the program to remain financially solvent. I remember discussing evaluations for the Canada Council with Victor Feldbrill and others. Some of the candidates we failed for the Faculty of Music at the University of Toronto had already been accepted by Galamian at Juilliard, so long as the Canadian Government paid the tab. After all, one needs a lot of milk to produce a little cream. This is the situation one finds almost everywhere; schools and individuals recruit and delude for basic economic reasons. And as with all competitions and auditions, there are fat years and lean years for those who are selling and those buying, but the same game is played from year to year and from school to school with only minor variations in the rules.

"Often name teachers are interested only in the solo star and can't teach the others because of their own limitations; however, through their good fortune in finding star pupils they are able to solicit and attract more business to the studio. If the teacher is unlucky and doesn't land the equivalent of a Menuhin, Perlman, Ricci, or Rabin, he is usually not very successful. It is simple to teach those who already play well. And the students themselves, or the students in conjunction with their parents, are guilty of playing the system by searching out star teachers, who are more obviously star politicians. Those whose egos require soloist status will need to spend more time on matters pertaining to the 'games people play' in life rather than on music.

"The naive or politicized student hoping to enter the promised concert circuit will pay, it is said, hundreds of cash dollars 'in an envelope' for a private lesson with one of our most prominent star teachers. Those who pay up are not seeking information about interpretation but rather connections to open doors in the music business. As a teacher, I am not interested in that individual who has entered the particular institution in which I teach for its reputation, and who has subsequently been assigned to me in a lean year to fulfill my contracted work load. The student I hope to meet in my studio is the well-informed and inquisitive one, hopefully talented, who, knowing my work, seeks me out.

"Institutions are much of a 'muchness.' One could be assigned someone who is well over the hill, or sitting on their tenure, and the institution itself, a collection of individuals, may be collectively over the hill. Institutions will present frustrating paper-chases and other distractions to serious students of the violin: somewhere between *My Fair Lady* and *Schenkarian analysis* comes the violin at the University of Washington.

"The student should judiciously search out individuals with orchestral experience, since some of the most popular pedagogues of the violin have never played in an orchestra and can do little or nothing to help prepare students for this role. This situation is the more ludicrous when one considers that 95% of the violinists leaving an institution and seeking work will be fortunate if they land an orchestral career. The area of orchestral preparation is unquestionably the weakest area of violin performance represented in institutions.

"If we take the largest music school in the world as our study group, we find that of the six violin teachers in the school, five have never played in a professional orchestra and the sixth, who does have substantial orchestral experience, has specialized in Baroque Music; nobody is teaching the orchestral excerpts in depth. By mutual consent, this failure to address practical realities is calmly and knowingly overlooked by teachers and administrators. With this in mind, I would stress that those majoring in performance should seek out the individual. In turn, when sending a student elsewhere for instruction, the teacher must take seriously the responsibility of guiding and advising their students. Either we, as teachers, know well who we are recommending, or the research must be done. The consequences of a negative experience, even to the most talented, are serious enough, but for the less talented, the loss of time could dampen or kill any motivation."

Auditioning

Sir Adrian Boult once wrote, "A memory as long as mine cannot forget the enormous advance in orchestral virtuosity through the last fifty years. It is a commonplace that no orchestral player could deal really adequately with Wagner's string parts at the time they were written. Now they are played with ease."[116] Staryk feels that most string players still experience difficulty in playing Wagner, but completely agrees with the changes that have occurred in the level of orchestral playing; the competition for placement is fierce and the need for guided audition preparation has never been greater. "The subtleties of high-level orchestral playing," he says, "will never be conveyed to students through their youth orchestras, and the attitude toward orchestral preparation summarized by the quip 'learn how to sightread' is outdated. Recent major orchestral audition results provide us with evidence of a general neglect in this area. Hundreds of very good fiddlers are summarily dismissed after the first few minutes of the first round of the audition process."

Fiddlers are simply not easily converted to orchestral musicians. *High Fidelity* reported in 1964 that "a solo-oriented string player who fails to make the grade is not necessarily a convertible item. Quite aside from the psychological readjustment involved, he is faced — possibly for the first time — with such practical matters as familiarity with the repertoire."

Staryk points out that "even the otherwise well-informed Norman Lebrecht, author of *Who Killed Classical Music?* and *The Maestro Myth* — books I highly recommend — isn't aware that the unsuccessful soloist does not simply pick up an orchestra job! The notion that unsuccessful soloists take orchestra jobs as consolation prizes is a very outdated mentality. What, in fact, this group preferred, and did, was to take teaching jobs in colleges, conservatories, and universities.

"There are already countless frustrated soloists in all the orchestras who are not always too anxious to let another 'earn as they learn.' Compared with a normal performance, if such a thing exists, or even solo competitions, an orchestral audition requires more immediate positive conviction in a much shorter time span. The excerpts or passages are short and rough, demanding highly developed reflexes in all areas and an ability to switch styles and techniques from one minute to the next. It's similar to a concertmaster having to play a short but demanding 'lick' — one note out of place is more crucial than ten notes here or there in a concerto.

"As for the required concerto, usually one of Mozart's, I recommend the Concerto No. 5 in A Major, since it is probably the most immediately revealing in many aspects. Juries listening to many applicants prefer immediate revelation for an obvious reason: it saves time.

"When entering into an audition situation, there are a multitude of uncontrollable variables. The auditioning committees of which I have been a member often contained weak players who were not always favorably disposed toward the idea of too many stronger players entering the orchestra. Also, some committees contain representatives from all sections of the orchestra. There can at times be more votes in the hands of those who play other instruments and have little understanding of the violin's problems, and these individuals often do not realize that what they are hearing is better than what is in the orchestra. The conductor may have the power to overrule the committee recommendations for many surprising reasons. Some young conductors feel more secure with younger players. Old conductors may need young players; the age factor alone is intriguing, to say the least.

"Despite disputable procedures and results, it is important, if one is truly qualified, to simply continue auditioning. There are countless variables coupled with luck and one must be as objective as possible in order to learn from the experience of each audition. The important thing is to gain experience and a level of comfort by taking as many auditions as possible. When preparing for and taking them, be aware that the disqualifying problems in an audition are generally lack of dynamics, acceptable fingerings, rhythmic sub-divisions, and subtle bow strokes, including intelligent bow sub-division. It is taken for granted that the auditionee will play all the notes, exhibit good intonation, and play with a 'pleasing sound.' But the 'pleasing sound,' and even musical inflection, are matters of musical taste reflecting the aesthetics and traditions of a geographic area. One additional disqualifying problem which is again dependent upon locale: lack of *style*."

The problem of style

"Musical style is one of the chief criteria by which a violinist is evaluated in an orchestral audition," says Staryk. "That is, if the technical aspects of playing are all in place and if the jury itself is sufficiently aware! It is a sense of style and the ability to differentiate between the styles and periods of individual composers that is largely lacking in today's players."

An explanation for this is difficult to pinpoint. One answer might be that style in Western art music is under pressure from the ongoing globalization of culture, and from the overwhelming and numbing predominance of the music and attitudes of popular culture in the media, films, and advertising and thus in the everyday existence of the young.

The globalization of culture, as evidenced in the increasingly uniform sound of the top orchestras, is necessarily a step away from the refinement attained by regional orchestras playing the music of their region's composers or composers who wrote with that particular orchestra's sound in mind. The sound and stylistic traits of these groups were rooted in traditions supposedly passed down from the composer or from the composer's milieu and retained the inflections of the local dialect. The first Mahler festivals were with the Concertgebouw, and Strauss's *Heldenleben* was written for Mengelberg, erstwhile conductor of that orchestra. What is developing in the place of the vanishing local sound of regional orchestras is a universal conception of sound which, under the right circumstances, will raise itself to its own summit of perfection, but something will have been lost in the process.

"I have taught many very talented professional violinists," remarks Staryk, "who were preparing for their initial orchestra auditions or upgrading from an orchestra in which they were currently employed. What I found in general was sweet facile playing without the traditional stylistic imprint. What often passes for style — the incidental effects of personal idiosyncrasy and temperament, or the habits picked up at this or that school of playing — is so entrenched that it is often impossible to create immediate substantial results."

Nikolaus Harnoncourt offers a concise solution: "The more musicians familiarize themselves with the specific style characteristics of various historical periods and various nationalities in Western music, the better they will recognize the profound interrelationships between a given type of music and its interpretation, both then and now."[117]

Aptitude, talent, industry, and curiosity

"Music must be *practiced*," Staryk emphasizes. "You must have control of it, while allowing for spontaneity and inspiration; it is not a thing you can leave to fate. Calculate and experiment and gamble at home until you reach the optimum."

Direction and insight into the raw materials of the trade form the core of Staryk's teaching methodology. He chooses those specific exercises which apply to a given problem and explains how it is to be practiced and where in the repertoire it will be applied. These brief and to-the-point exercises allow the violinist to maintain or continue developing all areas of technique over time, and are practiced in addition to work on repertoire.

Staryk encourages the cultivation of an active curiosity to supplement talent, aptitude, and industry, and to carry the student beyond his or her student years and into an independent career. A jingle he quotes from Rudyard Kipling tells the story perfectly: "I keep six honest serving men/(They taught me all I know)/Their names are What Why and When/ And How and Where and Who." Staryk suggests that students "practice inventively" and solve their problems directly by creating, out of difficult spots in the literature, exercises that approach the problem in a variety of ways: addressing the right and left hands separately, for example, or increasing the difficulty of a given problem by exaggerating the motions involved, "but with the music always dictating these physical motions," he emphasizes.

During his ten years at the University of Washington, Staryk encouraged individuals in his class to work with Margriet Tindemans, the University of Washington's viola da gambist *par excellence,* to improve both their understanding of Baroque performance practice and their general musicality. Several former Staryk students, including Dan Stepner of the Boston Museum Trio and Lydian Quartet, and Kim Zabelle of the Seattle Baroque Orchestra, have embarked on successful careers in Early Music.

Flexibility and inventiveness are part of the formula of success in Staryk's approach to teaching. One of his recent graduate students, Kyung Sun Chee, summarized the approach this way: "People are built differently, shaped differently, think differently, and work differently. What works for the teacher may not work for the student and giving the right individual diagnosis and treatment is the most challenging aspect of teaching."[118]

A former pianist for Staryk's class, Laurent Philippe, once related his view that "Staryk is a good chef; he is able to bring a number of dishes to completion at the right moment without allowing anything to burn." Promptly returning the compliment, Staryk feels that a pianist and musician of Philippe's caliber is "found only in a five fork-and-spoon Michelin-rated kitchen." Philippe added an element of real-world intensity to Staryk's master classes, and the two made an effective team, one address-ing various problems on a personal level during rehearsals, the other fulfilling the formal role of instructor and diplomatic referee. Staryk observes that "maintaining a healthily competitive studio is a difficult juggling act. There is a tendency for things to become venomously com-petitive at one extreme, or a mutual admiration club on the other; hu-man nature, under competitive stress, tends toward one or the other."

In Staryk's approach there is an emphasis on general musicianship that goes beyond the assimilation and regurgitation of orchestral excerpts. "In the comprehensive approach I try to convey," he explains, "one ab-sorbs information from a variety of sources: recordings, performances, biographical and historical writings on the specific subject, and as much literature and art as possible. All of this is undertaken to mold a sense of good taste and the accepted traditional style.

"In my experience of teaching on three continents, I have encoun-tered a marked difference between European students of the violin and their North American or Asian counterparts. The Europeans' sophisti-cated musical background compensates for a lack of technical proficiency, but the lack of sophisticated musical background in a North American or Oriental player with abundant technique still hinders the best music-making.

"I often exhort students to 'speak the correct musical language.' Which, needless to say, necessitates going beyond the musical notation on the page." Kyung Sun Chee summarized the approach in this way:

> Common wisdom relates that 'music is a universal lan-guage;' however, there are languages within the language. Berlioz is not Beethoven and Rachmaninoff is not Copland. The wide range of musical cultures, each with its historical context and concomitant style, require a great deal of study and acquaintance; the nuances and inflections of each must be digested and distinguished one from the other, as in the study of linguistics.[119]

"My advice in one word to students is *overqualification*," Staryk affirms. "Then, hope for the best and expect the worst." When more than one word is called for, he keeps a stock of pithy sayings for use in the studio: "The sound in Beethoven should be 'Lean and Mean,' as exempli-fied by the playing of the Berlin Philharmonic; neither harsh nor lush.

'Loose but tight' refers to the texture, sound, and inflections in Mozart, tight rhythm but loose sound — it's not Rossini! Beware of 'Paralysis from analysis,' or mental overkill leading to physical paralysis. Seek out intelligent guidance in 'sophisticated taste,' not only in music, but literature, art, and, in fact, most matters of life. Be able to verbally support, with researched information, your performance interpretation (needless to say, this will also help in teaching). The question of memory is part of the traditional solo syndrome mentality: if an advanced or professional player is constantly repeating passages or phrases just to memorize, time and energy are wasted. A realistic reminder: at least ninety-five percent of professionals are reading music in an orchestra. Nothing need be lost musically. Remember the following well-known story: 'Maestro Klemperer, you have conducted all this repertoire so many times, why do you use the score?' Klemperer's response: 'Because I can still read music!'"

Staryk points to a quote once pinned to the information board in his office. "*That*, finally, is what practicing is all about," he says. The quote? It's from Anton Chekhov: "Any idiot can face a crisis — it's the day to day living that wears you out."

From studio to stage

For the serious student seeking to make the transition to a professional career, Staryk stresses the benefits of engaging oneself in the activity of collective music making: "There is nothing that replaces the continued education and practical experience of playing in a first class orchestra with the better conductors for at least five years. Hopefully one is able to achieve this early on in a career. The best insights into the bread and butter of music, Bach and Mozart for example, are found in the *St. Matthew Passion, Don Giovanni* and other large scale works of major composers. One can't perform these alone; listening and watching help but are not quite like doing. As Baryshnikov once said to an overanalytic student, 'just do, dear.' As with everything else in this world, we have to 'do' with others — even when performing as a soloist."

Student tributes

"The most significant news from the String Division is quality growth," reported the University of Washington's 1991 School of Music newsletter, "Students have been coming from as far off as the People's Republic of China, Korea, Taiwan, New Zealand, the USSR, Alaska, Michigan, and Canada. Professor Steven Staryk's studio is one of the largest and best ever in enrollment and quality." By 1996, the list of nations represented in Staryk's class had expanded to include the United Kingdom, Germany, Switzerland, and Brazil.

Students made the journey to Seattle on the basis of Staryk's reputation. Once in his studio, the tangible results of working closely with their mentor often lead to responses on student evaluation forms that satisfyingly close the circle of the teacher/student relationship: "I appreciated your extensive knowledge and experience as a player . . . you also encourage me to *think* about my playing. It is a well-rounded, balanced approach to violin playing. Also, I like your honest, realistic, yet uncompromising attitude toward music. You make a good role model for us because you do and play what you teach. Thanks for your integrity."

"I learned two important lessons about teaching," wrote student Catherine Shipley. "First, I observed the importance of demonstrating in class. It seemed that no matter how good a verbal explanation was, a demonstration of the concept helped it immensely. Secondly, it seems that sometimes a teacher need not say anything at all in the way of constructive criticism. . . . [Sometimes] it was enough to say 'good,' nothing else was called for." Gwen Hoebig, Concertmaster of the Winnipeg Symphony, told *The Strad* in June, 1997 that "She found her experience with Staryk 'a major breakthrough — he took me off all my pieces and put me on technique . . . When I teach I draw constantly from Staryk . . .'" Staryk, for his part, responds that "it was most gratifying to witness Gwen warming up with the tried and proven formula, which I continue to teach, having found no better. This was at yet another Mostly Mozart festival in Monterey, California in 1991. Then, as she sat with me on the first stand asking if everything was right, I assured her that there were many she could replace in the major league."

Concertmaster of the Taipei Symphony and 1997 University of Washington graduate Keh-Shu Shen writes: "Staryk is unique in that he teaches every aspect of music and violin performance. If there are technical weaknesses, these will always be addressed in conjunction with the music. In fact, through music you are shown where your technique is deficient. The study of orchestral repertoire and audition preparation in minute detail, confirms for me that there is no one doing it as successfully as Staryk."

Nachum Erlich, professor of violin at the Musikhochschule in Karlsruhe, Germany, developed a collection of technical studies on the model of Staryk's method material and "daily dozen," which he refers to as *Die Robinson Crusoe-Violinschule, oder Was mache ich auf einer einsamen Insel?* [*The Robinson Crusoe School of Violin, or What Would I do on a Lonely Island?*] Staryk recalls, "My first contacts with Nachum came in the late 1970s when his father, a professional violinist, phoned me from Israel regarding the possibilities of Nachum studying with me. They had heard of my reputation in Europe and my recordings. There were, and are, surprisingly many instances when unknown colleagues, collectors, potential students call inquiring about my recordings or the possibility of studying with me. I refer to this as the 'initial recognition of speaking the same musical language.' If it goes beyond the music (as it did with Nachum) then we begin to get closer to the situation described by Unamuno: 'For men love one another with a spiritual love only when they have suffered the same sorrow together . . .'[120]

"Nachum and I finally connected in Seattle in 1995. I was very impressed by this master fiddler but shortly after we began working, as if it was meant not to be, I was hospitalized for pneumonia and internal bleeding. However, Nachum persisted trip after trip, and even convinced me to collaborate in a recital with him that included Wieniawski's Op. 18, which I had not performed since 1960. This plan was also ill-fated. A very rare Seattle snowstorm, especially for mid-November, kept me on the phone all day trying to resolve that age-old question, 'to cancel or not to cancel.' We eventually played to a handful of brave, loyal, and obviously very curious students."

Nachum Erlich was a graduating student of Max Rostal, 1975-81, who continued master classes with Nathan Milstein and Henryk Szeryng, taught at the Sibelius Academy in Helsinki, performed and gave classes in Western and Eastern Europe and Japan, and since 1991 has been a professor at the Karlsruhe Hochschule. Erlich wrote at length of his studies with Staryk:

> Staryk really opened new horizons for me. His whole approach is to present in a most incredible way, violinistically and musically, the student's situation and his or her very unique problems. He cuts away the non-essentials and drives to the center of each problem with everything in just the right proportion. Because he himself is such an incredible violinist, his solutions are unmatched. Concerning the aspects of musicality and stylistic understanding, my background, the Rostal-Flesch-German tradition is certainly one with a deep foundation. Staryk keeps with

the tradition, and takes it much further, much deeper. In this, he is unique. Certainly his background as concertmaster and as soloist with some of the greatest conductors and orchestras has helped mold his incredibly deep understanding of music and the violin. When he plays a Beethoven sonata, a Mozart concerto, or whatever, it doesn't sound just like a violin piece well-played; it sounds like a total entity, and has a depth of feeling and understanding that I have never before heard in any other teacher or performer.

The orchestral studies field is a very neglected one. From the soloists you will not get any advice. From those teachers who have had orchestral experience you can get some advice but usually not enough. Watching Steven Staryk teach a Mozart symphony or a Strauss tone poem, I felt the whole string section of a great orchestra, it's all there, clear and understandable to the highest degree. Staryk has an incredible knowledge of the orchestral violin literature.

Every teacher, every performer has something to offer. But Steven Staryk is a truly exceptional combination of life-experience, technical capabilities, and a musical mind in a wonderful, understanding human being. Any person who has had the good fortune to study with him, should consider themselves very lucky.[121]

Writing to nominate Staryk for a teaching award at the University of Washington, one student encapsulated the prevailing sentiments of Staryk's class: "I have not, in all my years of study in all areas of academia and at a variety of institutions, come across a more competent, challenging, and thought-provoking mentor."

On this final period of his teaching career Staryk writes: "The lack of any consequential P.R. from the School of Music made this a secretive period in my career; colleagues and potential students had no idea where I was. Tracking me down was accomplished by word of mouth, the proverbial grapevine, or resolute research. To some degree this obstacle was positive, as I then knew that they really came to the institution to study with me. The negative aspect is hearing about those who are still looking for my whereabouts! [The original title of the May 1994 *Strad* cover story on Staryk was: "Steven Staryk, Seattle's Best Kept Secret."] But except for my last period in Toronto [1975-87] where the rewards arose from both teaching and performing, my decade at the University of Washington was one of the most satisfying."

In the opinion of some of his friends, Seattle was an unlikely place for Staryk to hang his hat. "Vot are you dooink here?" asked Alexander Schneider during a visit, "They are payink you a meellion dollars, or you luv feesh."

Students who took part in this final stage of Staryk's career benefited from the practical orientation which long years in the trenches had instilled in their mentor. "The healthy environment we created in the studio was due to a variety of reasons," says Staryk. "To begin with, I convinced a body of normal, sensitive, and, for the most part, talented violinists that we were not gods! Then we openly addressed the issue of hyperbole through discussion and by posting articles and reviews to remind us of the unrealistic hype and P.R. (at whatever level) that many begin to believe. Though there were potential solo talents in the class, the reminder that talent is only one of the ingredients in the manufacturing of a solo career kept us out of the clouds.

"Role modeling included having the courage to demonstrate and 'blow it' myself. Teaching, for me, meant giving of my intellect, emotion, experience, and time: the hour lesson was not the institutional fifty minutes, it was a full hour or until the next student arrived in the studio. An effort was made to make-up for those who had to leave for orchestra rehearsals. Two classes per week covered performance of either solo, orchestral, or occasionally chamber repertoire, as well as pedagogy and any other subject or problem relating to the performance of music on the violin, including comparisons of instruments and bows and what to be aware of in seeking to purchase. Performances in class were on a voluntary basis unless individuals were registered for orchestral excerpts for credit.

"The rotation of violinists in the student orchestra was implemented to the extent that it was realistic considering the disparity of levels of playing. It was gratifying to see, and I sincerely hope this was not for appearance's sake, the subtle adjustments which took place as each found their step in our class hierarchy. If there were struggles, they were not brought to my attention, and I trust there were no victims. As with any group, there are individuals with characteristics most suitable for peace-keeping. In this respect I was most fortunate to have my first and last Teaching Assistants, Richard Stout and Kyung Sun Chee.

"There were numerous rewarding playing experiences with former and present students, the most recent being a 1996 performance of the Henk Badings Concerto with Kui He, who graduated as I retired. There were also many mixed emotions experienced during a very trying personal decade. I thank the many students individually, and as a collective body throughout this period. Fortunately they are among the select few where "classical music is dead amond the young" is not true.[122] Unaware of the major role they played in lifting my spirits, my hope, and my trust in youth, they may have sensed a facade in my derisive 'Class 101: Sarcasm.' But as Nietzsche said, 'Cynicism is the only form in which common souls come close to honesty.'[123] Or in Lily Tomlin's words, 'No matter how cynical you become, it's never enough to keep up.' I felt our interaction was warm, informal, honest, and full of humor. I will also never forget the many touching and humorous moments in the unofficial retirement party in June of 1997, held at the home of conductor Peter Erös, an old colleague from the Concertgebouw days, with whom I developed a good rapport and friendship. We fell to telling anecdotes that evening; one was relayed by my student Kelly Jeppeson:

> I was very diligently working on the *Scherzo* from Prokofiev's Sonata in D Major, Op. 94a during the Christmas break because — out of my entire recital program — it posed the most difficulties for me. The bowing articulations and 'runs' within this movement created a lot of nervous anxiety for me. When I took it to Mr. Staryk for my first lesson of Winter Quarter, the anxiety took control and caused me to 'bomb' the movement. Being very disappointed in myself, I worked even harder on the movement the following week. I so desperately wanted to please Mr. Staryk and show him that I could overcome the difficulties of this movement. I taped myself on a few runthroughs and had decided that it actually sounded pretty good. This provided me with a lot of confidence that carried over to my next lesson. I played the movement for Mr. Staryk and was quite happy with how I was sounding. I felt like everything was coming off with conviction and accuracy. Upon concluding the movement I looked at Mr. Staryk, expecting him to have some good things to say. With a very serious look on his face, the first thing he said to me was, "Your fly is open."

Staryk will continue to contribute to the musical life of the university as Professor Emeritus of Music, but considers himself essentially retired: "Old musicians never die, they just fake away: and that is why I am retiring, whilst it is still not noticeable. After a lifetime of measuring eleven inches of fingerboard, I have discovered that there are so many things to do which take less time."

AFTERTHOUGHTS

Steven Staryk is a self-described loner whose only affiliations were with orchestras, schools, and chamber groups. Whether this is due in part to his early experience as one of the Symphony Six isn't clear. Although his path eventually followed a course of great depth and breadth of orchestral experience, there were individuals in Staryk's career who hindered his progress in the short term and made advancement seem impossible. In contrast, others assisted him in ways that he couldn't have imagined and salved, with their generosity, the bitterness chafing in his memory. While recognizing inevitable set backs, compromises, and disappointments, Staryk's brief summary of his career reflects a sense of his own good fortune: "I have experienced, to a lesser or greater degree, the best of violins, concert halls, orchestras, opera, chamber music, and talented students; that is as close to ideal as it gets.

"For one who detests inefficiency and irresponsibility, it has been a very stressful and frantic life. I am retiring exhausted and primarily concerned that I do not find myself as described in this excerpt on life's last season by the revered Ukrainian poet Taras Shevchenko:

> Cry not for Spring, it will not come.
> It will not enter at thy door,
> Nor make thy garden green once more,
> Nor cheer with hope thy withered age,
> Nor loose thy spirit from her cage . . .
> Sit still, sit still! Thy life is spent;
> Nought art thou, be with nought content.[124]

"Of this memoir project, each topic covered could have been a book in itself. Those who know me well, also know how much was left out. In searching, filing, deciphering, given my lack of filing systems I found most reviews mixed with programs, correspondence, unrelated articles, and even recipes. This portrays my lack of concern for collecting career trophies or mementos. I have no rogues' gallery of inscribed photos and hardly any collected of my own career, not even photos of great instruments owned, with the exception of the Hochstein and Barrere: what's done is done.

"Oistrakh's words could have come out of my mouth: 'You cannot imagine how hard and tiring my life is, with more obligations and less strength every new year.' And Mark Twain's words, spoken after completing A Connecticut Yankee, sum up my feelings on my contribution to this book: 'Well, my book is written — let it go. But if it were only to write over again there wouldn't be so many things left out. They burn in me; and they keep multiplying and multiplying; but now they can't ever be said.'"

Staryk continues to do selective teaching and playing, collecting occasional reviews in such odd locations as Spokane, Washington, where he performed in May of 1997 in a recital with pianist Kendall Feeney. The program revealed both the virtuoso and the musician: Prokofiev's Sonata in D, Leclair's D Major Sonata, Brahms's Sonatensatz, and Mozart's K. 516 Quintet.

"Steven Staryk sure can play the violin," the Spokane critic announced at the opening of his review. "Leclair's simple, clear style allowed the violinist a chance to stake his musical territory." Several of the critic's remarks were familiar rehearsals of what is commonly said of Staryk's playing:

> Unlike many soloists who sound like themselves no matter what composer they are propped up to play, Staryk showed a lot of latitude in styles. Like having the right tool for the job, the violinist selected the suitable elements from all those available to him to enhance the music. Prokofiev brought on snapping crisp articulations, big soaring melodies and Staryk's continued absolute control from delicate to gutsy . . . Mozart's K. 516 quintet comprised the second half of the concert. Staryk took the lead and the Spokane String Quartet filled in the rest. The performance was thoroughly enjoyable with Mozart at his incredible best and great playing all around.[125]

Staryk remembers observing his aging colleagues as a young man of twenty and wondering when their playing would wind to a halt. Now, at the age of sixty-seven, he notes that the mechanics of his playing are still functioning and wonders the same of himself. The why of playing remains reassuringly constant: "Music has a higher function than just to occupy one's spare time," wrote Georges Enesco. "It will be an enchanted universe where the tribulations of life do not enter, and where your dreams will find a refuge. It will bring to you those priceless gifts — serenity of mind and forgetfulness of the cruelty of men." A 1975 article in the Port Hope *Evening Guide* offers another reflection on music's higher function:

> PCBs in the fish, nitrates in the bacon, terrorists in the Olympics, Moslems fighting Christians, union battling management, and killings everywhere.
>
> Constantly we are made aware of all the bad man can do, (and he can and has done a lot). Occasionally we get an opportunity to see some of the summits as well as the depths.
>
> Last night at the Port Hope United Church, Steven Staryk played his violin. It was music that would have soothed the most savage beast. Nothing we can say here would be able to transmit the beauty of his playing, the experience of music that he shared with his audience.
>
> We would like to thank Mr. Staryk for coming to our little burg, and thank the Friends of Music for bringing him. We need more artists like Mr. Staryk these days to remind us that we are more than desperate beings struggling with the ills of a society which at times appears to have soured. Indeed Mr. Staryk and his music are required more now, perhaps, than ever.[126]

From Port Hope, Ontario to Seattle, Washington. The students in Row N, sitting in the University of Washington's Roethke Auditorium on that mid-June afternoon near the end of a tedious week of finals, knew Staryk's music making from the insider's perspective, but could hardly have been more aware of its importance. Music, approached honestly, is always what wild strawberries were for Ingmar Bergman, an enclave of the ideal. The acceptance speech for his Distinguished Teaching Award was predictably stylish and concise, ending with a tongue-in-cheek reference to its own brevity. In his public life, as in his music, Staryk believes in keeping things moving along seamlessly to the end.

NOTES

[1] Collective farms

[2] Wasyl Hryshko, *The Ukrainian Holocaust of 1933*, ed., trans., Marco Carynnyk (Toronto: Bahrians Foundation, 1983), 77.

[3] Ibid., 72.

[4] Some estimates place the figure as high as 9 million. Ibid., 108.

[5] Ryszard Kapuscinski, *Imperium*. (Warszawa: Czytelnik, 1993).

[6] From Mary Paidak-Staryk's obituary.

[7] Gwenlyn Setterfield, "Introduction," *Without Compromise*, 6.

[8] Ibid., 6.

[9] Ibid., 7.

[10] Setterfield, "Introduction," 12.

[11] Hugh Thomson, Toronto *Daily Star*, May 4, 1949.

[12] Gerald Hannon, "The Big Chill," Toronto *Globe and Mail*, 29 February 1992, sec. D, 5.

[13] Ibid., 5.

[14] Setterfield, "The Symphony Six."

[15] Ezra Schabas, *Sir Ernest MacMillan: The Importance of Being Canadian* (Toronto: University of Toronto Press, 1994), 231.

[16] Sir Ernest MacMillan, ed., *Music in Canada* (University of Toronto Press, 1955).

[17] Schabas, *Sir Ernest*, 235.

[18] Setterfield "The Symphony Six," 10-11.

[19] Frank Tumpane, "Some Nerve," *Globe and Mail*, May 23, 1952, 3.

[20] Norman Hillmer, "The Second World War as an (Un) National Experience," in *On Guard for Thee: War, Ethnicity, and the Canadian State, 1939-1945*, Norman Hillmer, Bohdan Kordan, Lybomyr Luciuk, eds. (Canadian Committee for the History of the Second World War, 1988), p. xiv.

[21] Ibid, p. xiv.

[22] Bohdan Kordan, Lybomyr Luciuk, "A Prescription for Nationbuilding: Ukrainian Canadians and the Canadian State," *On Guard for Thee*, xiv.

[23] Ibid., 86.

[24] Barbara Tuchman, *The March of Folly* (Ballantine Books, 1985), 386.

[25] Pearl McCarthy, *Globe and Mail* (Toronto), n.d.

[26] Margaret Atwood, *Cat's Eye* (New York: Bantam, 1989), 13-14.

[27] Barbara McDougall, "Orchestral Star Turned Teacher," *The Strad* May 1994, vol. 105, no. 1249, 465-467.

[28] Harold C Schonberg, *The Great Conductors* (Simon and Schuster, NY, 1967), p. 298.

[29] Ronald Crichton, "Sir Thomas Beecham," in *The New Grove Dictionary of Music & Musicians*, vol. 2, 349.

[30] Casals

[31] From the IMG/BBC/Teldec video, *The Great Conductors*.

[32] Neville Cardus, *The Saturday Review of Recordings*, October 28, 1950,

[33] London *Times*, November 25, 1956.

[34] London *Times*, May 27, 1956.

[35] Beecham's emphasis should be explained here: specifically *British* orchestral mores were being transgressed. And it is interesting to note that while Staryk's language and directness clashed with British institutional norms, Beecham, with his titles, breeding, and fortunes, himself cultivated roguery and bad manners (to nearly everyone's delight).

[36] A similar situation arose when members of the London Philharmonic Orchestra decided, after Beecham's extended absence during the Second World War, that they couldn't abide Beecham's dictatorship after several years without a full-time conductor and after having adopted a system of collective stewardship over financial matters. Violist Frederick Riddle was then a member of the LPO — he protested against Beecham's move to resume control by resigning his position.

[37] "Krachmalnick arrived with all his furniture, appliances, plus a Cadillac, got settled, then for some reason decided to leave," recalls Staryk. "Everything was shipped back again and a big fuss arose about a refrigerator that went astray."

[38] J. Kasander, "Who Wields the Baton?", The *Holland Herald*, Vol. 13, Number 7.

[39] The standard Reiner yarn is this exchange; Q: "How do we know where to come in?" A: "Third button down the shirtfront."

[40] Claudia Cassidy, Chicago *Tribune*, February 28, 1964.

[41] Brandenburg No. 4 was issued in 1997 on compact disc, a souvenir of the Martinon/Staryk era.

[42] *Musical America*, November 1964.

[43] Intermezzo, 60

[44] Roger Dettmer, *The American*, June 2, 1967.

[45] Setterfield, "Time and Tune," 52-60.

[46] Jaak Liivoja-Lorius, *The Strad*, March 1983, Vol. 93, No. 1115.

[47] *Maclean's*, April 19, 1982.

[48] Gaynor Jones, *The Toronto Star*, September 22, 1983.

[49] from interview with Shona McKay, "The Return of a Roving Virtuoso," *Maclean's*, 19 April, 1982, 14-16.

[50] Helen Epstein, *Music Talks* (New York: McGraw Hill Book Co., 1987), 206.

[51] Alexander Inglis, *Fugue*, November 1977.

[52] Report by Earl Rosen and Associates Ltd, cited in the *Winnipeg Free Press*, Dec. 5 1981.

[53] Toronto *Globe and Mail*, November 28, 1986.

[54] Arnold Edinborough, *Financial Post*, February 16, 1987.

[55] Keith MacMillan, *Musicanada*, September 1969, No. 22, 2.

[56] Murray Ginsberg, *International Musician*, November 1987.

[57] Eric McLean, Montreal *Star*, December 1, 1969.

[58] Pat Kellog, "Steven Staryk: No Profit in His Own Country," *Performing Arts*, Winter 1978, 22-24.

[59] David Suzuki, *The Nature of Things* (Toronto: CBC documentary).

[60] Epstein, *Music Talks*, 200.

[61] Virgil Thomson, "Modernism Today," *Music Reviewed 1940-1954* (New York: Vintage Books, 1967), 233.

[62] Gordon Epperson, "Recordings, The Splice of Life," *American Music Teacher*, Feb/March, 1996.

[63] *Music Magazine*, May/June, 1978.

[64] Two such live performances were issued by *Masters of the Bow*. The Paganini Concerto No. 1, with the Norddeutscher Rundfunk Symphony conducted by Hermann Michael (January 16, 1969), and a recital in Toronto with pianist Robert Linzon, recorded in 1982.

[65] Claudia Cassidy, Chicago *Tribune*, March 14, 1965.

[66] George Jellinek, "A Remarkable Debut: Violinist Steven Staryk," *HiFi/Stereo Review*, September 1968.

[67] *American String Teacher*, Fall 1968.

[68] William Littler, "A Brilliant Record Album by a Canadian Violinist," Toronto *Daily Star*, 22 February 1971, 23.

[69] Murray Adaskin, *Stereo Review*, Summer, 1974.

[70] Setterfield, "Round and Round," pp. 36-37; and James Creighton's record notes, *Staryk Plays Paganini*, Masters of the Bow Series (MBS 2003).

[71] John Kraglund of the Toronto *Globe and Mail*: "The brilliance of his playing of Shostakovitch's Concerto Op. 99 makes it seem quite possible he has never sounded better . . a chance to display his virtuoso technique,

it also reveals the lyrical and interpretive subtlety of his art . . . an out-standing release."

[72] *Musicanada*: "Undoubtedly the most remarkable recent release of classical recordings in Canada." *Music Magazine*: "Their high level of artistry earns a rightful place among such notable interpretations as the Perlman/Ashkenazy and Heifetz/Bay recordings . . . Steven Staryk and John Perry have proven themselves to be of world class." *The Strad*: "The Staryk-Perry duo is a partnership which fully measures up to the kinds of standards set by the foremost duos of our time." The New York *Times*: "They played superbly from beginning to end, their playing was irreproachable — technically, tonally, and musically."

[73] *The Strad*, December 1985.

[74] Setterfield, "Solo Songs," 10.

[75] London *Times*: "It would be difficult to imagine closer teamwork . . . they had everything, virtuosity, range of colour and dynamics, rich cantabile, classically disciplined emotion."

[76] Otto Friedrich, *Glenn Gould: A Life and Variations* (New York: Vintage Books, 1989), 214.

[77] Glenn Gould, "We Who Are About to Be Disqualified Salute You!" in *The Glenn Gould Reader* (New York: Vintage Books), 252.

[78] Gould, "We Who Are About to Be Disqualifed," 252.

[79] Ulla Colgrass, "Music Competitions — Glory or Agony?" *Music Magazine*, May/June, 1978, 11.

[80] Y. Soroker, *David Oistrakh* (Jerusalem: Lexicon Publishing House, 1982),

[81] Colgrass, "Music Competitions — Glory or Agony?" 11.

[82] Epstein, *Music Talks*, 193.

[83] Ibid., 193.

[84] Richard Dyer, "David Helfgott Loses His Shine at the Piano," reprinted in the Seattle *Post-Intelligencer*, 6 March 1997, sec. C, 6.

[85] Alan Rich with Abigail Kuflik, "How Stars Are Made," *Newsweek*, 24 February 1986, 74-75.

[86] Donna Perlmutter, "Stern Sounds Youthful Note," Los Angeles *Times*, 9 September 1984, Calendar sec., 42.

[87] Setterfield, "Solo Songs," 13.

[88] Ibid., 18.

[89] Rich, "How Stars Are Made," 75.

[90] Norman Lebrecht, *Who Killed Classical Music? Maestros, Managers, and Corporate Politics* (Carol Publishing Group, 1997), 421.

[91] Entire exchange from Setterfield, "Solo Songs," 22.

[92] Seymour Bernstein, *With Your Own Two Hands* (New York: G. Schirmer,

1981), 209.

[93] Epstein, *Music Talks*, 211.

[94] Dyer, "David Helfgott Loses His Shine at the Piano," C6.

[95] Mordecai Richler created this fictitious company in his 1997 novel *Barney's Version* (New York: Alfred Knopf, 1997).

[96] "Spivakov: Athelete With Violin," *Ogonëk*, no. 22, May 1996, 74.

[97] Todd Brewster, *Strings*, May/June 1994, 42.

[98] Ibid., 40.

[99] R. M. Campbell, "Violinist Needs to Get Grip On Mannerisms," Seattle *Post-Intelligencer*, 14 May 1997, sec. D, 7.

[100] Epstein, *Music Talks*, 13.

[101] Setterfield, "Solo Songs," 55.

[102] Ibid., 54-55.

[103] Setterfield, "Round and Round," 54-55.

[104] Setterfield, "Solo Songs," 55.

[105] Ibid., 53.

[106] from student dissertation

[107] Reviews in the above two paragraphs are quoted in Setterfield, "Solo Songs." 46-55.

[108] Igor Stravinsky, *Poetics of Music* (Boston: Harvard University Press, 1970), 124-25.

[109] T. S. Eliot, *Selected Prose of T. S. Eliot*, ed. Frank Kermode (New York: Harcourt Brace Jovanovich, 1975), 37-44.

[110] Epstein, *Music Talks*, 15.

[111] *Sergei Prokofiev*, (Moscow: Foreign Languages Publishing House).

[112] Andrea Olmstead ed., *The Correspondence of Roger Sessions* (Boston University Press, 1992), 165.

[113] Perlmutter, "Stern Sounds a Youthful Note," 42.

[114] "Fiddlers Born," *BBC Music Magazine*, May 1995.

[115] Samuel R. Delany, "Eric, Gwen, and D. H. Lawrence's Esthetic of Unrectified Feeling," *Atlantis: Three Tales* (New Haven: Wesleyan University Press, 1995), 128.

[116] Adam Carse, *The Orchestra from Beethoven to Berlioz: A history of the Orchestra in the first half of the 19th century, and of the development of orchestral baton-conducting* (Cambridge: W. Heffer & Sons Ltd., 1948).

[117] Nikolaus Harnoncourt, *Baroque Music Today: Music as Speech: Ways to a New Understanding of Music*, trans. Mary O'Neill (Portland: Timber Press Inc., 1995), 76.

[118] Kyung Sun Chee, doctoral student at the University of Washington.

[119] Kyung Sun Chee, doctoral student at the University of Washington.

[120] Miguel de Unamuno, *A Tragic Sense of Life* (New York: Dover, 1954),
[121] Nachum Erlich, interview by author, Tape recording, Seattle, Washington, 22 May, 1997.
[122] Allan Bloom, *The Closing of the American Mind* (Touchstone Ed. Simon & Schuster inc. 1988 New York)
[123] Friedrich Nietzsche, *Beyond Good and Evil*, trans., R.J. Hollingdale (London: The Penguin Group, 1972).
[124] Taras Shevchenko, "Winter," *Poems* (Munich: Molode Zyttia Press, 1961), 112.
[125] William Berry, "Violinist Steven Staryk Dazzles With Style," *The Spokesman-Review*, 14 May 1997, sec. D, 5.
[126] editorial, "The Better Side," Port Hope *Evening Guide*, 21 October 1975, 2.
[127] The title "Hart" applied to Francescatti's Strad, or "David" to Heifetz's del Gesù, is a moniker that identifies the particular instrument and its lineage. If the original owner is known, as in the case of the "Tuscan" Strad (after Cosimo de Medici, the Grand Duke of Tuscany), the appellation draws on the reference. Often Strads are named after the renowned violinists who played them. For instance, the "Alard" Strad, after Jean-Delphin Alard, a nineteenth century French violinist, or the "Ysaÿe," Belgian virtuoso Eugene Ysaÿe's instrument. A few exceptional instruments, like the "Messiah" Strad, or Paganini's "Canon" del Gesù, have been given titles associated with authority or deity.
[128] Stradivari's main innovation, and that which differentiates his instruments from those of Amati, Stainer, and Seraphin, was the flattening of the arch in coordination with an increase in the overall dimensions. Almost three hundred years later, this evolutionary aspect of construction allowed Staryk to satisfactorily project his sound in any circumstance; the choice Strads have carrying power. The details of dimension of Stradivari's instruments vary from instrument to instrument, but there were general periods in which he experimented with larger and smaller instruments; hence the "long pattern" Strad, or the bold late period examples. Neil Grauer, writing for *Cigar Aficionado*, summarized the effect of Stradivari's work this way: "Through constant experimentation — varying by a fraction of an inch the arching of one instrument's back, another's length, the overall dimensions of yet another — he created . . . 'the violin of the future,' capable of producing not only delicate, sweet sounds but powerful, crystalline tones, strong and clear enough to perform brilliantly with the orchestras of today."
[129] dei Gesù: the plural form of del Gesù.

[130] *Science Digest*, December 1988.

[131] Staryk has continued to perform extensively on this violin. His recordings on the "Barrere" are as follows: The *Complete Violin and Piano Sonatas of Beethoven* (with the exception of No. 4, recorded on a 1740 del Gesù), originally released on CBC's Digital series, SM 5023-5; Strauss's *Ein Heldenleben* solo with the Toronto Symphony, on SM 5036; the Shostakovitch Concerto No. 1, with the Toronto Symphony, on SM 5037; the William Walton Sonata and Harry Freedman's *Encounter*, on SM 342; the sound track from the CBC Television production of *Vivaldi*, on MV 1020; the violin solos in Nos. 4 and 5 of the complete Bach Brandenburg Concerti, SM 5028-2 (Nos. 1 and 2 were recorded on a 1740 del Gesù); a live recording of a recital that included works of Corelli, Locatelli, Wieniawski, Vieuxtemps, Paganini, Kreisler, and others on the Discopedia *Masters of the Bow* series, MBS 2020; and televised performances, filmed by the CBC, of the Tchaikovsky Concerto and other repertoire. This listing alone speaks of the "Barrere's" versatility.

[132] The exact number of Strads in existense is also a point of contention. The brothers Hill list 540 Strads with which they had personal acquaintance; a few others have probably been unearthed since the publication of that figure.

[133] Arthur Alfred and W. Henry Hill, *The Violin Makers of the Guarneri Family* (London: Holland Press, 1965), 105.

APPENDIX A
Staryk on Violins: In Search of an Ideal

Antonio Stradivari (1644-1737)
Giuseppe Guarneri del Gesù (1698-1744)

Ye, who to wed the sweetest wife would try,
Observe how men a sweet Cremona buy!
New violins, they seek not from the trade,
But one, on which some good musician play'd:
Strings never try'd some harshness will produce;
The fiddle's harmony improves by use.

- Anonymous

My affair with violins was in many respects the most satisfying aspect of my career. Given sufficient musical talent and a specific aptitude for a particular instrument, one sets out forever searching for that ideal voice, that magical sound that defies total analysis or scientific explanation. This is more true of the violin than any other instrument. Ultimately the combination of one's temperament, physical makeup, and that "special" instrument produce a very distinct and personal sound. Some violinists can project their sound through vastly different instruments and still bring out each instrument's unique character. Others produce a sound that is relatively constant, regardless of the violin being played.

It has been my experience that players with heightened physical reflexes (and a range and facility on the instrument that enables them to manipulate extremes of dynamics and shading), have the ability not only to project their own personal sound, but also to bring out the maximum in every respect from any given violin. There are those with the lighter, "Amatise" touch, and those with the heavier, "late Strad or del Gesù" approach. These two ways of playing are described, though rather generally, by Ruggiero Ricci in the liner notes accompanying his recording, *The Glory of Cremona*. Many violinists, of course, fit in between the two extremes. The challenge would be to mix the most refined and expressive interpretive abilities of a violinist with the extreme parameters possible in the instrument, and thus approach an ideal.

It has always been puzzling to me why so few violinists develop a desire for substantial knowledge of this enigmatic instrument; especially considering the sophistication of musical awareness and sound perception that develops through the process of searching. Today, cost is an obvious obstacle. Most passable Strads are now valued at a minimum of $800,000 to an upper range of around $3.5 million or more. But there was a time when even a poor freelance fiddler could, through spartan living, purchase a quality instrument. Those more desperate resorted to theft, as in the case of Erica Morini's $3.5 million Strad, taken from her bedroom closet as she was dying, and the more recent case of Huberman's 1713 "Gibson" Strad. This instrument was stolen from the artist's dressing room in Carnegie Hall and, after being used professionally for years, was finally returned and given its day in court in November of 1996. And this is not fiction! There are many instances of stolen violins past and present.

I observed musicians around me whose priorities, given our common goal of perfection, seemed confused. Then, as today, there were many toys to be had: cars, stereos, televisions etc. These toys give immediate gratification. But acquiring a fine Italian violin meant foregoing toys, and even bypassing certain investments, such as that of a home, for the one all-consuming investment. Of those who did purchase a fine instrument, some were convinced of the merits of their particular choice — often becoming so accustomed to a particular violin that they became limited in their scope.

Jacob Krachmalnick, for example, had a "box" (as insignificant violins are known in the profession) to start with, then a Gagliano, and finally a del Gesù with which he was very happy. Francescatti was similar, upgrading from his Sanctus Seraphin to the "Hart" Strad, with which he struggled for a time until player and instrument became compatible. Heifetz had the Tononi and then the "ex-David" del Gesù, which became *his* fiddle.[127] In my case, this did not happen. I would get one, then another, learning that there were both subtle and vast differences from one instrument to another in the same price range. Admittedly, when I got my first del Gesù I thought it was also going to be my last.

Diary of a violinist

I wanted the sound of a del Gesù, or a dark sounding Strad. Disastrously, my first purchase was a most pleasing Sanctus Seraphin. Pleasing *to the eye* that is. I fell for the violin at least in part because of cosmetic considerations. It really was a very beautiful violin to look at. And, of course, it had other good qualities, but as with much beauty, the beauty of this instrument turned out to be, in my opinion, primarily only "skin deep."

This Seraphin was not the violin I should have chosen, but I was both too young and too inexperienced to discern this. Switching from a modern instrument to a highly sensitive old Italian was simply too great a change. Seraphin, a former student of Nicolaus Amati, produced instruments of the type generally termed Amatise, i.e., more soprano and lighter in response. In character and design, his instruments are much like the instruments of his teacher, or those of the Austrian luthier Jacob Stainer. This type of violin cannot be played in a heavy or aggressive manner as the sound will break.

I love to be able to dig into a fiddle, and need one with tremendous depth and range that will take a lot of robust playing. Also, I have always tended toward instruments that have a darker timbre. For two years I suffered with the Sanctus Seraphin, and it suffered with me.[128]

As a student, I had played on a few very fine violins, including a long pattern Strad, a Francesco (son of Antonio) Strad, and was in possession of a Joseph *filius* Andreas Guarneri when I experienced my first real revelation. This was in 1956 in Geneva, at the shop of Pierre Vidoudez. The nature of the revelation was not unlike first discovering sex. "It's even better than sex!" is the common consensus among "natural" fiddlers who have experienced a really great violin. The violin was the "ex-Kreisler," "ex-Huberman" (and now also "ex-Martzy") Stradivari of 1733. At that point in my life the instrument was totally unaffordable, since I was wandering in Europe jobless. However, only three months later, a del Gesù was offered to me by none other than Hill's of Bond Street. It was affordable, first because it lacked the original scroll, and secondly because I had just been appointed concertmaster of the Royal Philharmonic by Sir Thomas Beecham. So I bought it.

While I wallowed in this titled fiddle (the Lord Coke of 1744), Hill's had me play a number of other fine examples to ensure that the fit was right. I went through the motions and the fiddles, including the "Alard" Strad of 1715, one of the finest examples of Stradivari's work, though I was unaware of this at the time. At that young and inexperienced age I was captivated neither by the sound nor tactile sense of this instrument. Without question, I was drawn to the dark, dramatic, resistant type of violin, and probably would have stayed there for some time had the Lord Coke not possessed an incurable wolf tone. After appointments with all the 'specialists' in London and Paris, I realized I would have to live with the del Gesù's wolf tone or part with it.

I parted. The decision to change instruments was influenced by Milstein. After an entire afternoon of comparing his Strad to my del Gesù in his London hotel room, Milstein announced in his most direct and sarcastically charming manner, "If you want to play a del Gesù, then play viola; del Gesù is not a violin sound!" I thought to myself, "Maybe so, but even with the wolf, I wouldn't trade my del Gesù for your Strad." But then I was only twenty-six and had time to try a few before I settled down. As violin dealer Jacques Francais said years later, "Stevie, we all changed wives, but you changed fiddles, you clever son of a gun." Jacques is still a friend after much buying and selling. I would say that from my experiences with most of the major firms in the world, including Vidoudez, Möller, Wurlitzer, Moennig, Lewis, Warren, Weisshaar, Bein and Fushi, etc., Francais probably had as subjective and sympathetic a relationship with his professional customers as is possible for a dealer. On an even more personal level, this was also the case with my very first purchase and many later transactions with Canada's major firm, George Heinl and Sons (father, sons and grandson) of Toronto..

While searching to replace the Lord Coke, I was able to borrow and try seemingly everything available to play, as London was fertile ground. Interest in collecting was a very English trait, and the *per capita* of colleagues with excellent instruments was very high. I became familiar with collectors and dealers and eventually sold my del Gesù to a collector who loaned the "ex-Wieniawski" Strad (1719) to me on numerous occasions. From this source I borrowed and played and recorded on several fine instruments, including a 1721 Strad, a Guarneri del Gesù, and an Amati.

Needless to say, my desire and curiosity were ignited to a feverish pitch by then, and I continued to burn through approximately forty Strads, twenty-six dei Gesù,[129] and numerous good and bad instruments of all makes and degrees of monetary value. I recorded extensively on four del Gesù: the 1744 "Lord Coke," the 1739 "Papini" (or "Vieuxtemps" as described in the *Glory of Cremona*), the 1731 "Baltic," and 1740 "Steinhardt." Also on four Strads: the 1715 "Hochstein," the 1719 "Wieniawski," the 1736 "Muntz," and the 1727 "Barrere." With the exception of the Wieniawski, I owned the others at one time or another in my life and recorded on four other makers, a Hieronymus Brothers Amati, a Francesco Rugieri, a Joseph *filius* Andreas Guarneri, and a Petrus Guarneri of Mantua.

A rose is a rose is a rose

Although all "name" instruments have a characteristic nature, this nature is not always, by any means, positive or uniform across the scope of a single maker's output. Stradivari was a known experimenter, and not all of his concoctions met with equal tonal success; "a Strad is a Strad is a Strad," doesn't always hold true, unfortunately. The same is true of del Gesù and the other Italian masters and their instruments.

There have been lesser makers who have, on occasion, outdone themselves in creating an instrument that sounds as though it came from the hand of a top master but, unable to repeat this often enough, remain lesser names. I found just such a masterpiece for my wife, a Landolphi, outstanding with respect to specimen, condition, and sound.

Some violins have been literally used up, or played out. Others never possessed exceptional tonal qualities to begin with. There are those instruments so much in repair that they hang together by parchment and a measure of goodwill; one must discriminate between repair jobs since there are both fine repairs by masters and botched repairs by bunglers. Some fiddles have fallen victim to accidents in which one part or aspect survives while another is lost — the "Windsor" Strad, for instance. This violin went singing in the rain, and the voice got a permanet cold. Another Strad, the "Red Diamond," went for a dip in the Pacific, by way of a flashflood. The "Servais" Stradivarius cello fell off a dogsled in the Russian hinterland one winter, a fact Servais didn't discover until hours later, long after nightfall, when he finally arrived at the next village. When he went back the next day, he found his cello, thankfully intact, though the leather case had been gnawed by wolves during the night.

Varnish

Stradivari may have left the recipe for his varnish on the title page of a family Bible; his great-great grandson, Giacomo Stradivari claims to have found it there. Giacomo apparently wrote down the recipe, destroyed the Bible, and vowed to pass the secret only to members of the family, if, and when, they shouldered the yoke of their ancestor's trade. The secret, if there was one, died with this latter Stradivari.

"The secret is in the varnish" is, in my experience, a myth. I owned the "ex-Steinhardt" del Gesù of 1740, which had its original varnish stripped at some time in it's past and replaced by Sacconi's. The monetary value was affected, but certainly not the sound. Many believe that

212

the formula for the oil-based varnish was common knowledge among Stradivari's contemporaries and that it was devoid of any magical ingredients or combinations of ingredients that would in and of itself enhance the quality of an instrument's sound.

There are old wive's tales, both past and present, which hover somewhere between fact and fiction in their attempt to explain the "secrets" of great instruments. These attempts — often whimsical, like the music world itself, and as wide-ranging in their conclusions as the telling and retelling of history — reveal our dissatisfaction at not knowing, but bring us no closer to the creation of violins of a similar quality. To cite an example, the following is from an article in *Science Digest*: "What is it about a 300-year-old Stradivarius that makes musicians drool? What is the secret behind the unmatched tone of these revered string instruments? We had heard it was the varnish, or perhaps the wood, but now chemists at the University of Cambridge have come up with another possibility. Analyzing a Stradivarius cello with an electron microscope and a special x-ray device, they discovered a thin layer of material between the varnish and the wood comprised mainly of a volcanic ash found in the Cremona region of Italy where Stradivari lived. The researchers suspect the ash was part of a solution used to prime the instrument for varnishing, and now plan to test other instruments to determine if the ash is indeed the secret to Stradivari's success."[130]

The collector: a Strad on holiday

Many Strads and del Gesù have been spared excessive wear and tear through the guardianship of the church, the state, and wealthy amateurs. These collectors are generally happy with instrumental qualities which tickle their ears in private drawing or music rooms and never place on an instrument the extreme demands of a professional performer. As long as they don't tinker with an instrument (as some have), they can and have preserved many fine fiddles which might otherwise have suffered normal wear and tear, or even abnormal abuse.

Certain collectors and corporations have constructed foundations through which they loan instruments to deserving and aspiring players — players who through their playing can, on occasion, elucidate the tonal properties of the instrument for them. A current example of this is Japan's Fuji film and camera company, which bought the "Jupiter" Strad and loaned it to Midori.

The physical preservation and tonal confirmation of an instrument's value is a most interesting and elusive aspect of the business. A violin's physical condition, especially with present technology, can readily be confirmed; however, the ethereal and momentary impressions of an instrument's tonal quality remain difficult to assess. Many dealers, in fact, do not bother to assess the tonal quality, depending largely on foundations or collectors to purchase the "name" specimen, find the right period, determine the condition, and assess what the market price will be. This is why a professional performer can still hope to find a fiddle that sounds.

Making the choice

The quantity and quality of the sound of an instrument must be evaluated through a certain amount of greatly varied professional playing. The inner drive to seek out the ideal multi-purpose instrument is the result of (and results in) sophisticated musical growth. Only the stresses and demands of a professional career can create the conditions for this growth and the true testing ground for the instrument and player; indeed there is a vast difference between "fiddling around" with your fiddle colleagues, and making serious music with other instrumentalists and conductors, musicians who do not see all music through the f-holes of a violin.

The act of comparison is not unlike judging competitors in the highest class of any competition. As with competing violinists, the particular instrument must prove itself in good and bad concert and recital halls — in recording studios, large and small ensembles, and in different periods and styles of music. The violin must even work well when someone else plays it without knowing its subtleties. It should be blind-tested in a situation where it is compared with other instruments, in different spaces, played by a variety of players. It should be stable through climatic changes. In short, the violin must prove itself a thoroughbred that performs under any conditions, a violin for all seasons!

To arrive at the point where it is possible to judge such qualities, one must have accumulated much knowledge about both the obvious and the scarcely perceptible. It demands many years and many fiddles, uncounted performances, and endless discussions with makers and specialists in setup. It requires many changes of bridges, posts, and string labels. One must also develop a sixth sense for guessing right a high percentage of the time about the potential of a particular fiddle. A violin that appears right in every respect, but does not sound as expected, may have an abnormal and inappropriate setup, or *require* an abnormal setup (abnormal generally, yet appropriate to the specific instrument).

Finally, when all the excitement and pressure of choosing is past, comes the moment of reward for one's discernment, the pleasure of actually playing the violin. To begin with, if you have chosen well, you immediately sound better (instant gratification!). A great instrument will suggest infinite subtleties and inflections. This will improve your playing, which, with any luck, should improve your income from playing.

Ultimately, the greatest perk from finally owning the greatest of instruments is that it is just you and the violin in the privacy of your home or studio, acting the part of the wealthy collector. You play in an atmosphere of unadulterated pleasure, devoid of fickle critics, deaf recording engineers and producers, unsophisticated audiences, frustrated orchestras, deadening halls, disgruntled accompanists, all of whom are surely intent on messing things up and spoiling your fun. Here then is that fantasy time where we can drop our intellect a few notches and wallow in the sound like an *aficionado*. In the meantime, as long as you have a reputable maker or repairer to do the normal periodic examination, are adequately insured with an established firm which specializes in musical instruments, and don't literally sit on the instrument, it's capital appreciation in every way.

The "Barrere" Strad of 1727

As mentioned, many unusual variants on the Strad exist, and the one I ended up with, and which heads the list, is the "Barrere" Strad of 1727. My discovery of this instrument ended my lifelong search. The decision to purchase the "Barrere" was made in one afternoon. My only other immediate commitment to a purchase was at Wurlitzer's in 1969 with the "Muntz" Strad of 1736.

The "Barrere" is a choice Strad and sounds like none other that I have played before or since. (Admittedly, comparisons are odious — however, much of everything in life is judged on a comparative basis, and in most instances there are yardsticks.) One of the documents that accompanies the violin states, "It has always been noted for its exceptional tone." I have found this instrument to be extremely flexible, full of variety of color (both dark and bright), complex, multilayered, free of wolf tones, capable of a great range of dynamics, amiable and responsive in execution, and perennially stable. The "Barrere's" certificates also attest to its health, remarking that it is "unusually well-preserved" and "in splendid condition."

The state of preservation of an instrument has much to do with its general stability. With the "Barrere," the bridge and post, after the usual experimenting, were set during the first year and, after minimal alterations, remain largely in the same position all these many years later. The strings, at first selected by coincidence (in the same manner that Janos Starker discovered strings for his cello), are not of a set, but four different makes and materials. The soundpost setup is of normal tension and "user friendly" to both player and violin.

The violin is listed in Herbert K. Goodkind's *Violin Iconography of Antonio Stradivari* (1972). The photographs of front, side, and back are on page 614 of that work and information on ownership is listed at the end of the volume. The instrument was used professionally by the Los Angeles violinist Louis Kaufman in many performances, recordings, and movie sound tracks.[131] I have never owned or played on a more giving or forgiving instrument, Strad or del Gesù, in a career that now spans over fifty years, forty-three of which were spent oscillating exclusively between the Strad and del Gesù camps.

Dale Clevenger, principal horn of the Chicago Symphony, remarked during a rehearsal for a performance of the Brahms Horn Trio (in August 1996), "I have never heard this passage played so softly!" Further into the rehearsal, Dale said "there are a couple of places where I'll drown you out, can't help it." After these couple of places he responded, "I take that back!" Needless to say, the instrument will not perform on its own — which reminds me of a story attributed to Heifetz, where an admirer states after a performance, "Mr. Heifetz, your violin sounds beautiful," to which Heifetz replied, "Really? I don't hear anything."

What I had believed was virtually impossible in one instrument, I found in the "Barrere."

The "Muntz" Strad of 1736

This instrument is referred to in the novel *The Violin Hunter*, by William Alexander Silverman, as well as in William Henry Hill's *Antonio Stradivari*, Doring's *How Many Strads?*, Goodkind's *Violin Iconography of Antonio Stradivari*, Henley's *Antonio Stradivari*, and more recently in Charles Beare's *Antonio Stradivari: The Cremona Exhibition of 1987*. This is a violin in pristine condition. It has a silvery sound, though thicker than the more typical golden period soprano sound. (Stradivari's so-called "golden period" spanned the years between 1700 and the mid-1720s, with some of his best work produced in the year 1716.) The lower register of the fiddle is full but lean, and it has incredible carrying or projecting power. It is generally of a neutral quality of sound — neither nasal nor totally open. The instrument required calculated and focused playing through its initial period of resistance, a period of approximately one year, after which the flexibility greatly improved. The "Muntz" is extremely stable in all respects, and at the time I played it, had no wolf tones. I recorded a number of albums on this violin, including works by Paganini, Bartok, Hindemith, Satie, and Mozart.

It is common knowledge that for an instrument to sound it must be played. I can confirm this through my experience with the "Muntz." In perfect condition, the "Muntz" had received very little playing. Its annual solo performance was for a few years given by my colleague Jacob Krachmalnick, while he was concertmaster of the San Francisco Symphony. Jake's comment on the instrument, in his usual no-nonsense manner, was, "It sounds like the back fell off." I also found it stiff and unyielding, though still in three dimensions. Jacques Francais and others who also knew the instrument before I played it, assured me that the violin had undergone a dramatic transformation of sound after a year in my hands. Comparing it with the many other Strads I've played, the identifying characteristic of the "Muntz" was its capacity to project through the worst of acoustic conditions. A recent quote for it by Bein and Fushi Inc. of Chicago was four million dollars.

The "Hochstein" Strad of 1715

This instrument is included in Doring's *How Many Strads?*, as well as the works of Henley and Goodkind. Visually, it is one of the most beautiful Strads I have seen or owned. The table was extensively repaired, and the scroll, a point of inquiry during another of my sessions with Milstein, was later confirmed to have originated from a 1703 Strad. This fact was discovered by Max Möller, who noticed a slight discrepancy in the size cited in the "Hochstein's" Hill document when compared to other documents from that firm. After inquiring at Hill's, we discovered that a single, very relevant, line had been cleverly deleted without noticeably altering the description. The sound has a beautiful quality; neither too dark nor too bright. The instrument offers a resilient tactile response, not overly soft or stiff, hides no wolf tones, and is very even. As a partial list, I recorded on this instrument the traditional etudes in Every Violinists' Guide, the solo sonatas of Pisendel, Geminiani, Prokofiev, and Hindemith, and most of the all-Wieniawski album.

The "Wieniawski" Strad of 1719

This violin can be found in the work of Goodkind and its photograph is on the cover of the EMI release (HQS 1139) of my all-Wieniawski recording. (The notes on the back cover contain a misprint: the date reads 1717 instead of 1719.) The "Wieniawski's" voice is deep and thick, velvety but clear, and slightly darker than one associates with the typical golden period instrument. The tactile feeling was extremely pliable and flexible. I used this instrument on many occasions, including the EMI Wieniawski recording. During the period of this recording, which was the longest time I consistently played the instrument, it suffered from fatigue. Fatigue is a condition similar to any stress, but which is particularly noticeable in "thinned-out," badly repaired, overly repaired (too many cracks, breaks, etc.), and/or older work requiring renewal. I completed the project on my "Hochstein" Strad, which, even with an extensively repaired table, was renewed and structurally sound.

The "Kyd" Strad of 1714

The "Kyd" is similar in feel and sound to the 1719 "Wieniawski;" in fact, these would have been an ideal pair for a performance of the Bach Double, or for other significant two-violin repertoire. I often borrowed this violin from a Chicago collector, and used it for the Tchaikovsky Concerto in my first solo performance with the Chicago Symphony. It was later acquired by Itzhak Perlman and was his concert instrument for some time.

Other Strads

In addition to the Strads mentioned above, there were many others of which I had extensive use: the "Darnley," 1712; the "Macmillan," 1721; and "Rode," 1722. There were brief encounters with the "Wilmotte," 1734; the "Milanello," 1728; the "Kiesewetter," 1731; and the "Scotland University," 1734. Another 1721 example I often borrowed in London, with characteristics similar to the "Kiesewetter," proved to be a most interesting comparative experience. I owned and was performing on the 1739 "Papini-Vieuxtemps" del Gesù. Experiencing conditions similar to those that led Michael Rabin to turn to me during a rehearsal in the

Royal Festival Hall and exclaim "it sounds like I still have the practice mute on!" I began looking for an alternative instrument. I ended up borrowing this 1721 Strad, to the delight of the collector, and, I must admit, to my own. There were many other del Gesù and Strad comparisons which proved very educational from every point of view, especially the practical.

One of each, please!

Needless to say, it is extremely difficult to find a violin ideally suited for Bach or Mozart, Tchaikovsky or Sibelius. While leading the Royal Concertgebouw Orchestra, for instance, I always borrowed a particular del Gesù for the "Erbarme dich" solo in the *Saint Matthew Passion* of Bach, rather than play it on the "Hochstein" Strad. However, years later, when I simultaneously owned the "Barrere" Strad and the "Steinhardt" del Gesù, I used both at successive performances of the *Passion*.

I managed to own both instruments for a number of years, a situation which, though luxurious, was physically and economically very taxing. When some of the repertoire could be played on either instrument, I would end up practically doubling my hours of practice deciding which fiddle to use. I felt like the horse with two riders; one rider would mount just as the other dismounted. Usually, with a typical Strad or del Gesù, the choice of instrument for a particular piece of music is obvious. In my case, the character of the "Steinhardt" del Gesù was obviously better suited to certain works, while the "Barrere" Strad could cross many boundaries.

Investing practically all of my capital in two expensive instruments was not, and would not be, highly advised by any money manager. Only a subjective fiddler would feel he is diversifying! Of course, some fortunate individuals are "happily married" to a fortune which provides no end to the choices; though even in that situation, frustrations can continue. By way of example, Mr. Balakovic once arrived with two great fiddles, the 1737 "Swan" Stradivarius and the 1735 "King" del Gesù to perform with the Royal Philharmonic in Festival Hall. He played and I listened, I played and he listened, before the rehearsals, during intermissions, and after rehearsals. The "giant mute" of Festival Hall seemed to be the only winner, and I cannot recall which violin was used.

In most cases, del Gesù have a darker, dryer, and more veiled sound than Strads. Performing in an acoustically dead hall with an orchestra inevitably produces great problems of projection, even for the confirmed "del Gesù only" performers. There are a few of the full dimension, late examples which are less dry, less veiled. There are also more soprano, metallic examples that *will* project; but in my experience from years of listening and playing, in good and bad halls, there are simply more Strads that successfully carry or project quality and quantity of sound in acoustically unsympathetic halls. This is in part due to the fact that there are more Strads than del Gesù to choose from.

Violinists are often typecast by their preference in instruments. For example, Elman, Oistrakh, Milstein, and Francescatti favored Strads; as did Menuhin and Fuchs, and more recently, Perlman and Anne-Sophie Mutter. Heifetz, Stern, Ricci, and Zukerman all found their ideal in the del Gesù. Kreisler played both and others besides. Perlman has changed to del Gesù, as had Menuhin. One of each would be ideal. However most players would be only too happy to borrow, let alone own, a violin by either maker!

I feel very fortunate to have had the opportunity to play so many del Gesù (a total of twenty-six), as there are less than one half as many del Gesù as Strads in existence. The total numbers always vary depending on the source. A common round figure is 700 Strads and 300 del Gesù, with some sources citing either lower or higher figures for the del Gesù.[132]

The "Lord Coke" del Gesù of 1744

The "Lord Coke" del Gesù was my first great violin, purchased in 1956 from Hill's. This instrument was affordable because it did not have the original scroll (or any period del Gesù scroll). It was one of the few full size models that Guarneri made, and embodied a very full, dark, and dramatic tone, though not a veiled tone, as is typical with del Gesù. As mentioned earlier, this violin had an incurable wolf tone, a condition that prompted me to sell it two and a half years later. With a maximum investment of effort, it would respond incredibly well. My first recordings, which included the *Scheherazade* and *Heldenleben* solos with Beecham and the Royal Philharmonic Orchestra, were made on this instrument — as well as Bartok's *Two Portraits* (the first movement of which was originally the first movement of Bartok's First Violin Concerto), recorded with Kubelik and the Royal Philharmonic Orchestra.

The "Papini-Vieuxtemps" del Gesù of 1739

The "Papini" is a prime example and twin to the 1739 del Gesù owned by Grumiaux. It exhibits a most beautiful tone quality which, unfortunately, included the veiled characteristic, and was therefore not always successful in acoustically weak halls. However, it was excellent for recording. Visually, it was a striking instrument, with rubies and diamonds set in the pegs, tail piece, and end button (which would tend to rattle and buzz and require re-gluing). The violin's stately genealogy stretches back to a noble Russian family and continues to the present; now it is in the possession of one of the most acclaimed violinists, who does not play on it, preferring to play on another del Gesù which is more capable of projecting. I recorded a considerable amount of repertoire on this violin including four sonatas of J.S. Bach, sonatas of Nardini, Veracini, Locatelli, and Corelli, as well as the two Prokofiev violin and piano sonatas.

The "Baltic" del Gesù of 1731

This del Gesù (photographed for the cover of my Paganini Concerto No. 1 and Caprices recording) came immediately after the "Muntz," and, needless to say, faced an incredible challenge. To my great relief it worked well enough. Though slightly veiled, it possessed the "metallic" edge which projected under most circumstances. This instrument also possessed extreme clarity (a drier ambiance between notes) and a slightly nasal quality. These characteristics are the necessary ones in my experience for a "concert hall" del Gesù. Recordings on the "Baltic" include an album of twelve works by Kreisler, a contemporary Canadian concerto by Kenins, the Hoffert Concerto for Contemporary Violin, Stravinsky's L'Histoire du Soldat, the Bach E Major Concerto, and Prokofiev's D Major Concerto.

The "Steinhardt" del Gesù of 1740

This is a very fine-playing del Gesù with a mix of characteristics prevalent in the "Baltic" and the "Lord Coke." One of the easiest to play, the "Steinhardt" displayed wonderful response and a color that was not overly dark. The hole for the end button was slightly off-center, and the varnish, as mentioned, was not original, but that of Sacconi; so much for another "old wives' tale." Some of my recorded work on this instrument includes the Beethoven Sonata No. 4 (from the complete recordings), Bach's Brandenburg Concerti Nos. 1 and 2, the violin solos from the Vier letzte Lieder of Richard Strauss, and Bach's "Erbarme Dich, Mein Gott" from the Saint Matthew Passion with Maureen Forrester in the film of the

221

memorial service for Glenn Gould.

The "ex-Huberman-Ricci" del Gesù of 1734

This violin is still played by Ricci and, as set up by him, is quite dark and very responsive. He is one of the very rare breed of violinists who has played and tried many violins (more than are accounted for on the *Glory of Cremona* recording), and who dares to move post, bridge, and whatever else to satisfy his personal needs. I found the setup too loose for my liking, though this characteristic made it extremely easy to play (for a del Gesù).

Ricci and I taught together at a well-known summer music festival; the experience was memorable for more than one reason. This was the place and time I was thinking of changing from the "Muntz" Strad to the "Macmillen" Strad. I had both on stage (one on a table), and was intending to switch instruments between movements as part of my comparison formula, when a string broke. Naturally, I picked up the fiddle waiting on the table, but not before I heard, in that Brooklyn accent, "Like a real pro, always ready for an emergency." The switch that Autumn was from the "Muntz" Strad to the "Baltic" del Gesù.

As with the Strads, there were more del Gesù played for longer or shorter periods. These included the "ex-Balakovic-Becker," 1732; the "ex-Kortschak," 1739; the "ex-Sainton," 1741; the "ex-Dushkin," 1741; the "ex-Carrodus," 1743; the "ex-Sennhauser," 1735; the "ex-Parlow," 1735; the "ex-Rodriguez," 1730-31; and others, some with names attached, others with only birth dates.

Conclusions

In total, there were still more Strads, del Gesù and other makers which I played upon, compared in fiddle shops, concert halls, homes, and hotel rooms. In recalling and describing this partial list, it was interesting to compare notes, with Hill particularly, on the del Gesù. I am certain that some of the priorities of those buying or trading have changed with the times, as have some of the violins, for better and for worse. I have taken into consideration that some of the violins were not set up as I would have them, and therefore could sound and respond differently. As stated at the beginning of this survey, the ultimate sweetener of any violin remains in the fingers of its player.

Aside from those I owned, with the fiddles that I borrowed for longer periods I would get permission to make adjustments to the violin, be it strings, bridge, and/or post. This of course is the only way to truly test a violin unless by coincidence it is set up very closely to what you are comfortable with and believe is best for the violin.

Before concluding, I would like to mention that there is at least as much that can be written about the finest violin bows, without which no violin, good or bad, can sound. I have been very active in collecting bows, including the "ex-Huberman" Francois Tourte, the "ex-Dancla" Paul Simon, and other fine examples. Suffice it to say that a great bow can alter the sound of a violin to such a degree that one becomes convinced that the violin itself has been changed for another.

> In the elder days of Art,
> Builders wrought with greatest care
> Each minute and unseen part;
> For the Gods see everywhere.[133]

APPENDIX B
Steven Staryk's Discography

Updated from James Creighton's
Discopaedia of the Violin

ALBINONI

Adagio in g (org, strs & c)
with A. de Klerk (org) & chamber orch.-
Rieu
CNR RS041

BACH, J.S.

Concerto no. 2, in E, BWV.1042
(1717/23)
(vln, strs & c) with Toronto Chamber
Orch.- Neel
Umbrella UMB-DD 9

Brandenburg Concertos nos. 1, 2, 4, 5
CBC Vancouver Orch. - Bernardi
CBC SM 5028-2

Brandenburg Concertos no. 4
(Live performance, Chicago Symphony)
(June 1966)
CSO CD 97-2

(6) Sonatas, BWV.1014/9 (1717/23) (vln
& clav)
Sonato no. 4, in c, BWV.1017
with V. Weeks (hpsi)
Masters of the Bow MVS 2004

Sonata in g, BWV.1020 (vln & clav)
(NOTE: Of doubtful authenticity. Possi-
bly by one of Bach's sons or pupils.)
with K. Gilbert (hpsi)
Baroque BC 1858, BCS 2858
Everest (in set SDBR 3203)
Saga STXID 5300

Sonata in F, BWV.1022 (vln & hpsi)
(NOTE: Of doubtful authenticity. Pos-
sibly by one of Bach's sons or pupils.)
with K. Gilbert (hpsi)
Baroque BC 1858, BCS 2858
Everest (in set SDBR 3203)
Saga STXID 5300

Sonata in e, BWV.1023 (1714/7) (vln &
c) with K. Gilbert (hpsi)
Baroque BC 1858, BCS 2858
Everest (in set 3203)
Saga STXID 5300

Sonata in G, BWV 1021
(vln. & c)
Baroque BC 1858, BCS 2858
Everest (in set SDBR 3203)
Saga STXID 5300

BARTOK

(2) Portraits, op. 5 (1907) (vln & orch)
with Royal Philharmonic Orch.-Kubelik
(1958)
Capitol G 7186, SG 7186
Electrola E 91064, STE 91064
HMV ALP 1744, ASD 312, ASDF 221,
ASDW 312,
FALP 655, WALP 1744

(6) Rumanian folk dances (1915)
(pf-arr. vln & pf Székely)
with R. Pannell (pf) (1984)
Duke Records DBR 31003

Sonatina in D (on 2 Transylvanian peasant themes)
(1915) (pf-transcr. for vln & pf in 1931
by André Gertler.)
with J. Schwarz (pf)
CBC SM 172

BEETHOVEN

(3) Sonatas, op. 12 (1797/8) (vln &pf)
Sonata no. 1, in D with J. Perry (pf) (17
Jan. 1982)
CBC (in set SM 5023-5) (1 A)

Sonata no. 2, in A
with J. Perry (pf) (24/25 May 1982)
CBC (in set SM 5023-5) (1 B)

Sonata no. 2, in A
with L. Boucher (pf)
RCA CC 1016, CCS 1016

Sonata no. 3, in E flat
with J. Perry (pf) (20/21 Jan. 1980)
CBC (in set SM 5023-5) (2 A)

Sonata no. 4, in a, op. 23 (1800) (vln &
pf)
with J. Perry (pf) (12 Feb. 1980)
CBC (in set SM 5023-5) (4 B)

Sonata no. 5, in F, op. 24 (1800/1) "Spring"
(vln & pf)
with J. Perry (pf) (20/21 Jan. 1980)
CBC (in set SM 5023-5) (2 B)

(3) Sonatas, op. 30 (1801/2) (vln & pf)
No. 1. Sonata no. 6, in A, op.30
with J. Perry (pf) (26 May 1982)
CBC (in set SM 5023-5) (3 A)

No. 2. Sonata no. 7, in c, op.30
with J. Perry (pf) (23 May, 1982)
CBC (in set SM 5023-5) (3 B)

No. 3. Sonata no. 8, in G, op.30
with J. Perry (pf) (27 May, 1982)
CBC (in set SM 5023-5) (5 A)

Sonata no. 9, in A, op. 47 (1802/3)
"Kreutzer"
(vln & pf)
with J. Perry (pf) (12 Feb. 1982)
CBC (in set SM 5023-5) (4 A & B)

Sonata no. 10, in G, op. 96 (1812) (vln
& pf)
with J. Perry (pf) (24/25 May, 1982)
CBC (in set SM 5023-5) (5 B)

BONPORTI

(10) Concerti a quattro, op. 11 (1727)
(strs & c)
Concerto no. 8, in D
with G. Leonhardt (hpsi) &
Amsterdam Chamber Orch. - Rieu
Telefunken AWT 9415, SAWT 9415

BRAHMS

(21) Hungarian Dances (1852/1869) (pf
duet)
Hungarian Dance no. 4, in f
(arr. vln & ens Salzedo)
with Royal Tziganes - Staryk
Monitor MFS 715
Philips 870 034 BFY
World Record Club SP 929, TT 929

Hungarian Dance no. 17 in f sharp
(arr. vln & ens "in f" Salzedo)
with Royal Tziganes-Staryk
Monitor MFS 715
Philips 870 034 BFY
World Record Club SP 929, TT 929

Sonata no. 3, in d, op. 108 (1886/8) (vln
& pf)
with M. Bernardi (pf)
CBC SM 39

Sonata (1853) "Frei aber Einsam"
(vln & pf)
Allegro (Scherzo) in c (3rd mvt)
"Sonatensatz"
with E. Niwa (pf)
Everest (in set SDBR 3203)
Orion ORS 7027
Orion Naxos-7805 CD

Symphony no. 1, in c, op. 68 (1855/76)
(orch)
with Royal Philharmonic Orch. - Kletzki
Columbia CX 1573

CORELLI

(12) Sonatas, op. 5 (1700) (vln & c)
Sonata no. 2, in B flat
with K. Gilbert (hpsi)
Baroque BC 2874
Columbia HRS 1012 EV
Everest (in set SDBR 3203)

Sonata no. 2, in B flat
(NOTE: Arranged by Geminiani as a concerto grosso which, in this recording, serves
as an accompaniment for the violin, thus
becoming a violin concerto.)
with Baroque Chamber Orch. - Staryk
Baroque BC 1880, BC 2880

Sonata no. 12, in d "La follia"
(NOTE: Original version.)
with R. Linzon (pf) (Apr. 1982 "live" performance from a Toronto recital)
Masters of the Bow MBS 2020

DANCLA

(24) Caprices, op. 52 (solo vln)
Caprice no. 9, in c (Allegro agitato)
Everest (in set SDBR 3203)
HMV HQS 1124
Imperial ILX 1015
Virtuoso VIR 1002
RCM 8601

Caprice no. 16, in b flat (Allegro vivace)
Everest (in set SDBR 3203)
HMV HQS 1124
Imperial ILX 1015
Virtuoso VIR 1002
RCM 8601

DELIBES

Sylvia (1876)-ballet (orch)
Pas de deux (Act III)
with Royal Philharmonic Orch. - Irving
Capitol G 7245, SG 7245
Electrola SME 73956
HMV CLP 1239

DINICU

Hora staccato (1906) (vln & pf-arr. vln &
ens)
with Royal Tziganes - Staryk
Monitor MFS 715
Philips 870 034 BFY
World Record Club SP 929, TT 929

DONT

(24) Caprices, op. 35 (solo vln)
Caprice no. 2, in a (Moderato)
Everest (in set SDBR 3203)
HMV HQS 1124
Imperial ILX 1015
Virtuoso 1002
RCM 8601

DVORAK

Concerto in b, op. 104 (1894/5) (vlc & orch)
with M. Rostropovich (vlc) &
Royal Philharmonic Orch. - Boult
Capitol G 7109
HMV ALP 1595, ASD 358
Seraphim S 60136

FALLA

(La) Vida breve (1913)-opera
Danza española (orch-arr. vln & pf Kreisler)
with E. Niwa (pf)
Everest (in set SDBR 3203)
Orion ORS 7027
Orion Naxos 7805 CD

FARNON

Rhapsody (vln & orch)
with London Festival Orch. - Farnon
Polydor 2382 008

FAURE

Berceuse in g, op. 16 (1880) (vln & orch)
with J. Perry (pf)
CBC RCI 438

Berceuse in g, op. 16 (1880) (vln & orch)
with R. Linzon (pf) (Apr. 1982 "live"
performance from a Toronto recital)
Masters of the Bow MBS 2020

FIOCCO

Suite no. 1, in G (hpsi)
Allegro (10th mvt) (arr. vln & pf Bent & O'Neill)-
with E. Niwa (pf)
Everest (in set SDBR 3203)
Orion ORS 7027
Orion Naxos 7805 CD

Suite no. 1, in G (hpsi)
Allegro (10th mvt) (arr. vln & pf Bent & O'Neill)
with M. Bernardi (pf)
CBC SM 39

FIORILLO

(36) Etude-caprices, op. 3 (solo vln)
Caprice no. 3, in C (Allegro)
Everest (in set SDBR 3203)
HMV HQS 1124
Imperial ILX 1015
Virtuoso 1002
RCM 8601

Caprice no. 8, in G (Largo)
Everest (in set SDBR 3203)
HMV HQS 1124
Imperial ILX 1015
Virtuoso 1002
RCM 8601

Caprice no. 14, in g (Adagio)
Everest (in set SDBR 3203)
HMV HQS 1124
Imperial ILX 1015
Virtuoso 1002
RCM 8601

Caprice no. 28, in D (Allegro assai)
Everest (in set SDBR 3203)
HMV HQS 1124
Imperial ILX 1015
Virtuoso 1002
RCM 8601

Caprice no. 28, in D (Allegro assai)
(July 1972 "live" performance from a Toronto recital)
Master of the Bow MBS 2020

FREEDMAN

Encounter (1974) (vln & pf)
with H. Bowkun (pf)
CBC SM 342

GEMINIANI

(6) Sonatas, op. 5 (1738) (solo vln)
Sonata in B flat (ed. Corti)
Baroque BC 1851, BC 2851
Everest (in set SDBR 3203)
Hispavox HBR(S) 380-03
Orion 7809-2 CD

GROFE

Grand Canyon (1931)-suite (orch)
On the trail (3rd mvt)
with Capitol Symphony Orch. - Dragon
Capitol P 8523, SP 8523

HANDEL

(15) Sonatas, op. 1 (ca. 1731) (fl/vln & c)
Sonata no. 9 in b: Andante (6th mvt)
(arr. vln & pf as "Larghetto" Hubay)
with E. Niwa (pf)
Everest (in set SDBR 3203)
Orion ORS 7027
Orion Naxos 7805 CD

HAYDN, F.J.

Sonata no. 1, in G, H.XV, no. 32 (1794)
(vln & hpsi)
with L. Boucher (pf)
CBC Transcription Program 243
Sonata no. 1, in G, H.XV, no. 32 (1794)
(vln & hpsi) with L. Boucher (pf)
Orion ORS 7027, Select CC 15069
Orion Naxos 7805 CD

Symphony no. 103, in E flat, H.I, no. 103
(1795)
"Drum roll" (orch)
with Royal Philharmonic Orch. - Beecham
HMV ASD 341

HINDEMITH

(6) Sonatas, op. 11
(NOTE: Only sonatas 1 & 2 are for
vln & pf.
Number 3 is for vlc & pf; no. 4 is for vla

& pf; no. 5
is for solo vla and no. 6 is for solo vln.)
Sonata no. 1, in E flat (1920) (vln & pf)
with J. Schwarz (pf)
CBC SM 172

(2) Sonatas, op. 31 (1924) (solo vln)
Sonata no. 2
Baroque BC 1851, BC 2851
Everest (in set SDBR 3203)
Hispavox HBR(S) 380-03
Orion 7809-2 CD

HOFFERT

Concerto (1976) (vln & orch)
with orch. - Hoffert
Sine Qua Non ULDD 12, MQS 145

HUBAY

(14) Scenes de la Csarda (vln & pf/orch)
No. 4. Hejre Kati, op. 32 (1887)
(arr. vln & ens)
with Royal Tziganes - Staryk
Monitor MFS 715
Philips 870 034 BFY
World Record Club SP 929, TT 929

KALMAN

Grafin Maritza (1924)-operetta
Komm' Zigany (arr. vln as "Play, gypsy play"
Brammer & Grunwald - arr. vln & ens
Grey & Foley) with Royal Tziganes -
Staryk
Monitor MFS 715
Philips 870 034 BFY
World Record Club SP 929, TT 929

KAYSER

(36) Elementary and Progressive Studies,
op. 20 (solo vln)
Study no. 4, in C (Allegro)
Everest (in set SDBR 3203)
HMV HQS 1124
Imperial ILX 1015, Virtuoso VIR 1002
RCM 8601

KENINS

Concerto (1975) (vln & orch)
with CBC Vancouver Chamber Orch.-
Avison
CBC SM 293

KREISLER

Caprice viennois, op. 2 (vln & pf)
with J. Corwin (pf)
CBC SM 299

Gypsy caprice (vln & pf)
with J. Corwin (pf)
CBC SM 299

Liebesfreud (vln & pf)
with J. Corwin (pf)
CBC SM 299

Liebesfreud (vln & pf)
with R. Linzon (pf) (Apr. 1982 "live"
performance
from a Toronto recital)
Masters of the Bow MBS 2020

Liebesleid (vln & pf)
with J. Corwin (pf)
CBC SM 299

Liebesleid (vln & pf)
with R. Linzon (pf) (Apr. 1982 "live"
performance from a Toronto recital)
Masters of the Bow MBS 2020

Schön Rosmarin (vln & pf)
with J. Corwin (pf)
CBC SM 299

Tambourin chinois, op. 3 (vln & pf)
with J. Corwin (pf)
CBC SM 299

--(in the style of other composers)--
Chanson Louis XIII et Pavane (L.
Couperin), (vln & pf)
with J. Corwin (pf)
CBC SM 299

(La) Chasse (Cartier) (vln & pf)
with J. Corwin (pf)
CBC SM 299

Praeludium e Allegro (Pugnani) (vln &
pf)
with J. Corwin (pf)
CBC SM 299

(La) Precieuse (L. Couperin) (vln & pf)
with J. Corwin (pf)
CBC SM 299

Scherzo (Dittersdorf) (vln & pf)
with J. Corwin (pf)
CBC SM 299

Sicilienne et rigaudon (Francoeur) (vln
& pf)
with J. Corwin (pf)
CBC SM 299

KREUTZER, R.

(42) Etudes. op. 16 (solo vln)
(NOTE: Originally 40 Etudes.)
Etude no. 2, in C (Allegro moderato)
Everest (in set SDBR 3203)
HMV HQS 1124
Imperial ILX 1015
Virtuoso VIR 1002
RCM 8601

Etude no. 8, in E (Allegro non troppo)
Everest (in set SDBR 3203)
HMV HQS 1124
Imperial ILX 1015
Virtuoso VIR 1002
RCM 8601

Etude no. 15, in B flat (Allegro non
troppo)
Everest (in set SDBR 3203)
HMV HQS 1124
Imperial ILX 1015
Virtuoso VIR 1002
RCM 8601

Etude no. 35, in B flat
(July 1982 "live" performance from a To-
ronto recital)
Masters of the Bow MBS 2020

LECLAIR

(12) Sonatas, op. 9 (1738)-Book IV (vln
& c)
Sonata no. 3, in D
with L. Boucher (pf)
CBC Transcription Program 243

Sonata no. 3, in D
with L. Boucher (pf)
Orion ORS 7027
Select CC 15069
Orion Naxos 7805 CD

LOCATELLI

(24) Caprices, op. 3 (1733) (solo vln)
(NOTE: The caprices are usually performed
as cadenzas, two per Concerto, to the set of
Concerti,
op. 3, which are entitled "L'Arte del
Violino".)
Caprice no. 2, in D
(Apr. 1982 "live" performance from a To-
ronto recital)
Masters of the Bow MBS 2020

Caprice no. 2, in D
Caprice no. 3, in C
Caprice no. 20, in F
Caprice no. 23, in D, "Il laberinto
armonico"
RCM 8601

(12) Sonatas, op. 6 (1737)
Sonata no. 1, in g
Baroque BC 1874, BC 2874
Columbia HRS 1012 EV
Everest (in set SDBR 3203)

MAHLER

Symphony no. 4, in G (1900) (orch)
with S. Stahlman (s) &

Concertgebouw Orch., Amsterdam - Solti
Decca LXT 5638, SXL 2276
London CM 9286, CS 6217

MARCELLO, B.

(12) Concerti, op. 1 (1708) (vln, vlc obb,
strs & c)
Concerto no. 1, in D
with Baroque Chamber Orch. - Staryk
Baroque BC 1880, BC 2880

MASSENET

Thais (1894)-opera
Meditation
with Chicago Symphony Orch. - Martinon
RCA 940 040, LSC 2939, SB 6741, VICS
1358

MATHIEU

(3) Etudes modernes "Monologues" (1924)
(solo vln)
Etude no. 5
CBC Transcription Program 243

Etude no. 6
CBC Transcription Program 243

Etude no. 8
CBC Transcription Program 243

MONTI

Csardas (1904) (vln & pf-arr. vln & ens)
with Royal Tziganes - Staryk
Monitor MFS 715
Philips 870 034 BFY
World Record Club SP 929, TT 929

MOZART, W.A.

Concerto no. 3, in G, K. 216 (1775) (vln
& orch)
(cadenzas: Franko (1st mvt); Ysaye (2nd
mvt)
with National Arts Centre Orch. -
Bernardi
CBC SM 174

Concerto no. 5, in A, K. 219 (1775) "Turkish"
(vln & orch)
(cadenzas: Joachim)
with National Arts Centre Orch. - Bernardi
RCA KRL1-007
ANALEKTA (BMG) CD-AN 2 7201-2

Serenade no. 7, in d, K. 250 "Haffner" (1776) (orch)
Rondo (4th mvt) (arr. vln & pf Kreisler)
with E. Niwa (pf)
Everest (in set SDBR 3203)
Orion ORS 7027
Orion Naxos 7805 CD

NARDINI

(7) Sonatas "Sonates avec les Adagios brodes"
(undated) (vln & c)
Sonata no. 2, in D
with K. Gilbert (hpsi)
Baroque BC 1874, BC 2874
COLUMBIA HRS 1012 EV

NOVACEK

(8) Concert Caprices, op. 5 (1889) (vln & pf)
No. 4. Perpetuum mobile
with E. Niwa (pf)
Everest (in set SDBR 3203)
Orion ORS 7027
Orion Naxos 7805 CD

PAGANINI

(24) Caprices, op. 1 (ca. 1805) (solo vln)
Caprice no. 1, in E
(15 Aug. 1969)
Musical Heritage Society MHS 1122
Select CC 15076

Caprice no. 2, in b
(15 Aug. 1969)
Masters of the Bow MBS 2003

Musical Heritage Society MHS 1122
Orion 665 (cassette)
Select CC 15076

Caprice no. 5, in a
(15 Aug. 1969)
Musical Heritage Society MHS 1122
Select CC 15076

Caprice no. 9, in E
(15 Aug. 1969)
Masters of the Bow MBS 2003
Musical Heritage Society MHS 1122
Orion 665 (cassette)
Select CC 15076

Caprice no. 13, in B flat
(15 Aug. 1969)
Musical Heritage Society MHS 1122
Select CC 15076

Caprice no. 14, in E flat
(15 Aug. 1969)
Masters of the Bow MBS 2003
Musical Heritage Society MHS 1122
Orion 665 (cassette)
Select CC 15076

Caprice no. 16, in g
(15 Aug. 1969)
Masters of the Bow MBS 2003
Musical Heritage Society MHS 1122
Orion 665 (cassette)
Select CC 15076

Caprice no. 16, in g
(Apr. 1982 "live" performance from a Toronto recital)
Masters of the Bow MBS 2020

Caprice no. 17, in E flat
(15 Aug. 1969)
Musical Heritage Society MHS 1122
Select CC 15076

Caprice no. 19, in E flat
(15 Aug. 1969)
Masters of the Bow MBS 2003

Musical Heritage Society MHS 1122
Orion 665 (cassette)
Select CC 15076

Caprice no. 20, in D
(15 Aug. 1969)
Masters of the Bow MBS 2003
Musical Heritage Society MHS 1122
Orion 665 (cassette)
Select CC 15076

Caprice no. 21, in A
(15 Aug. 1969)
Masters of the Bow MBS 2003
Musical Heritage Society MHS 1122
Orion 665 (cassette)
Select CC 15076

Caprice no. 24, in a
(15 Aug. 1969)
Masters of the Bow MBS 2003
Musical Heritage Society MHS 1122
Orion 665 (cassette)
Select CC 15076

Concerto no. 1, in D, op. 6 (1817) (vln
& orch)
(cadenza: Sauret & Wilhelmj - arr. Staryk)
with Norddeutscher Rundfunk Symphony
Orch.
Michael (16 Jan. 1969)
Masters of the Bow MBS 2003
Orion 665 (cassette)

(6) Sonatas, op. 3 (ca. 1805) (vln & gtr)
No. 6. Sonata no. 12, in e
with E. Niwa (pf)
Everest (in set SDBR 3203)
Orion ORS 7027
Orion Naxos 7805 CD

PAPINEAU-COUTURE

Aria (1946) (solo vln)
Baroque BC 1851, BC 2851
Everest (in set SDBR 3203)
Hispavox HBR(S) 380-03
Orion 7809-2 CD

(3) Caprices (1965) (vln & pf)
Caprice no. 1 "Nadia" (Allegro)
with L. Boucher (pf)
CBC Transcription Program 243

Caprice no. 2 "Ghilaine" (Adagio)
with L. Boucher (pf)
CBC Transcription Program 243

Caprice no. 3 "Francois" (Scherzando)
with L. Boucher (pf)
CBC Transcription Program 243

Sonata in G (1944 - rev. 1953) (vln &
pf)
with J. Perry (pf)
CBC RCI 438

Suite (1956) (solo vln)
RCA CC 1016, CCS 1016

PISENDEL

Sonata in a (solo vln)
Baroque BC 1851, BC 2851
Everest (in set SDBR 3203)
Hispavox HBR(S) 380-03
Orion 7809-2 CD

PREVOST

Sonata (1960/1) (vln & pf)
with J. Schwarz (pf)
CBC SM 172

PROKOFIEV

Concerto no. 1, in D, op. 19 (1916/7) (vln
& orch)
with Vancouver Symphony Orch. -
Akiyama
CBC SM 235

(5) Melodies, op. 35bis (1921) (vln & pf)
(NOTE: Composed in 1920 for v & pf -
rewritten in
1921 for vln & pf.)
No. 2
with E. Niwa (pf)

Everest (in set SDBR 3203)
Orion ORS 7027
Orion Naxos 7805 CD

(5) Melodies, op. 35bis (1921)
(vln & pf)
(NOTE: Composed in 1920 for v & pf -
rewritten in 1921 for vln & pf.)
with J. Perry (pf)
CBC RCI 438

Sonata in D, op. 115 (1947) (solo vln)
Baroque BC 1851, BC 2851
Everest (in set SDBR 3203)
Hispavox HBR(S) 380-03
Orion 7809-2 CD

Sonata no. 1, in f, op. 80 (1938/46) (vln
& pf)
with M. Bernardi (pf)
Ace of Diamonds SDD 2152
Musical Heritage Society MHS 1135

Sonata no. 2, in D, op. 94bis (1944) (vln
& pf)
(NOTE: Origianlly composed for fl and
pf.)
with M. Bernardi (pf)
Ace of Diamonds SDD 2152
Musical Heritage Society MHS 1135

RACHMANINOFF
(6) SONGS, OP. 38 (1916) (v & pf)
No. 3. Daisies
(arr. vln & pf as "Albumblatt-Marguerite"
Kreisler)
with R. Pannell (pf) (1984)
Duke Records DBR 31003

RAVEL

Berceuse sur le nom de Gabriel Faure (1922)
(vln & pf), with J. Perry (pf)
CBC RCI 438
Daphnis et Chloe (1910) - ballet (orch)
Suites 1 & 2
with Chicago Symphony Orch. - Martinon
RCA A 635 061, A 645 061, LM 2806,
LSC 2806

RIMSKY-KORSAKOV

Capriccio espagnole, op. 34 (1887) (orch)
with Royal Philharmonic Orch. - Kurtz
HMV ALP 1632

Easter Overture, op. 36 "Grand Peque
russe" (orch)
with Royal Philharmonic Orch. -
Rodzinski
HMV ALP 1711
Seraphim 60074

Scheherazade, op. 35 (1888) (orch)
with Royal Philharmonic Orch. - Beecham
Angel 35505, S 35505, Rl 32027
HMV ALP 1564, ASD 251, ASDF 536,
FALP 536,
SXLP 30253
EMI CDC 7 47717 2

Scheherazade, op. 35 (1888) (orch)
The sea and Sinbad's ship (1st mvt)
with Capital Symphony Orch. - Dragon
Capitol P 8547

RODE, P.J.J.

(24) Caprices (en forme d'etudes) op. 22
(ca. 1813)
(solo vln)
Caprice no. 2, in a (Allegretto)
Everest (in set SDBR 3203)
HMV HQS 1124
Imperial ILX 1015
Virtuoso VIR 1002
RCM 8601

Caprice no. 8, in f sharp (Moderato assai)
Everest (in set SDBR 3203)
HMV HQS 1124
Imperial ILX 1015
Virtuoso VIR 1002
RCM 8601

Caprice no. 17, in A flat (Vivacissimo)
Everest (in set SDBR 3203)
HMV HQS 1124, Imperial ILX 1015
Virtuoso VIR 1002, RCM 8601

Caprice no. 21, in B flat (Tempo giusto)
Everest (in set SDBR 3203)
HMV HQS 1124
Imperial ILX 1015
Virtuoso VIR 1002
RCM 8601

ROUSSEL

Bacchus et Ariane, op. 43 (1930) - ballet
(orch)
Suite no. 2
with Chicago Symphony Orch. - Martinon
RCA A 635 061, A 645 061, LM 2806,
LSC 2806

RUSSO

The English Concerto
with London Jazz Orch. - Russo
GM 3017 CD

SAINT-SAENS

Danse macabre, op. 40 (1874) (orch)
with Royal Philharmonic Orch. - Collins
HMV ALP 1649

Introduction et Rondo Capriccioso, op. 28
(1863)
(vln & pf/orch)
with London Festival Orch. - Gamley
Orion ORS 7027
Select CC 15069
Orion Naxos 7805 CD

SARASATE

Introduction et Tarantella, op. 43 (1899)
(vln & pf)
with R. Linzon (pf) (Apr. 1982 "live"
performance
from a Toronto recital)
Masters of the Bow MBS 2020

Zigeunerweisen, op. 20 (1878) (vln & pf/
orch)
(NOTE: Part 1 only.)
with Royal Tziganes - Staryk

Monitor MFS 715
Philips 870 034 BFY
World Record Club SP 929, TT 929

Zigeunerweisen, op. 20 (1878) (vln & pf/
orch)
with London Festival Orch. - Gamley
Orion ORS 7027
Select CC 15069
Orion Naxos 7805 CD

SATIE

Choses vues a droite et a gauche (sans
lunettes)
(1912) (vln & pf)
with J. Schwarz (pf)
CBC SM 172

SCHUMANN, R.

(3) Romances, op. 94 (1849)
(ob/vln/vlc/cl & pf)
Romance no. 2, in A   (arr. vln & pf
Kreisler)
with E. Niwa (pf)
Everest (in set SDBR 3203)
Orion ORS 7027
Orion Naxos 7805 CD

SHOSTAKOVITCH

Concerto no. 1, in a, op. 99 (1955) (vln
& orch)
with Toronto Symphony Orch. - Davis
(12/3 Jan. 1984)
CBC SM 5037
SMCD 5037

(3) Danses fantastique, op. 5 (1922) (pf)
with R. Pannell (pf) (1984)
Duke Records DBR 31003

SOMERS

Sonata no. 2 (1955) (vln & pf)
with L. Boucher (pf)
RCA CC 1016, CCS 1016

STAMITZ, J.W.A.

(2) Divertimenti (1762) (solo vln)
Divertimento no. 2, in G: Allegro
moderato
(1st mvt); Minuetto (3rd mvt)
Baroque BC 1851, BC 2851
Everest (in set SDBR 3203)
Hispavox HBR(S) 380-03
Orion 7809-2 CD

STRAUSS, R.

Don Juan, op. 20 (1888) (orch)
with Concertgebouw Orch., Amsterdam -
Jochum
Fontana 894 119 ZKY
Philips PHC 9106

(Ein) Heldenleben, op. 40 (1898) (orch)
with Royal Philharmonic Orch. - Beecham
Capitol G 7250, SG 7250
HMV ALP 1847, ASD 421
Seraphim 60041
World Record Club ST 664, T 664
Seraphim 4XG 60493

(Ein) Heldenleben, op. 40 (1898) (orch)
with Toronto Symphony Orch. - Davis
(3/4 June 1983)
CBC SM 5036
SMCD 5036

Till Eulenspiegel's lustige Streiche, op. 28
(1895)
(orch)
with Concertgebouw Orch., Amsterdam -
Jochum
Fontana 894 119 ZKY
Philips PHC 9106

STRAVINSKY

(L') Histoire du Soldat (1918)
(narrators, cbs, tbn, cl, vln, bsn, cor,
pcn, vln & cbs)
with unid. soloists
Sine Qua Non ULDD 12
MQS 145 ERAD 145 CD

Suite italienne (on themes of Pergolesi)
(1932)
(vln & pf)
(NOTE: From the ballet "Pulcinella"
1919/20.)
with J. Perry (pf)
CBC RCI 438

SZYMANOWSKI

King Roger, op. 46 (1926) - opera
Chant de Roxane (arr. vln & pf
Kochanski)
with E. Niwa (pf)
Everest (in set SDBR 3203)
Orion ORS 7027
Orion Naxos 7805 CD

TCHAIKOVSKY, P.I.

(12) Morceaux (difficulte moyenne) op.
40 (1878) (pf)
No. 2 Chanson triste in g (arr. vln &
ens)
with members of the Concertgebouw
Orch., Amsterdam - Staryk
Imperial IPE 5084

Quartet no. 1, in D, op. 11 (1871)
(2 vlns, vla & vlc)
Andante cantabile (2nd mvt) (arr. vln &
ens)
with members of the Concertgebouw
Orch., Amsterdam - Staryk
Imperial IPE 5084

Sleeping Beauty, op. 66 (1888/9) - ballet
(orch)
Pas de deux (Act III)
with Royal Philharmonic Orch. - Irving
Captiol G 7245, SG 7245
HMV CLP 1239

Souvenir d'un lieu cher, op. 42, (1878)
(vln & pf)
No. 3. Melodie in E flat (arr. vln & ens)
with members of the Concertgebouw
Orch., Amsterdam - Staryk
Imperial IPE 5084

Swan Lake, op. 20 (1875/6) - ballet (orch)
Dance of the queen of the swans (Act II)
with Concertgebouw Orch., Amsterdam -
Fistoulari
Decca LXT 5648, SXL 2285
London CM 9287, CS 6218

Pas de deux (Andante: Black swan vari-
ations)
(Act III)
with Concertgebouw Orch., Amsterdam -
Fistoulari
Decca LXT 5648, SXL 2285
London CM 9287, CS 6218

TORELLI

(12) Concerti, op. 8 (1709)
(1/6: 2 vlns, strs & c - 7/12: vln, strs &
c)
Concerto no. 8, in c
with Baroque Chamber Orch. - Staryk
Baroque BC 1880, BC 2880

VERACINI

(12) Sonatas, op. 2 (1744) "Sonate
accademiche"
(vln & c)
Sonata no. 8, in e
with K. Gilbert (hpsi)
Baroque BC 1874, BC 2874
Columbia HRS 1012 EV
Everest (in set SDBR 3203)

Sonata no. 11, in E: Menuet e Gavotte
(3rd mvt)
with K. Gilbert (hpsi)
Baroque BC 1874, BC 2874
Everest (in set SDBR 3203)

VIEUXTEMPS

Suite in D, op. 43 (1871) (vln & pf)
with R. Linzon (pf) (Apr. 1982 "live"
performance
from a Toronto recital)
Masters of the Bow MBS 2020

VIVALDI

(12) Concerti, op. 3 (1712) "L'Estro
armonico"
(var. cbns, strs & c)
Concerto no. 9, in D: Allegro (1st mvt)
RV.230,
F.I, no. 178, P. 147, R. 414 (vln, strs & c)
with Vivaldi Players of Montreal (1987)
Musica Viva MV 1020
MVCD 1020

Concerto no. 11, in d: Largo e spiccato
(3rd mvt)
(2 vlns, vlc, strs & c)
with A. Robert (vln) C. Bogenez (vlc) &
Vivaldi Players of Montreal (1987)
Musica Viva MV 1020
MVCD 1020

(12) Concerti, op. 4 (1715) "La
Stravaganza"
(vln, strs & c)
Concerto no. 2, in e, RV.199, F.I, no. 181,
P.98, R.419
with Baroque Chamber Orch. - Staryk
Baroque BC 1880, BC 2880

(12) Concerti, op. 8 (1725) "Il cimento
dell'armonia
e dell'invenzione" (nos. 1/4: Le quattro
Stagioni)
(vln, strs & c)
Concerto no. 1, in E: Allegro (1st mvt)
RV.269
with Vivaldi Players of Montreal (1987)
Musica Viva MV 1020
MVCD 1020

Concerto no. 2, in g: Presto (3rd mvt)
RV.315,
F.I, no. 23, P.335, R.77 "L'estate"
with Vivaldi Players of Montreal (1987)
Musica Viva MV 1020
MVCD 1020

Concerto no. 3, in F: Allegro (1st mvt)
RV.234,
F.I, no. 24, P.257, R.78 "L'autunno"
with Vivaldi Players of Montreal (1987)
Musica Viva MV 1020
MVCD 1020

Concerto no. 4, in f, RV.443, F.I, no. 25,
P.442,
R.79 "L'inverno"
with Vivaldi Players of Montreal (1987)
Musica Viva MV 1020
MVCD 1020

Concerto in D: Allegro (1st mvt) RV.212a,
F.I,
no. 136, P.165, R.312, op. 35, no. 19 "Fatto
per la
solennita della S. Lingua di S. Antonio"
(1712)
with Vivaldi Players of Montreal (1987)
Musica Viva MV 1020
MVCD 1020

Concerto in A: Allegro (1st mvt) RV
532, F.V,
no. 2, P.133, R.194, op. 2, no. 1
(2 mands, strs & c - arr. 2 vlns, strs & c)
with G. Hoebig (vln) C. Bogenez (vlc) &
Vivaldi Players of Montreal (1987)
Musica Viva MV 1020
MVCD 1020

VLADIGEROV

Vardar (Rapsodie bulgare) op. 16 (1922)
(vln & pf - arr. vln & ens)
with Royal Tziganes - Staryk
Imperial ILPT 117
Metronome HLP 10082
World Record Club TP 339

WALTON

Sonata (1939) (vln & pf)
with H. Bowkun (pf)
CBC SM 342

WIENIAWSKI

(L') Ecole moderne (10 Etudes) op. 10
(1854)
(solo vln)
(NOTE: Etude no. 10 comprises a trill
exercise on Wieniawski's "Souvenir de
Moscou" and a trill exercise on a a ca-
denza to the Beethoven Concerto. It has
yet to be recorded.)
Etude no. 1, in C "Le sautille"
Everest (in set SDBR 3203)
HMV HQS 1124
Imperial ILX 1015
Virtuoso VIR 1002
RCM 8601

Etude no. 5, in E flat "alla saltarella"
Everest (in set SDBR 3203)
HMV HQS 1124
Imperial ILX 1015
Virtuoso VIR 1002
RCM 8601

Etude no. 5, in E flat "alla saltarella"
(Apr. 1982 "live" performance from a To-
ronto recital)
Masters of the Bow MBS 2020

Etude no. 7, in A flat "La cadenza"
Everest (in set SDBR 3203)
HMV HQS 1124
Imperial ILX 1015
Virtuoso VIR 1002
RCM 8601

(8) Etude-Caprices, op. 18 (1863)
(vln, 2nd vln acc)
Etude-caprice no. 1, in g
(playing both parts)
Everest (in set SDBR 3203)
HMV HQS 1139
Imperial ILX 1016
Musical Heritage Society MHS 1131
Virtuoso VIR 1001

Etude-caprice no. 2, in E flat
(playing both parts)
Everest (in set SDBR 3203)

HMV HQS 1139
Imperial ILX 1016
Musical Heritage Society MHS 1131
Virtuoso VIR 1001

Etude-caprice no. 3, in D
(playing both parts)
Everest (in set SDBR 3203)
HMV HQS 1139
Imperial ILX 1016
Musical Heritage Society MHS 1131
Virtuoso VIR 1001

Etude-caprice no. 4, in a
(playing both parts)
Everest (in set SDBR 3203)
HMV HQS 1139
Imperial ILX 1016
Musical Heritage Society MHS 1131
Virtuoso VIR 1001

Etude-caprice no. 5, in E flat
(playing both parts)
Everest (in set SDBR 3203)
HMV HQS 1139
Imperial ILX 1016
Musical Heritage Society MHS 1131
Virtuoso VIR 1001

Etude-caprice no. 6, in D
(playing both parts)
Everest (in set SDBR 3203)
HMV HQS 1139
Imperial ILX 1016
Musical Heritage Society MHS 1131
Virtuoso VIR 1001

Etude-caprice no. 7, in c
(playing both parts)
Everest (in set SDBR 3203)
HMV HQS 1139
Imperial ILX 1016
Musical Heritage Society MHS 1131
Virtuoso VIR 1001

Etude-caprice no. 8, in F
(playing both parts)
Everest (in set SDBR 3203)
HMV HQS 1139

Imperial ILX 1016
Musical Heritage Society MHS 1131
Virtuoso VIR 1001

Legende in d, op. 17 (1860) (vln & pf)
with A. Kotowska (pf)
Everest (in set SDBR 3203)
HMV HQS 1139
Imperial ILX 1016
Musical Heritage Society MHS 1131
Virtuoso VIR 1001

(2) Mazurkas, op. 12 (1853) (vln & pf)
Mazurka no. 2, in g "Le menetrier/
Dudziarz"
with A. Kotowska (pf)
Everest (in set SDBR 3203)
HMV HQS 1139
Imperial ILX 1016
Musical Heritage Society MHS 1131
Virtuoso VIR 1001

Polonaise brillante no. 1, in D, op. 4
(1853)
(vln & orch)
with A. Kotowska (pf)
Everest (in set SDBR 3203)
HMV HQS 1139
Imperial ILX 1016
Musical Heritage Society MHS 1131
Virtuoso VIR 1001

Scherzo-tarantelle, op. 16 (1856)
(vln & pf)
with A. Kotowska (pf)
Everest (in set SDBR 3203)
HMV HQS 1139
Imperial ILX 1016
Musical Heritage Society MHS 1131
Virtuoso VIR 1001

WILLAN

Sonata no. 2, in E (1923) (vln & pf)
with L. Boucher (pf)
CBC Transcription Program 243

APPENDIX C
Conductors With Whom Steven Staryk Worked

Kazuyoshi Akiyama
Karel Ancerl
Alfredo Antonini
Kees Bakels
Ernesto Barbini
Sir Thomas Beecham
Jiri Belohlavek
Sir Adrian Boult
Semyon Bychkov
Myung Whun Chung
Sir Andrew Davis
Franz Paul Decker
James De Priest
Victor De Sabata
Antal Dorati
Arthur Fiedler
Peter Erös
Jean Fournet
Anatole Fistoulari
Piero Gamba

John Elliot Gardiner
Vittorio Gui
Carlo Maria Giulini
Bernard Haitink
Walter Hendl
Gunther Herbig
Irwin Hoffman
Jascha Horenstein
Robert Irving
Antonio Janigro
Eugen Jochum
Herbert Von Karajan
Rudolphe Kempe
Paul Kletski
André Kostelanetz
Joseph Krips
Emmanuele Krevine
Rafael Kubelik
Efrem Kurtz
Ferdinand Leitner

Erich Leinsdorf
Eduardo Mata
Jean Martinon
Hermann Michael
Pierre Monteux
Boyd Neel
Vittorio Negri
Vaclav Neumann
Seiji Ozawa
George Pretre
André Previn
Sir John Pritchard
Fritz Reiner
Helmut Rilling
Artur Rodzinski
Hans Rosbaud
Mstislav Rostropovitch
Gennady Rozhdestvensky
Paul Sacher
Kurt Sanderling
Sir Malcolm Sargent
Wolfgang Sawallisch
Hans Schmidt-Isserstedt
Tulio Serafin
Constantine Silvestri
Giuseppe Sinopoli
Stanislau Skrowacevski
Sir Georg Solti
Laszlo Somogyi
William Steinberg
Leopold Stokowski
Simon Streatfield
Walter Susskind
Hans Swarowsky
Dr. George Szell
Klaus Tennstedt
Michael Tilson Thomas
Heinz Unger
Wolf-Ferrari
Victor Yampolsky

Canadian conductors

John Avison
Raffi Armenian
Jean Marie Beaudet
Dwight Bennet
Mario Bernardi
Alexander Brott
Boris Brott
Jean Deslauriers
Victor Feldbrill
Laszlo Gati
Ruben Gurevitch
Pierre Hétu
Elmer Iseler
Arpad Joo
Eugene Kash
Sir Ernest MacMillan
Yuri Mayer
Ettore Mazzoleni
Paul Scherman

List to the best of my memory

APPENDIX D
Composers With Whom Steven Staryk Worked

Aaron Copland
Robert Farnon
George Fialla
Harry Freedman
Srul Irving Glick
Hans Henkemans
Paul Hoffert
Talivaldis Kenins
Lothar Klein
Frank Martin
Darius Milhaud
Jean Papineau-Couture
André Prévost
William Russo
Harry Somers
Igor Stravinsky
Sir Michael Tippett
Sir Ralph Vaughan Williams
Sir William Walton

APPENDIX E
Steven Staryk In Print

Bender, Peter Urs, *Leadership from within* (North York: Stoddart Publishing Co., Ltd. 1997)

Campbell, Margaret, *The Great Violinists* (Strad Publications, 2000)

Canadian Who's Who

Careers in Music (Oakville: The Frederick Harris Music Co., Ltd. 1986)

Dictionary of International Biography

Discopaedia of the Violin

Encyclopaedia Canada

Ginsberg, Murray, *They Loved to Play* (Toronto: eastend books, 1998)

International Who's Who in Music

International Who's Who of Intellectuals

International Who's Who of Professionals

The New Grove Dictionary of Music and Musicians.

Ukrainians in North America

UW Showcase: "A Century of Excellence in the Arts, Humanities, and Professional Schools at the University of Washington" (Seattle, 1997)

Who's Who in America

Who's Who in Music and Musicians International Directory

Who's Who in Toronto

APPENDIX F
Steven Staryk: Center Stage
"The Unparalleled Versatility of Steven Staryk"

"...should reawaken an appreciation of what solo violin playing meant to a generation ago."

— *Gramophone*, London

This token collection of recordings gives a sampling of the incredible versatility of Steven Staryk. Staryk, like no other violinist before or since, can convincingly run the stylistic gamut from ethnic to jazz; from baroque to classical to romantic. "His successful diversity of styles is not equalled by any other violinist," wrote James Creighton, author of *The Discopaedia of the Violin*.

Handel's *Largo* from Sonata Op. 1, No. 15 on track 2 is from a recording of Bach, Handel, Pergolesi, Tartini, and Leclair sonatas which was never released. The Rimsky-Korsakov is from a live television production, while the Faure *Berceuse* Op. 16 and the Paganini *Concerto* No. 1 are from a live concert and studio broadcast respectively. The Hoffert *Concerto for Contemporary Violin* is a direct-to-disc recording and, as such, a live performance. Most of the recordings, including the Complete Beethoven Violin Sonatas, were never released on CD, and the handful of CDs that do exist are not adequately representative of Staryk's total output on disc. (A number of excellent digital or monolog masters still exist with some of his finest recorded performances).

Through this sampling from the late 1950's to the late 1980's, Staryk can once again be rediscovered.

Titles contained in the Accompanying CD
"The Unparalleled Versatility of Steven Staryk"

1. Locatelli   - Caprice No. 23, Op. 3 "Il Laberinto Armonico" solo violin

2. Handel   - Sonata Op. 1, No. 15 - Largo, with Valerie Weeks Harpsichord

3. Sarba Pomperilor - (Rumanian Dance)
   Hora Lui Timosca - (Rumanian Dance), with the Royal Tziganes

4. Beethoven Sonata - Op. 12, No. 2 - Allegro Piacevole

5. Hoffert   - Concerto for contemporary Violin - Excerpt (Blues, Jazz, with Paul Hoffert Conducting)

6. Mozart   - Concerto No. 3, K. 216 - Rondo Allegretto, with the National Arts Centre Orchestra, Conductor Mario Bernardi.

7. Faure   - Berceuse, Op. 16, with Robert Linzon Piano

8. Rimsky-Korsakov - Flight of the Bumble Bee (Arr. Heifetz), with Linda Lee Thomas Piano

9. Beethoven   - Sonata Op. 96 - Adagio Espressivo, Scherzo Allegro, with John Perry Piano

10. Paganini   - Concerto No. 1, Op. 6 - Adagio Espressivo, with the Norddeutscher Rundfunk Symphony Orchestra, Conductor Hermann Michael

11. Strauss   - Ein Heldenleben - Excerpt with The Toronto Symphony Orchestra, Conductor Andrew Davis

12. Shostakovich   - Concerto No.1, Op. 99 - Cadenza - Burlesque (Allegro con brio), with the Toronto Symphony Orchestra, Conductor Andrew Davis

13. Kreisler   - Gypsy Caprice, with Jane Corwin Piano

14. Paganini   - Caprices Op. 1, No.s 14, 19, 16, Solo Violin

15. Prokofiev   - Concerto No. 1, Op. 19 - Moderato, with the Vancouver Symphony Orchestra, Conductor Kazuyoshi Akiyama

Compilation Engineer, Gary Louie

BIBLIOGRAPHY

Carse, Adam. *The Orchestra from Beethoven to Berlioz: A history of the Orchestra in the first half of the 19th century, and of the development of orchestral baton-conducting.* W. Heffer & Sons ltd, Cambridge, 1948.

Cremer, Lothar. *The Physics of the Violin.* MIT Press, Cambridge, 1984.

Farga, Franz. *Violins and Violinists.* Rockliff, Salisbury Square, London, 1950.

Feuerlicht, Roberta Strauss. *Joe McCarthy and McCarthyism: the Hate that Haunts America.* McGraw-Hill, New York, 1972.

Gross, Jan T. *Revolution from Abroad: The Soviet Conquest of Poland's Western Ukraine and Western Belorussia.* Princeton University Press, Princeton, 1988.

Hill, Alfred, Aurthur and W. Henry. *The Violin-Makers of the Guarneri Family (1626-1762).* The Holland Press Ltd., London, 1965.

Hill, W. Henry. *Antonio Stradivari: His Life and Work (1644-1737).* Dover Publications, Inc., New York, 1963.

Hryshko, Wasyl. *The Ukrainian Holocaust of 1933.* Ed., trans., by Marco Carynnyk, Bahrians Foundation, Toronto, 1983.

Jalovec, Karel. *Italian Violin Makers.* Crown Publishers Inc., New York.

Kahn, Gordon. *Hollywood On Trial.* Boni & Gaer, NY, 1948.

Krawchenko, Bohdan, ed. *Ukrainian Past, Ukrainian Present.* St. Martin's Press, New York, 1993.

Lubachko, Ivan S. *Belorussia Under Soviet Rule, 1917-1957.* The University Press of Kentucky, 1972.

MacMillan, Sir Ernest ed. *Music In Canada.* University of Toronto Press, 1955.

Martynowych, Orest T. *Ukrainians in Canada.* University of Alberta, Edmonton, 1991.

Oshinsky, David M. *A Conspiracy So Immense.* MacMillan, New York, 1983.

Petryshyn, Jaroslav. *Peasants in the Promised Land: Canada and the Ukrainians.* James Lorimer and Company, Toronto, 1985.

Sahaydak, Maksym. "Ethnocide of Ukrainians in the USSR," *The Ukrainian Herald*, Issue 7-8. Smoloskyp Publishers, Toronto, 1976.

Schabas, Ezra, *Sir Ernest MacMillan: The Importance of Being Canadian,* University of Toronto Press, Toronto, 1994.

Swyripa, Frances. *Ukrainians in Canada.* University of Alberta Press, Edmonton, 1978.

Swyripa, Frances and John Herd Thompson. *Loyalties in Conflict: Ukrainians in Canada During the Great War.* University of Alberta, Edmonton, 1983.